Negotiating Power and Privilege

This series of publications on Africa, Latin America, Southeast Asia, and Global and Comparative Studies is designed to present significant research, translation, and opinion to area specialists and to a wide community of persons interested in world affairs. The editor seeks manuscripts of quality on any subject and can usually make a decision regarding publication within three months of receipt of the original work. Production methods generally permit a work to appear within one year of acceptance. The editor works closely with authors to produce a high-quality book. The series appears in a paperback format and is distributed worldwide. For more information, contact the executive editor at Ohio University Press, Scott Quadrangle, University Terrace, Athens, Ohio 45701.

Executive editor: Gillian Berchowitz
AREA CONSULTANTS
Africa: Diane M. Ciekawy
Latin America: Thomas Walker
Southeast Asia: William H. Frederick
Global and Comparative Studies: Ann R. Tickamyer

The Ohio University Research in International Studies series is published for the Center for International Studies by Ohio University Press. The views expressed in individual volumes are those of the authors and should not be considered to represent the policies or beliefs of the Center for International Studies, Ohio University Press, or Ohio University.

Negotiating Power and Privilege

IGBO CAREER WOMEN
IN CONTEMPORARY NIGERIA

Philomina E. Okeke-Ihejirika

Ohio University Research in International Studies
Africa Series No. 82
Athens

The books in the Ohio University Research in International Studies Series
are printed on acid-free paper ⊚ ™

Earlier versions of parts of this book were published as:

Portions of "Negotiating Social Independence: The Challenge of Career
Pursuits for Igbo Women in Postcolonial Nigeria," adapted from *"Wicked"
Women and the Reconfiguration of Gender in Africa*, ed. Dorothy L. Hodgson
and Sheryl A. McCurdy. Copyright © 2001 by Dorothy L. Hodgson and
Sheryl A. McCurdy. Published by Heinemann, a division of Reed Elsevier,
Inc., Portsmouth, NH. All rights reserved.

"Female Wage Earners and Separate Resource Structures in Post Oil Boom
Nigeria," *Dialectical Anthropology* 22, nos. 3–4 (December 1997): 373–87.
With kind permission of Kluwer Academic Publishers.

"Bringing up the Domestic Rear: Nigerian Working Mothers and the
Structure of Gender Relations in the Family and Society," in *Silent Voices*,
ed. Doug Newsom and Bob Carrell, 95–116. Lanham, MD: University
Press of America, 1995.

Library of Congress Cataloging-in-Publication Data

Okeke-Ihejirika, Philomina E. (Philomina Ezeagbor)
  Negotiating power and privilege: Igbo career women in contemporary Nigeria /
Philomina E. Okeke-Ihejirika.
    p. cm. — (Ohio University research in international studies. Africa series ; no. 82)
  Includes bibliographical references and index.
  ISBN 0-89680-241-8 (pbk. : alk. paper)
    1. Women, Igbo—Social conditions. 2. Women, Igbo—Economic conditions.
3. Women, Igbo—Employment. 4. Women employees—Nigeria. 5. Working mothers—
Nigeria. 6. Sex role—Government policy—Nigeria. 7. Women—Government policy—
Nigeria. 8. Sexual division of labor—Nigeria. 9. Nigeria—Social conditions.
10. Nigeria—Economic conditions. I. Title. II. Research in international studies.
Africa series ; no. 82.
DT515.45.I33O586 2004
    305.48'8963320669—dc22

2004015379

To my late father, James Okeke, who gladly negotiated power and privilege with my mother every day of his married life, and my husband and buddy, Chiemeka, who embodies this legacy.

Contents

Preface

This book, I hope, will generate significant debate, not because of any dramatic claims within but because of the challenge its contents present to scholars. The voices of Igbo women in this volume force us to rethink what existing literature tells us about schooling and paid employment as weapons for social liberation and viable assets for women's social mobility. This book looks at the link between Igbo women's access to these assets and their socioeconomic status. It highlights, in particular, patriarchal continuities and contradictions that shape the experiences of one group of African women—Igbo career women. Given the envied status female groups like them occupy across Africa, it is important to me that this volume expose both the prospects and the limitations of formal education and wage employment for them. Current debates among scholars, policymakers, and politicians in the continent also call for critical assessments of how far education and paid work can take African women.[1] In these assessments, the following questions, among others, need to be asked: What factors affect African women's access to schooling and paid work, especially in the professional ranks? How do African women fare relative to their male counterparts? In what ways do their academic and professional attainments mediate relations of gender in various social spheres?

At every stage of my academic career I have been motivated to ask questions about the representation of Africans in existing literature. I am continually challenged by a limited database that does little justice to the diversity of female experiences in Africa. This is perhaps the most important factor that inspired me to write this book. Obviously, this volume is only one contribution to a tiny database that needs to rapidly grow, for at least one important reason: What scholars say and how they say it is, at present, still largely structured by Western-oriented theories and methodologies which inform our analyses. Hence any efforts at developing valid analytical frameworks for African studies need to be grounded in the diverse experiences of Africans.

In reviewing the existing literature on Africans, I am also forced to ask questions about those who study African women. For a group vastly diverse, yet largely understudied, African women's own voices are barely audible in the forums where their concerns are discussed.[2] I believe that female African scholars bring a crucial ingredient to this data bank: their position as subjects and scholars in many instances. As both subject and scholar of this book, I could relate to the experiences shared by Igbo career women. I easily identified with them as mothers, aunts, sisters, cousins, friends, and sisters-in-law. In fact, the important cultural elements shaping their lives were familiar territories to me. I had amassed a wealth of information about African women, Nigerian and Igbo women, before proceeding to field work, but my own perspective as an insider in this culture was the main starting point of my inquiry.

Of course it is one thing to live in a culture and another thing to look at how that culture has shaped one's life, especially the relations of domination and subordination enmeshed in daily life, which are often taken for granted. As I probed into the lives of these career women, I came close on many occasions to my own lived experiences. Although as a scholar I knew I had to maintain a "critical" distance from my "data," it was also clear to me that the commonalities we shared inspired some of the useful connections I came up with in my analysis. They were also a source of encouragement which strengthened my conviction of the need to tell these women's stories.

I believe that my coming to this study from two cultures made a difference. On the one hand, doing graduate work in North America afforded me the opportunity to distance myself from my own culture and critically examine a way of life I was born into and raised in. This quest exposed me to useful insights by both insiders and outsiders to this culture and thus provided a base for an informed critique. On the other hand, I was well aware that I was addressing a wider readership of scholars. In other words, my presentation was to a "mixed" audience. I have to be careful about my interpretations of social relations in my culture, knowing full well that the conception of oppression differs in time and space.

As much as I celebrate the birth of this book, I am also concerned about the prevailing controversy surrounding the study of African women. I had hoped that the tumultuous debate on the political economy of knowledge production in African and gender studies would generate a deeper appreciation of African women's voices as both scholars and subjects in the field. But it has, instead, created a visible dividing line between indigenous insiders (African women scholars) and foreign outsiders (Western women scholars). The former emphasize their interconnectedness with the social arrangements and bodies of experiences under study, while the latter make their own claims as scholars in a field of knowledge they helped to develop and must sustain. In defending their positions, each side has, at various times, spurred a tendency for dragging issues to extremes. The explosive nature of the debate has also put scholars on both sides on guard, creating a climate for what I refer to as *praise-singing* scholarship. Under the probing eyes of one another, we may become too careful about what we say, to a point where the goal is to avoid being hounded by the "other" rather than to meet the rigorous standards of good scholarship. Praise-singing becomes, in effect, the politically correct path to tread in feminist forums.

As long as our research is mediated by various social factors, including gender, class, ethnicity, and religious beliefs, the bases for creating divisions remain endless. My fear is that too much attention paid to the political economy of knowledge production could stand in the way of critical investigations that dare to probe the touchy facets of the present social arrangement that are inimical to African women's progress. It is of crucial importance that whatever knowledge is presented as feminist scholarship be critically interrogated and not accepted simply because of an author's social location. In this regard, we must ensure that knowledge produced and fed into our databases endures the rigors of assessment.

My hope is that this book will make a significant contribution to the growing database as scholars in the field wrestle with the challenge of providing to policymakers information that is sensitive to the diverse circumstances of African women. Given this book's focus on a specific group of African women, I cannot make any general claims based on their lives. Rather, I highlight valuable insights from my analysis which I believe will be useful in looking at similar groups. I have therefore organized the book in a manner that places the stories of these Igbo career women in wider social and historical contexts. The conclusions I draw emerge from my understanding of women's experiences. I hope that these insights will rejuvenate a healthy debate in the field and also present some pointers for policy-makers as they chart viable paths to African women's progress in the twenty-first century.

Acknowledgments

My gratitude goes to all the African female students in higher education, professionals, and social activists whose testimonies and desire to change society continually motivated me to write this book. I am especially indebted to the women who shared their experiences and views about schooling, paid work, and family life in Nigeria. Without your sacrifice of time and openness in telling your stories, this book would not have been written.

I needed the help of many, however, in order to make my yearnings to tell your stories a reality. For a book that was so long in coming, I owe its debut to the many hands that worked alongside with me to bring my efforts to fruition. I am deeply grateful to my mother, Caroline Okeke, and my siblings—Victor, Oddie, Chuks, Ngozi, and Nelo—all of whom supported and encouraged my childhood dream to study "abroad" and become a "doctor." I also cannot forget the extra encouragement I have received from Jane Parpart, one of my doctoral supervisors, who has always been there for her "Ph.D. baby." I am very thankful to Dallas Cullen, chair of the Women's Studies Program at the University of Alberta, for the solid support she threw behind the publication of this volume, and to my colleagues Lise Gotel, Denise Spitzer, and Karen Hughes, whose support, many times unspoken, helped to carry me through. I am also deeply grateful to the publishing team at Ohio University Press: senior editor Gillian Berchowitz, project editor Sharon Rose, and copy editor Bob Furnish, all of whom provided valuable advice and also accommodated my schedules, including a sabbatical trip abroad.

Of all the people who gave their valuable time toward the completion of this book, I reserve my special thanks to Professor Anthonia Kalu, who spent sleepless nights going through the drafts and endured my endless whining about reviewers and their corrections. I wish there were more mentors like you, who would sacrifice some of their valuable time, mobilizing other female scholars toward this crucial task of building a database on African women.

1

Placing Igbo Women within an African Context

Patriarchal Continuities and Contradictions

This book started with a story. It is my story as well as that of thousands of African women who either aspired to acquire higher education or found themselves in a postsecondary institution. After over fifteen years of living away from my home country, going through graduate school and becoming a university professor—with a doctoral degree, a husband, and two children—the incident described below remains fresh in my mind. It sustained my motivation to write this book and perhaps also charted my destiny as an African woman. Defying the potentially stiff cultural penalties that could be levied against me, I took a leap into a world I knew very little about simply to fulfill a childhood dream of acquiring the title Doctor.

My youngest sister and an older cousin stood beside me at the bus station. They had waited to make sure I found a vehicle in good shape for my trip to Lagos, Nigeria's commercial capital, where I would be boarding a flight to Canada. They had lingered for a few minutes to talk to me, but were beginning to cast a questioning glance at me, wondering, I guessed, why I was not making any move. After a few uncomfortable moments, my cousin said, "Philo, it's time. Get in the taxi." I still did not move. I was trying to shake off the feeling of foreboding that had descended on me the day before. Until then, I seemed to have been on an exciting roller coaster, from the time the letter bearing the news of my scholarship arrived and the warm handshakes from professors and students in my department followed, to the trips to the Canadian embassy and British Airways and the medical tests for immigration clearance. I could not believe that I, a young woman from an Igbo village, with no godmother or godfather, had been offered full sponsorship for a doctoral program at a Canadian university.

But as I reflected that night on the turn of events that had led to this journey, I feared that I might be making the wrong choice. Of course, I still had the burning desire to fulfill my childhood dream. I had just completed my master's degree, while teaching in the village. But I had also received a few marriage offers in the past year and knew the pressure was on. As an Igbo woman in her late twenties, I knew that I was not getting any younger, and with two younger sisters after me, I had little time to drag my feet. The normal social expectation is that I would marry and leave the scene for their suitors to emerge. As I contemplated my predicament that day at the bus station, my cousin, as if reading my thoughts, walked closer and held me by the shoulders. He had received his undergraduate degree in the United States and was the only one I'd confided in about the second thoughts that were creeping in. Earlier, we had discussed my fears and he had assured me they were normal. In a forceful voice this time, he said, "Philo, what are you thinking? Don't even think of abandoning your plans. Do you know how lucky you are?" I was looking at my sister. There were tears in her eyes. She probably had mixed feelings, I thought, about my leaving Nigeria. My cousin sensed my confusion and moved closer to hold me. He whispered gently, "Philo, don't worry about finding a husband. There are men everywhere. Go and get your Ph.D."

As a graduate student in Canada I met female university students from various parts of Africa who were struggling with a dilemma I thought was peculiar to Nigeria. In the course of my graduate work, I noticed the significant attention paid to African women's poor access to education. But over the years of researching African women, I also became aware of the increasing concern about the conditions of African women's lives expressed by African national leaders, policymakers, international organizations, and scholars.[1] There is certainly a growing emphasis since the 1990s on the need to position African women as equal partners with men in nation building rather than as victims of development.[2] In all the hue and cry about the plight of African women, schooling is perceived as that basic prerequisite around which the policies and plans for their advancement can be centered. I find it frustrating, however, that those who plan African women's future as equal partners with men ignore certain crucial factors which obviously influence African women's decisions about what to train for and how far they should go in school. These planners fail to acknowledge the limitations society places on their mobility. These limitations are clearly evident in the conditions under which African women receive and utilize educational training. The pressure to marry, the race to have children, and the demand for male heirs, among other factors, significantly shape African women's career ambitions. The stories of Igbo career women, which highlight many aspects of these experiences, motivated me at every juncture to write this book. But since I do not wish to spoil the reader's surprise, joy, and (sometimes) pain, these stories will be unveiled later in what I refer to as voice chapters.

The global database on policies and programs for development leads us to believe that with greater educational attainment, women in developing countries such as Nigeria can pursue careers in formal employment and ultimately advance their social status.[3] But the literature on African women suggests that the power and status conferred on them by formal education and paid employment are mediated by the social boundaries and expectations to which they must adhere.[4] Very little is known, however, about how specific female groups deal with these boundaries and expectations and how the particular circumstances of each group mediate its experiences.[5] I believe that without such critical investigations, the resources we invest in African women's formal training may not achieve the desired purpose. The experiences of Igbo career women in this book are proof of the fact that the value of formal training depends a great deal on the context within which it is gained and used.

For very good reasons, research on African women has placed considerable emphasis on the large majority outside the formal sector.[6] Despite its racist and sexist dimensions, this body of research celebrates African women's roles as farmers, traders, and guardians of culture. But I intend in this volume to highlight, instead, the experiences of a small minority whose life chances in any contemporary African nation greatly affect and define the prospects of the entire female population. Most African women who have made it to higher education can relate to the experiences shared by Igbo career women in this book. Their life stories raise very crucial questions about the kind, level, and utility of formal training available to African women. As I listened to their stories, I realized that beyond what they might see as a personal journey lie generally shared experiences that need to be analyzed within a much wider context.

The analysis I develop here is woven around two basic premises. First, social relations in contemporary Africa are structured within a hybridized social order where men and women must deal with both foreign and indigenous dictates that were brought together through Western influence. Second, women must negotiate their place within that social order—as persons subordinate to men. However, not all aspects of African traditions are patriarchal. In fact, men and women alike struggle to preserve many aspects of our cultures, such as respect for older people, the extended family support system, and some marriage customs. The same can be said of Western cultures. I am interested, however, in elements of these cultures that can illuminate our understanding of African women's status in contemporary society. Obviously, the exact interaction of foreign and indigenous elements during the historical passage is anything but clear. Colonization and capitalist expansion brought the African and the Western together to produce a hybrid, a term I apply loosely since the exact measures of this cultural mix can neither be ascertained nor generalized among Africa's diverse populations. One thing, however, is apparent. From the colonial period to the present, African women's status has suffered a significant decline. Over this period, women have been placed in a subordinate status to men in terms of establishing themselves both as individuals in their own right and as a group whose participation is central to developing and implementing initiatives for nation building.[7]

Based on these assertions, I argue that, just like other groups of African women, the lives of Igbo career women need to be understood in the context of the historical passage that generated patriarchal continuities and contradictions within Igbo culture. Traceable to both indigenous and foreign culprits, these continuities and contradictions have defined these women's lives with various degrees of intensity. They have introduced a pattern in the present hybridized social order in which women must struggle to find a place. Patriarchal continuities, in my view, are gender biases that are seemingly rooted in the indigenous social order of African societies.[8] These biases exist in the postcolonial social order in residual forms with a remarkable resilience that can also be attributed to a convenient and sometimes necessary symbiosis with Western sexism. For instance, formal politics in Africa is considered a male preserve, but much as it mirrors many sexist specifications of Western power structures, it also finds some resonance in the assumedly strong male presence in many precolonial regimes. Similarly, most legal systems in Africa presently uphold monogamy with various forms of enshrined polygamy. It is also the case that the domestic-public dichotomy in urban Africa and the current gendered division of labor within families are not easily separable from women's precolonial roles, especially in terms of the contributions of mothers and wives to family subsistence. It is also not surprising that contemporary African societies have tended to assume a rather loose interpretation of women's restriction to food farming and de facto access to land. These and other aspects of basic indigenous tradition are presently contested by women and, interestingly, have become amenable in some cases to the economic demands of contemporary life.[9] But as women in this book point out, the basis for denying women equal treatment with men, at any time, still has a significant cultural foothold.

Colonization and capitalist development, as major definable markers of Africa's historical transition, undoubtedly afforded men the foundation to build and legitimize new power bases and privileges.[10] These power bases and privileges have introduced new patriarchal patterns that in some cases are not even justifiable on indigenous grounds. The hybridized social order, with its fusion of Western and African features, also embodies contradictions that blur the boundaries of the old and the new.[11] Boundaries are blurred especially where Western features reinforce already established patterns. For example, men's tight grip on the production and sale of agricultural exports invaded gendered territories when it extended to "female" crops such as palm oil and peanuts. Similarly, women's subordination, as housewives, to civil servants did not exactly contravene an already established gender hierarchy. But their domestication as dependents to male breadwinners found little support in cultures where women's significant contribution to family subsistence also gave them some degree of economic autonomy. Imposed on African societies, Western domestic ideology normalized African women's subordinate status as housewives or paid workers restricted to pink-collar occupations. These positions were branded the perfect roles for respectable *ladies* in society. It is also the case that African contemporary legal systems, regardless of region, embed overt as well as covert sexist interpretations of customary law incorporated by African male authorities that served the colonial regimes.[12] Transposed on Western legal statutes, these sexist re-interpretations of African law obviously strengthen men's privileged status in the hybridized social order. Women, in contrast, are left to defend their economic niches and rights to property in marriage on very shaky legal grounds. The emergence of these Western patterns certainly played a role in the decline of women's supportive bases and avenues of resistance in the postcolonial society. But as Simi Afonja, a major contributor to the debates on the status of African women, insists, these Western patterns found a fertile ground to germinate on our indigenous soil. According to her, traditional gender stratification, which appeared to bestow upon women a degree of autonomy, "did not preclude inequalities," many of which are hardly perceived because they are "culturally legitimized."[13] The life stories of Igbo career women in this book vividly portray the dilemma of African women as they struggle to reconcile cultural norms with what may be seen as progress in modernity.

Patriarchal contradictions, just like continuities, are equally manipulated by society to serve some desired agenda. It seems that those contradictions that reinforce indigenous gender biases are held up to women to justify the limitations society places on their path. In contrast, new rights and opportunities for women are often seen as inconsistent with the cultural norms to which women should adhere. Access to landed property, for instance, is an important economic base the older career women in this book encourage their younger counterparts to take advantage of. Outside ancestral land, women who have the means are free to purchase land, build or buy their own houses, and rent such property. In the same manner, formal training and paid work, regardless of their limited prospects at present, remain the major avenues to social mobility for African women. Unlike the traditional bases, these two crucial assets could, in principle, place men and women on an equal footing through income and status that are not tied to any relations of gender.[14] It is not surprising, however, that the potential niches women could build with these new features are fiercely contested by society at every turn.

Obviously, African societies have reconstituted themselves in the postcolonial era without most of the culturally placed checks and balances that may have given women a foothold in the past. The present social hybrid appears to have rendered impotent the various openings through which African women previously made their voices heard. But African women have not settled calmly into a supine acceptance of their situation. Rather, both overtly and covertly, women across the continent not only contest the basis for their present social status but also exploit any viable cracks in the system to expand opportunities made available to them.[15] The motivation to write this book was also fanned by the gross dearth of in-depth qualitative studies on African women. If the debate over the past two decades on the political economy of knowledge production between "insiders" and "outsiders" has accomplished one thing, it is a solid critique of the often bold Western attempt to lump the whole of "Africa in one book."[16] Much of the existing data on social relations in Africa is hardly sensitive to gender issues and does not tell us much that we do not already know. These studies provide useful background data but say very little about individual female groups. The time has passed for studies that merely give us an overview of how African women are faring at present, with a dash of statistics on schooling and formal employment thrown in for good measure. My investigation is built around one group of recipients of female higher education—Igbo career women in Nigeria. On a personal level, access to higher education and paid work has given this group of women some degree of social mobility. In broader terms, their educational credentials provide a sound prerequisite for any tangible contribution to nation building. But the conditions under which these women acquire and utilize tertiary training clearly show how far these assets can take them. I do not seek in this volume to form any generalizations based on the stories of those sampled. Rather, my main objective is to search out the relevant patterns that speak to career Igbo women's experiences and, where possible, highlight aspects of these patterns that could illuminate the experiences of other Nigerian and African female groups. I believe that such critical reexaminations of African women's experiences are necessary at this time, given the questionable prospects of schooling for men and women in contemporary Africa.[17]

Moreover, my arguments clearly deviate from any simplistic perceptions of African women as either the daughters of indigenous female powerhouses or merely the victims of male domination. Igbo career women in this volume project themselves as agents of social transformation who, in many instances, are pushing the boundaries of social expectations. Their experiences as career women break the convenient separations of old and new, traditional and modern. On a daily basis, they confront many aspects of social relations (of gender, class, religion, etc.) that could unite, distance, or even pit women against one another. An in-depth investigation must examine how these women employ their privileged status to mediate the balance of power in various social contexts. What I provide below is therefore only an overview of the theoretical, historical, and social developments to enable the reader to place these women's experiences within a broader setting.

Explaining African Women's Current Social Status

African women's status and their place in national development do not seem to find a place in the usual conventional analytical frameworks, such as human capital theory and labor market segmentation. The human capital theory argues that investments made in humans through training significantly increase their productivity, improve individual standards of living, and expand society's stock of active contributors to development. Unlike men, the proponents claim, women's primary roles already curtail their extra domestic ambitions, providing little justification for extensive investments.[18] But in assessing the viability of such investments, the costs to individuals and society, this theory captures very little of the African experience which recognizes women's economic autonomy as a crucial factor in family subsistence. Alternatively, labor market segmentation attempts to explain the existence of two major sectors in paid work—a primary market with lucrative, stable, and promising employment opportunities and a secondary market characterized by low wages, job instability, and poor conditions of service. Segmentation is attributed to factors such as existing customs and traditions, labor market unionization, and established legal codes.[19] Besides the shallow gender component, such analytical frameworks cannot be easily carried over into African contexts, the social relations and institutions of which do not neatly fit into Western situations.

Explanations of African women's experiences of schooling and paid work may be better understood in the context of Western feminist theories of the continent's development. Western feminists built their early conceptions of gender relations in Africa around the modernization debates of the 1950s and 1960s, which shaped the development initiatives of new African states. After the Second World War, many African states emerged from nationalist struggles for political independence as full-fledged nations with dreams of joining the ranks of developed nations in a few decades. New African states embraced the promises of modernization as the major thrust for a wave of economic, social, and political change that would catapult the newly independent states onto the global center stage. Following the works of notable proponents of modernization—such as Walt Rostow and Theodore Schultz[20]—African intellectuals and policymakers of the day enthusiastically welcomed the rapid incursion of Western institutions of education, commerce, law, and government on indigenous soil. The emergence of these institutions marked a break from what may be seen as an already existing social order to a new social arrangement that spelled out the nature and direction of Africa's development along Western lines.

But even as a number of African nations showed promise of economic boom in the 1960s and 1970s, women as a social group remained in the shadows. Women's subordinate status in the domestic sphere, poor representation in public decision making, and low participation in the modern economy signified in bold terms their vulnerable stance. Western liberal feminists who entered the development debate in the early 1970s argued that the situation of women in the third world, including Africa, was a result of their poor integration into the emerging structures of postcolonial society. They stressed the need for women's full integration into modern institutions of education, law, government, and commerce. As many contributors to the women in development (WID) debate argued, the development process drew from women's labor and expertise but denied them a meaningful participation and a share of the proceeds. Although the unfolding debate focused on the female majority outside the modern economy, advocates of women's education in particular called for the expansion of available facilities to raise women's profile in both the school system and paid employment. As many of these scholars pointed out, women's capacity to embrace the challenges of modern society depended seriously on the nature and level of training attained.[21]

But WID's injunctions were largely extrapolations of Western conceptions of gender roles. Without a solid set of arguments grounded in the challenges women faced in the new African economies, these injunctions found little support, especially among African scholars. WID adopted modernization as a development model, drawing largely from neoclassical generalizations of Western capitalist expansion. It analyzed the impact of capitalist expansion in Africa with respect to gender roles and the division of labor. But WID paid little attention to the nature and diversity of social formations that mediated the process and presented different scenarios for different female groups.[22] In the specific case of Igbo and Nigerian women, for instance, WID explanations did nothing to address the following questions: What roles did women of different classes, ethnic groups, and religions play in the precolonial era? In what ways did colonization and the transition into an independent state accommodate existing differences? How far did women go in their struggle for emancipation after all the decades of decolonization as a social group with common as well as conflicting loyalties? In mapping the vision for Africa's future, how should women's place in the present social setting be reconfigured?

Subsequent feminist attempts to articulate African women's experiences in contemporary society provided further insights but did not come close to presenting a comprehensive account. For instance, Marxist-based analyses, under the rubric of women and development (WAD) debates in the early 1980s, conceptualized African women's status in terms of their access to and control of material resources. WAD suggested a more critical reference point, but did not completely escape the WID trap. WAD traced African women's subordinate status in contemporary society to their lack of direct access to critical resources, particularly land. The female minority in the modern economy were portrayed as both victims and perpetrators of an oppressive relationship. Where women's mobility is largely linked to their relationship with the male ruling class, this line of thinking maintained, the privileged female minority must hold on to vested interests that are likely to reinforce already existing gender inequalities.[23] Although Marxist-based analyses of class challenge the homogenization of female experiences, other forms of social categorizations were hardly captured. For instance, very little groundwork had been done toward examining the facets of a modern economy, which provides women with direct access to capital and income through education and paid work yet denies them any reasonable autonomy to act as equal citizens with men. Similar to those offered by WID, these explanations did not examine the historical transition of women in African farming systems who managed effectively to balance their constrained access to land with a primary responsibility for children, while also asserting a reasonable degree of individual economic autonomy.

The gender and development (GAD) debates of the mid-1980s attempted to provide a broader theoretical forum that could capture the diversity of social relations in the developing world. With respect to African women, GAD argued for critical analyses that recognized other social categories mediating the relations of gender and class.

But again, the ensuing debates over GAD conceptualizations exposed the peculiarities of various social configurations that cannot be subsumed within a universal analytical framework. A number of cogent contributions to the debate strongly suggest that the categories of analyses employed by GAD, which defined social roles and institutions, did not make visible the essence and peculiarities of African cultural contexts.[24] It may therefore be argued that, despite the exposure feminist writings have brought to African women's concerns, the existing literature has yet to confront in any substantive manner many fundamental questions about their lives at present. The potential for teasing out these basic structural components as historically configured in particular social formations has been seriously curtailed by the massive homogenization of female experiences. This is a pattern feminist analyses appear to have repeated in most of the third world.[25]

The flurry of postmodern and postcolonial discourses since the mid-1980s has come to stress the importance of critical studies of specific social contexts for building theory grounded in lived experiences. In the same manner, my analysis of Igbo career women's lives in this book challenges the previous approaches that conflate African women in a monolithic category that ignores their diverse experiences. This contribution, like my previous work, joins the voices of many scholars in the field that increasingly stress the need for critical analyses of African women's experiences that reflect the "specificities of plural and localized knowledge bases."[26] This vision needs to be nurtured with the voices of female African scholars as a distinct source for the database we are building. Scholars in the field can no longer afford to circumvent questions about social locations and theoretical fit if we are serious about unraveling the complexities and diversity of female experiences in Africa.

Igbo Women and Nation Building: Precolonial Contexts

Any serious reexamination of African women's current status must include retracing the origins of their weak presence in the formal power structures of society. Such a reexamination cannot overlook the dynamics of gender relations in the nation-building process. Although borrowed from Western civilization, the term *nation building* does not bear an exact symmetry to any indigenous process. It is therefore no surprise that nation building as a process is often peddled around in analyses of African social transformation without any clear understanding of what it really represents. The obscurity is further deepened by the difficulties scholars face in their attempts at naming precolonial African societies as nations and states. A nation may well be viewed as a well-defined geographical territory housing people of the same ethnic group who share a common history, language, and culture, but the modern state is, in contrast, generally viewed as a configuration of different social origins with a shared experience of Western capitalist intrusion and colonization.[27] Of course, scholarly debates have shown that precolonial Africa did not always maintain clear compartments of ethnic groups as nations. These debates cite examples of cases where political conflicts, commerce, and slavery created multi-ethnic geographical territories.[28] Igboland, for instance, can only be loosely described as a precolonial nation. While many parts of Igboland may claim a common history, language, and culture, a great deal of diversity exists in the way particular groups live out these traits.[29] In fact, among the principal characteristics of Igboland often showcased are the plurality of language dialects and the non-centralization of social and political governance. Compared to the present administrative structures of African nations (with their provinces and local governments), Igboland was constituted (as was the case in most of precolonial Africa) by much smaller groups—extended families, clans, villages, and towns. These groups interacted as separate entities with others outside their boundaries. They engaged in political overtures and conflicts, established commercial linkages, and came together as individual units for social ceremonies (e.g., marriage and funeral ceremonies). Seats of royalty were often confined to these borders and did not usually extend beyond the specified boundaries. As the Igbo saying goes, "Igbo enwero eze" (The Igbos have no king).

Historically, the Igbo social structure existed with varying degrees of social hierarchy. This hierarchy included groups that could currently be accorded elite status. Like other Nigerian ethnic groups, the social stratification within Igbo culture set some people apart from the larger population and accorded them economic, social, and political rights and privileges denied to others. Families and clans in Igboland were generally placed in two major ranks: the privileged free-borns (*diala*) and the ostracized *osu* (or *ume*) people.[30] The ostracized status of the latter can be traced to certain cultural trespasses committed by either individuals or groups within their lineage in earlier times.[31] Others, who for similar reasons were either sacrificed or handed over to an oracle, lost their status as citizens. Osu status was then conferred on them and their entire lineage in future generations. Although social transformation has weakened the impact of the osu and diala labels on individuals and families in many parts of Igboland, they still have strong currency in other instances that may even affect the actions of indigenes living outside the culture. This is especially the case in decisions about the choice of marriage partners and the conferment of traditional titles in many Igbo towns and villages.[32]

Beyond the broad categories of diala and osu, individuals and families in Igboland gained access to elite groups through various channels, including membership (by descent or appointment) in the religious ranks or organizations, blood or marital ties to royalty, and as holders of traditional titles. In matters of ranking, women generally came second to men in Igboland. The patrilineal family structure in Igboland endorsed women's subordinate status to men, and many traditional elite categorizations reflected this gendered hierarchy. Indeed, women continue to live in this fundamentally subordinate position as daughters, sisters, wives, and mothers, often requiring some form of male presence to assert their place, views, and claims within Igbo culture. It seems, however, that the culture made considerable allowance for both complementary relations and independent spheres of influence for men and women.[33] For instance, the *ndi inyem* (women married into an extended family, village, or town) could also speak with a common voice in family or community matters. Similarly, the *umuada* (female members born into an extended family, village, or town) had significant influence among the male members of their kin. Also, the *iyom nwanyi* (a major traditional female title common in many parts of Igboland) was highly revered in precolonial times, although her influence was substantively restricted to women's decision-making forums.

Apart from these well-defined but limited spaces of privilege and power, Igbo structures of authority within the precolonial setting allowed women other social platforms from which to exert their presence. For example, within the smaller geographical entities held together by ties, however broad (e.g., natal, marital, royal ties), women seemed less vulnerable to the patriarchal onslaughts than to those that broader social relations might have generated. Moreover, gendered social groupings, such as the umuada and ndi inyem, provided political platforms for women to address their concerns outside the glare of patriarchal authority. Furthermore, when circumstances justified or demanded it, women assumed and were socially recognized with clearly defined male status. The positions held by *male daughters* and *female husbands* were vivid examples.[34] Further, in their role as guardians of social health (e.g., midwives and female herbalists), women could assume positions of power, trust, and respect within their communities. In fact, as native doctors and chief priestesses of specific oracles, a tiny group of Igbo women were looked on as mediators between humans and the spirit world. The authority that age commanded in many African cultures, including Igboland, may also have tempered, to some degree, women's vulnerable social status. Moreover, Igbo women's economic status as farmers and traders in the precolonial era gave them some degree of space to manage their own affairs without the patriarchal checks and penalties with which economic dependents must deal.

But whatever freedom women enjoyed in the precolonial era did not seem to permit any bold or outright confrontations with the underlying patriarchal principles on which social relations rested.[35] While the level of power and privilege women derived from these indigenous roles cannot easily be assessed in a postcolonial setting, some of these positions certainly allowed women entrance into social arenas where men and women alike listened to them as individuals in their own right. Unfortunately, these spheres of influence have greatly diminished in recent times. For women, the structures of power embedded in precolonial social groupings seem to have lost most of their currency in contemporary society. For both men and women, some of the gendered social groupings continue to function mainly at the village level. But men have found ways to translate their dominance into established positions in contemporary formal institutions. Women's power bases, in contrast, appear to be buried in the weakened indigenous structures that survived colonization and Western transformation.

Elite Women's Struggles in the Colonial Era: Nigerian and Igbo Contexts

Membership in traditional elite circles may have facilitated African men's accumulation of wealth with the gradual penetration of capitalist relations across the continent, but, as noted earlier, distinct positions within the traditional hierarchy did not directly translate themselves into the contemporary elite social structure in most of Africa. In terms of access to economic opportunities, social prestige, and political power in the contemporary setting, formal education played a crucial role in the formation of a male ruling class supported by the wider circle of male elites. In an emerging social order that alienated its people from the familiar systems of social governance, Africans turned to the new male elite, a petite bourgeoisie that was to guide them into political freedom. This privileged group, with their British cronies, shaped the dictates and contours of the new society, making allowances for indigenous incursions that posed no threats to either camp in the new structures of power. As Georges Nzongola-Ntalaja argues, "The new African nation was born in the struggle against colonialism. It had its class base in the African *petite-bourgeoisie*, the class to whose interests it corresponded within the colonized society."[36] In Nigeria, for example, Britain succeeded in its gradual consolidation of power among ethnic groups by making viable and safe compromises to accommodate the structures of local authority. The colonial regime recognized and promoted mainly those structures of local authority controlled by men. By the turn of the twentieth century, the colonial government had established a male ruling class of caretakers to carry its agenda well into the grass roots.[37] The new ruling class, a superior group, along with the larger body of educated Nigerian men (including civil servants and those employed in the smaller private sector), largely constituted the new elite. Despite the considerable heterogeneity within that group, members shared an interest in issues, places, and ideas beyond the awareness of the masses, "[which drew] them together and [gave] them common ground for understanding and fellowship."[38] While wealth, family connections and political influence afforded many entrance into the various colonial circles, formal education and paid work, especially the civil service, provided the greatest access. Those with European education not only swelled the ranks of the elite but also dictated the criteria for membership and promotion. This group, especially those who studied abroad, was further privileged, having come into close proximity to the Western lifestyle.[39]

Evidently, the colonial regime's working arrangement with an indigenous class of caretakers was anything but stable. Nevertheless, the relationship nurtured a reasonable degree of congeniality that provided a political platform for national independence struggles. The political stakes for both parties encouraged the establishment of some common ground for association. Over time, Nigerian male elites increasingly pressed their political claims to the colony as *sons of the soil*, asserting in distinct ways their indigenous identity (e.g., dress, speech, and composition of social circles).[40] British colonization invoked its own conventions of a patriarchal tradition, which in many instances found an ally with the indigenous culture. It created an indigenous elite group that placed men at the helm of affairs and was officially authorized to dictate the conditions for and limits to women's mobility.

In terms of access to economic resources, social prestige, and political power, therefore, women's status in the emerging elite society was already severely undermined at the outset. As in other African countries, the new Nigerian female elite followed a clearly different path from the male elite. The colonial administration neither recognized any traditional female power bases nor established effective alternatives. For instance, Christian values that spread through schooling aborted women's social autonomy both within and outside the domestic sphere.[41] Moreover, the expansion of exports drew men into international markets but left women unprepared to assume the responsibility for food farming.[42] Western commerce ignored any indigenous prerequisites that favored women and consolidated power in the hands of men, excluding Nigerian women at the initial stages of colonization from any significant involvement in the nation's industrial development. Thus, the current identification of Igbo and other African women as subsistence farmers and petty traders is seen as a logical translation of a precolonial design. Alternative visions for enhancing women's status may therefore be seen as deviations from a long-established norm.

Archival evidence, as well as oral history, clearly recognizes the modes of resistance that Nigerian women have employed from the very beginnings of British colonization, in the early 1900s. For instance, the Aba women's riots in 1929 set Igbo women on a collision path with colonial policymakers, who invaded their economic space of petty trading in the local markets with the imposition of taxes. Women in much of West Africa continued to command a strong presence in the open-air markets, where they sell their wares. Although the authority of African women's organizations—such as the Igbo women's organization Mikiri, which made rules pertaining to farm and market affairs—has weakened over time, African women continue to mobilize themselves under influential female leaders to negotiate with public authorities for their control over this economic space.[43]

Nigerian women also played a significant role in national liberation struggles with the emergence of prominent female leaders, such as

Margaret Ekpo in southeastern Nigeria and Funmilayo Ransom-kuti in western Nigeria, in the 1940s and 1950s. Drawing on gender-based modes of women's mobilization across the ethnic groups and a common set of concerns about their place and well-being in the emerging postcolonial state, these female politicians established important links with women even at the grassroots level. They succeeded in drawing women into the struggles for political independence and earned national recognition for their accomplishments. But their political achievements did not earn them a place beside men in the partisan structure of postindependence Nigeria.

African Women in Contemporary Society: Igbo and Nigerian Contexts

Nigerian women may have emerged from the colonial era as second-class citizens, but their current social status remains a highly contested terrain. In their struggle to establish themselves in contemporary society, they contend with various colonial incursions on their social, economic, and political domains. The constant political upheavals that have plagued Nigeria since the first republic have deflected, to some extent, national attention from the "woman question." For over forty years of Nigeria's postcolonial history, the political climate has been shaped by a strong military presence with short interludes of civilian intervention. In 1966 the new civilian regime, borne out of decades of nationalist struggles, was overthrown, and the ensuing political crisis resulted in a civil war between 1967 and 1970. The military regime that took up the challenge of uniting the nation after the civil war flourished in the oil boom of the early 1970s but was overthrown in 1975. In its wake a series of coups and countercoups ensued, until the installation of the next civilian regime in 1979. Four years later that regime was ousted by a wave of military dictatorships. However, the repressive economic and political climate they generated kept up the unrelenting pressure from viable male-dominated human rights groups backed by the international community, culminating in the inception of the incumbent civilian rule, in 1999.

Nigeria's history of political upheavals may have helped to dampen women's efforts to mobilize themselves toward the common goal of advancing their status. But it is also evident that the rich history of women's social movements in Nigeria found little resonance in formal politics since the installation of the first republic. Apparently, the vision of the first generation of female politicians to insert women's concerns into national political debates was not sustained in subsequent female social movements. Their voices very soon gave way to elitist women's organizations that pursued charitable causes but avoided any confrontations with a ruling class that gave them material support.[44] The National Council of Women's Societies (NCWS), for instance, charted the path for Nigerian women's status in formal politics and ushered them in as cheerleaders. Established in 1959 as an umbrella for women's organizations across the country and with regular subventions from the government, NCWS has steered a neutral course with respect to debates about and campaigns against women's marginalization. Lodged in the machinery of the male ruling class, the NCWS has for the most part left unchallenged the existing gender ideologies that leave little room for women's assertion of their citizenship in formal political arenas. For instance, NCWS promotes Nigerian women's primary roles and responsibilities as mothers and wives in contemporary elite society as the basic rationale for improving their access to formal education.[45] It seeks women's support in the informal sector by drawing national attention to their role as food producers whose international profile has been on the rise since the 1970s.[46] NCWS initiatives attract the expected support of male leaders because they rarely challenge the status quo.

Compared to the experiences of women in other African countries, the Nigerian case is hardly unique. In fact, the resilience shown by women across the continent in the struggle to improve their life situations has not been matched by the capacity and political will of the state to effect fundamental change. After three decades of research and praxis, the declining status of African women should be clearly evident to national leaders and policymakers. African governments are not unaware of women's growing profile in global movements and development agencies. The international women's movement is perhaps the most important trend that has steadily favored women's causes globally. The second wave of the feminist movement in the 1960s catapulted women's issues onto public platforms in North America and Europe. From the 1970s onward, women's concerns have moved into the global arena. This movement gave the international community some early glimpses of African women's plight and continues to provide a strong voice for women across the world to contest their status. African governments initially ignored, for the most part, the impact of global feminism on the home front, especially the heated intellectual discourses about African women's declining status it elicited. With time, and mostly as a result of pressure from the international community, many of these governments began to respond to the rise of women's organizations in their countries. From the mid-1970s and increasingly into the 1980s, African governments sought ways to integrate women into formal state machineries and political forums. For instance, during the United Nations' Decade for Women (1975–85), African male leaders unanimously voiced their concern for the well-being of women across the continent and gave official support to the major policy declarations that followed. Over the past three decades, most African countries have created state portfolios to address women's issues (over fifty countries in Africa have established state mechanisms).[47] But whatever initiatives followed, these gestures have had little or no salutary effect on African women's plight.

The weak responses to women's concerns in African countries should not come as a surprise to anyone in the field. African governments have devised ingenious ways of deflecting whatever threats they face within and outside national boundaries. This has been a viable strategy in dealing with women's movements. A good number of African countries have deftly worked out a pattern of "political showcasing," invalid gestures, empty declarations, and deliberate trivialization of women's efforts at social advancement—all in a bid to present a good example to the world outside. Such moves are vividly portrayed in their approach to policy making and implementation. For instance, in 1990 African leaders and UN agencies convened a meeting in Arusha, Tanzania, to address the economic, social, and political crises that characterized a decade of structural adjustment programs (SAPs) across Africa. The forum, which was dominated by men, brought together nongovernment organizations (NGOs), women's collectives, and youth groups to initiate strategies for mobilizing groups and individuals for Africa's economic recovery through democratic nation building. Of the twenty-four declarations arrived at by Arusha delegates, only two specifically addressed the conditions of African women's lives. These declarations stress, as the excerpts below indicate, African women's crucial role in national development. But, in practical terms, they do not address those facets of gender relations in the present social arrangement that stand in the way of women's advancement and full participation in nation building.

12. In view of the critical contribution made by women to African societies and economies and the extreme subordination and discrimination

suffered by women in Africa, it is ... [our] consensus ... that the attainment of equal rights by women in social, economic and political spheres must become a central feature of a democratic and participatory pattern of development.

14. In view of the vital and central role played by women in family well-being and maintenance, their special commitment to the survival, protection and development of children, as well as survival of society, and their important role in the process of Africa's recovery, ... special emphasis should be placed on eliminating biases ... with respect to the reduction of the burden on women.[48]

These declarations invite a number of questions: How can African women participate as equal partners with men when they are hardly represented (in their own voices) in the forums where the substantive issues of social progress are deliberated? How will the burdens they carry be reduced when African women are continually placed in the role of sustainers, holding forth in the shadows and picking up the pieces of social destruction wrought by male ruling classes? The declarations above assert the need to move African women into the center of political mobilization and socioeconomic development in African nations, but not as equal partners with men. African women are recognized only in terms of their contributions as wives, mothers, and food farmers. The crucial contributions, and the social spaces within which women are expected to make them, are still rigidly tied to their subsistence roles. Narrowly defined, these roles reinforce the rigid social boundaries already drawn for women. Obviously, whatever social specifications these roles may have carried in the indigenous culture cannot be reproduced at present with certainty. But in their current forms they embrace obligations and boundaries that restrict women's entrance to the very public arenas in which African leaders seek to move them. Thus, women's entrance into contemporary public arenas remains selective, with existing openings allowing very limited access. For example, women enter the local markets with greater ease as petty traders rather than as commercial wholesalers. They are welcomed into formal political settings as cheerleaders on the sidelines rather than contestants with men. Africa's male leaders make empty promises that acknowledge the burdens women carry but are not prepared to confront the relations of gender that affirm this state of affairs. They echo in the right forums their strong intent to improve the situation, but are not prepared to tackle the structural and ideological barriers that militate against women's social mobility. More recent policy documents, such as the African Plan for Action (1995) and the New Partnership for Africa's Development in the twenty-first century (NEPAD, 2001), suggest a definite change in direction by African leaders but have yet to be followed up with the necessary directives for action.[49]

The wave of democratization that has been sweeping across Africa since the late 1980s seems to have added some momentum to women's mobilization. What appears to be emerging as fairly open political spaces in many African countries is propelling women's groups into public arenas where they can challenge the existing conservative political climate and assert women's political demands.[50] But the structure of public governance in Africa remains undeveloped, with women at the margins. The process, a renowned critic argues, is inherently crippled by the "inability of such new 'popular' governments to take full control of the state, to set up structures to mediate and contain opposition and contradictions, and to meet, at the very least, some of the immediate expectations of the electorate," a common scenario that "can set a process of rapid de-legitimization in motion."[51] Following a precedent set before the so-called democratic wave, African women's international profile continues to provide states with a mirror in which to polish their image.[52] As Amina Mama aptly puts it, "African governments have found it expedient to exploit the gender question so as to receive economic aid in an international climate that has become increasingly sympathetic towards women's demands for equality. The fact is that, despite the virtual absence of mass-based women's movements in most African countries, the majority of African states have, for one reason or another, begun to profess a gender politics that is couched in terms of encouraging women's integration into development."[53] Other critiques of this emerging gender politics clearly show that many African governments have, over the past three decades, succeeded in thwarting the efforts of women's organizations in the continent. In many cases, these governments either infiltrate the movements or create their own women's organizations to weaken the feminist surge. Many African states have installed their own brands of "state feminism," which are merely state-directed processes seemingly designed to advance women's status by integrating them into government machineries and the political system.[54] Obviously, the creation of spaces for women in public governance has neither expanded their sphere of collective action nor exerted much pressure on the state. If anything, state feminism in Africa has suppressed the voices of independent women's organizations outside its political grip. In most cases, Africa's governments, including the military regimes, are using these state-directed reforms to improve their human rights image with Western donors, while silencing the progressive elements within the women's movement in their countries.

State feminism in Africa appears to have bred a social climate in which African women are forced to build their political platforms strictly within the confines of state privilege. Many political regimes have substituted established women's machineries in the urban centers for new ones run by female consorts of men in power. As Lisa Aubrey points out in the case of Ghana and Kenya, state feminism "serves ultimately to maintain the status quo of the public life of politics, and to repress women's engagement in civil society."[55] In Nigeria, the two most recent military governments introduced the now common pattern of what I refer to as the first lady syndrome.[56] Using the offices of the first lady at the national, state, and local government levels, the Babangida (1985–93) and Abacha (1994–98) regimes carved out a female populist voice. These regimes encouraged the formation of cliques of followers for the first lady at the three levels of government. Using fund-raisers, exhibitions, and political rallies, these groups of highly privileged ladies built a massive support base for the office of the first lady. They mobilized other women both within their social circles and at the grassroots level to promote the Better Life Program for the Rural Woman (BLP), initiated by the first lady, Maryam Babangida. The BLP was managed by the wives of state governors and local government chairmen.[57] The BLP gave the wives of the military rank and file great latitude in mobilizing women, even at the grassroots level, but silenced any forces resistant to its message.[58] Over time, the first lady and her cliques took over the official administration of women's affairs in Nigeria. Gradually, however, the first lady's portfolio faced mounting pressure from radical groups at the edges of civil society over questions of efficiency and the ethics of its existence.[59] In response to this state of affairs, the civilian regime of President Olusegun Obasanjo, instituted in 1999, promised to reverse the trend. But five years into its inception, the regime has yet to dismantle the female bureaucracy it inherited. Obasanjo's government may have remodeled the focus and scope of the first lady's portfolio, but her female entourage at local, state, and federal levels continues to serve as an effective populist voice in a harsh economic climate.[60] This entourage not only still enjoys the economic support of the first lady but has credentials that command great currency with the larger community of women who are struggling for their daily bread.

The prominent radical organization Women in Nigeria (WIN), which could have provided a forceful opposition to the first lady syndrome, currently lacks the nationwide support for establishing its platform. Along with other women's organizations across Africa, WIN rode on the waves of third world women's rising profile since the UN Decade for Women (1975–85). The decade spurred a global discourse on women's experiences and progress compared to men, and generated policy analyses that demanded responses from national governments and the international community. But after three decades of social discourse and policy responses, women's organizations in Africa, such as WIN, are yet to generate a viable movement to fight their causes. Retracing the steps of female political heroes of the first republic, WIN attempts to identify with the female majority outside elite circles. The organization challenges the basis for Nigerian women's subordinate status within and outside the home, demanding a platform to voice women's concerns in national political debates. But WIN faces at least one major barrier. It is not socially located in any way to place Nigerian women in the center of national politics and public decision making. If the success attained by women in a number of African and Latin American countries provides any indication, women's organizations like WIN must command the broad membership (at national or state levels) required to negotiate their support for particular candidates and regimes.

WIN's militant stance is therefore dampened by the absence of coherent and unified women's movements that can be harnessed under a strong leadership capable of making political demands. The historically low female participation in schooling and paid work, coupled with the restrictive conditions for elite membership since the first republic, has widened the gap between an urban female middle class and their less privileged sisters in the rural and urban areas. The "elite" divide has, over time, been exacerbated by ethnic and religious tensions that Nigerian women might have successfully dealt with or circumvented in previous times. In addition, prevailing gender ideologies continue to project women's demands, mostly in their capacity as wives and mothers. Unlike in a number of Latin American countries, existing conservative gender ideologies in Nigeria have not so far been creatively deployed to further women's political causes. These gender ideologies inevitably modify women's claims to citizenship and weaken the premise for any assertions of gender equality. Not surprisingly, Nigerian women's representation in politics and urban governance has remained woefully low.[61] The decades of economic decline and political upheaval now make the task of mobilizing Nigerian women even more challenging.

This state of affairs challenges the authenticity of African democratic transitions, especially their viability in what many critics consider potentially unworkable situations. Democratic transitions in Latin America, in contrast, appear to have provided important political openings for women. In countries like Turkey and Chile women have managed to build very strong platforms on which to contest their marginalized social status.[62] The achievements of women in Latin America, however, remain a far cry from those made in the African context. Although the magnitude of political impact has yet to be fully assessed, many scholars watch with keen interest the relatively new developments in southern Africa. Women's organizations in southern Africa (especially South Africa) appear to be breaking through the structures of political patronage to make their voices heard.[63] The majority of these organizations are mobilizing African women around broader causes of social emancipation (education, legal rights, and formal employment), with the help of supportive NGOs (local and foreign). The entrance of NGOs into formal politics in this region differs significantly from the conventional "women's arm" of political parties, which rests heavily on established channels of partisan patronage. But as Aubrey points out, African women tend to be attracted to NGOs not necessarily as political platforms to air their grievances but as sources of material assistance. Aubrey argues that many elite African women and, to a greater degree, their less privileged sisters in urban and rural settings have yet to enter the arena of formal politics as full-fledged participants. Many of them shun formal political engagements, either to avoid threatening confrontations with the patriarchal state or even as a response to the paternal state that no longer dispenses favors.[64]

Whatever progressive trends have been identified in this region (however limited their political prospects), they have yet to emerge in the Nigerian political scene. Nigerian women remain deadlocked in the informal sector, with restricted access to economic opportunities in the formal capitalist sector. Education and paid work still constitute the major pathways to social mobility. However, these assets, especially for women, remain only prerequisites for accessing available opportunities. Placed in the context of Nigeria and Africa's history of development, the stories of Igbo career women in this volume resonate with many of the challenges discussed above. But more important, their experiences provide entrance into a deeper critical analysis of the specificities of one social setting.

African Women in a Specific Context: Igbo Career Women

I have chosen to focus on highly educated women, perhaps the most privileged among Nigerian women, because in their society's eyes they are best positioned to tap the full potential of formal education. They have managed to avoid the disfunctionalities associated with low-level and poor-quality female education in Africa. Given the declining employment opportunities in the formal sector, highly educated women are the only group left to reap most of the benefits associated with schooling.[65] These women's experiences also expose the challenges that even privileged elite women must grapple with in order to gain and maintain a niche in contemporary society. For a group regarded as a privileged minority, their struggles have important implications for the welfare of the larger female population, especially the younger generation.

As I noted earlier, one of the most important factors that attracted me to qualitative research was the desire to produce an impressive knowledge base that reveals the diversity of African womanhood, particularly the peculiarities associated with that diversity. I want to provide more than mere descriptions of who African women are and what they do in comparison to their Western counterparts. I firmly argue for critical investigations of African womanhood that interrogate their experiences within the context of the social structures that shape their lives. Such investigations would in many cases require a hands-on familiarity with these structures that other scholars cannot easily acquire by simply spending weeks and months in the field. In this respect, studies of Igbo and other African women remain incomplete without any appreciable contributions from the indigenes. As Claire Robertson admits, "Culturally specific knowledge is essential, and findings often cannot be generalized cross-culturally or across classes. Subjective consciousness is very difficult for outsiders (no matter how well-intentioned) to explore effectively. With more African women scholars becoming interested in studying African women, we may gain more knowledge in these areas."[66]

Many African female scholars would agree with Robertson, but with some reservations. I, for one, would argue that "culturally specific knowledge" is not merely essential but should remain the major defining element of this scholarship. A good number of African scholars make the point that African women's status has already been defined in relation to that of Western women as the norm. They argue that the problem is not merely a question of welcoming African female scholars into the field but also that of restructuring the unequal relations in the creation of feminist knowledge.[67] Feminist scholarship cannot afford to ignore the voices of scholars who from their own social location also help to create the experiential base for its investigations.

Igbo women stood out to me as the group to work with because my own experiences are not far removed from theirs. It was convenient for me to gain access and easily relate to women of similar social origins and status. Apart from chance meetings, I got in touch with them through friends and family relatives (a sister-in-law who is a school teacher, an old family friend who is a bank manager, or "that woman who lives in Papa Okeys's building"). As an Igbo woman, my familiarity with the culture, language, and traditions of my people provided me with crucial insights that otherwise could not be assessed. I was not merely a scholar in search of answers, but a *daughter of the soil* who could easily immerse herself in a familiar cultural milieu. This immersion was not simply a matter of walking into these women's lives with a pen and notebook. Arriving from "abroad" to begin my investigation, I knew I had to make certain changes with regard to what I said, did, and wore in order to blend in with the populace. I was familiar with the nuances of Igbo dialects, which are replete with bodily expressions of various kinds. I could also follow with ease the common shifts from one language or dialect to another. In a multilingual anglophone country such as Nigeria, English is spoken among people from every ethnic group, and there are also several dialects of indigenous languages. In a city like Enugu, where people of different ethnic and social backgrounds congregate, the *pidgin*, which combines English with indigenous expressions, is commonly used in public places, such as the local markets and bus stations. During our sessions the women meandered from one language or dialect to another. I had no problem following the trend of our discussions.

My access to Igbo culture and society also enabled me to keep track of the fluid use of Igbo and English terms by these career women to describe family relations such as brother, cousin, and sister-in-law; decipher the indiscriminate use of "he" and "she," a direct transliteration from the nongendered Igbo equivalent "o"; and follow the use of acronyms for places, events, and persons. Interviewees' sentences were often open-ended, and I knew that my interrupting at certain times would not be considered rude. I just had to recognize the right moment to barge in. At various times our discussions veered into unrelated topics such as the 1967–70 civil war and the first lady's wardrobe. Some degree of diplomacy was required to bring the interview back on course.

Enugu, the city where the research was carried out, was originally the capital of eastern Nigeria, which at present includes about five different states. Given its historical importance, Enugu remains one of the most promising spots for job seekers in Igboland and beyond. Although subsequent updates of the data, including a number of research trips to Nigeria between 1997 and 1999, were needed for the publication of this volume, the voices emerging from its pages belong to eighteen female university graduates in paid employment who volunteered for in-depth interviews between August 1991 and March 1992. I sought to reflect the existing female presentation in the formal sector by selecting twelve civil servants, including eight secondary school teachers. The six private-sector employees consisted of two accountants, three lawyers, and an economist. At the time of the interview, twelve of the women were married with children, while six were single. To reflect the proper historical and economic contexts, I selected women with more than ten years' working experience— whose educational training and employment status were undoubtedly shaped by the oil boom—and those with less than ten years' working experience, who joined the labor force in the postboom era.[68] Interviews with individual women were largely unstructured. These interviews explored in considerable detail their educational background, work history, and family life. Moreover, they identified the significant factors in their lived experience that had affected the translation of their educational training into socioeconomic status. (The format of the interviews can be found in the appendix.)

I also collected and analyzed the relevant official records and background data that were needed to place these women's experiences within a larger social context. This information, including national and international statistical surveys, was obtained from various institutions, including federal and state government ministries; the Women's Research and Documentation Center (WORDOC) at the University of Ibadan; the Nigerian Institute of Social and Economic Research (NISER) Library at Ojoo, Ibadan; the Nigerian Law School; and professional organizations for accountants, lawyers, medical doctors, architects, and teachers. Interviews were also held with the relevant personnel in these institutions. In-depth archival research on Nigerian women was carried out at the Library of Congress in Washington, D.C.

2

Gender Relations in Family and Society

The Crystallization of an Elite Female Class

African women entered the new society of colonial elites as the house-wives of civil servants and businessmen and therefore built their lives around marriage, family, and the household.[1] From these early begin-nings, they gradually acquired their identity as elite women, strug-gling to find their place in a new social order. In the case of Nigeria the female elite "class" had crystallized by the 1940s, when formal colonial rule was already in its fourth decade.

Marriage and Family among Colonial Elites: Igbo Women in the Nigerian Context

Early literature on Africa's colonial history inserted images of elite women as a privileged group whose status as the housewives of male breadwinners shaded them from the plight of their sisters outside the formal sector.[2] In fact, the few writings that specifically investigated the domestication of African women in the early stages of British colonization created the impression that a female elite enjoyed a life of blissful leisure, with a large pool of cheap domestic labor at her dis-posal. Janet Bujra, for instance, describes this experience in vivid terms: "In Africa, petty bourgeois wives seem rarely to be immersed in domestic concerns. To begin with, they almost universally em-ploy domestic servants to carry out all the dirty work of the house-hold, and to nurse and tend young children. . . . To some extent, this devolution of responsibility allows petty bourgeois wives more leisure to act as ornaments to their husband's success . . . [and to] utilize paid domestic help in order to free themselves to work in high-income white-collar or professional jobs."[3] Of course, Bujra's claims have been variously contested. Most of her critics argue that her assertions generalize, to a great extent, the experiences of elite African women in both time and space. In her historical review of Nigerian women's involvement in domestic and paid work, for instance, Jane Parpart insists that, although many elite women of the nineteenth century were not formally employed, "they certainly worked hard managing their households."[4] By the beginning of the twentieth century, she explains, many elite wives had to find ways to supplement household income because their husbands were not fully supporting them. But despite the evidence provided by critics such as Parpart, enviable impressions of elite African women as a highly privileged group survived well beyond the colonial era.[5]

The burden of oppression carried by rural African women and urban petty traders had never been in question. But interpretations of elite women's lives, especially in the colonial era, often generate controversy, rendering any notion of a critical assessment at best elusive. In my view, this controversy is well founded because scholars in the field have lumped together a group that may share certain experiences, but that evidence significant diversity across time and space. The debate, in effect, conflated the experiences of different groups of women under the nebulous term *elite women.* The experiences of women who speak in this volume clearly suggest that this term needs to be interrogated both in terms of the different groups who share the label and changes in their experiences over time.

For the most part, entrance into the elite circle was not something any group of African women was adequately prepared to embrace. Both indigenous and Western values (some of which rest on Judeo-Christian tenets) shaped the social expectations attached to the roles prescribed for them. In fact, the descriptions of social expectations by Igbo career women in subsequent chapters, as well as their varied responses to them, clearly reflect the foreign influence on Igbo culture.[6] Colonial influence tore through the social, political, and economic life threads that held precolonial societies together. However, it allowed the male elite to negotiate, to some degree, the translation of indigenous patriarchy into the new society. Nigerian women, Kristin Mann notes, were thrust into a new subordinate role in the emerging elite society by forces outside their control. She points to the social changes sweeping across West Africa at the turn of the twentieth century: "Colonial rule and the growth of international trade adversely affected [women's] . . . status. . . . The expansion of trade created new opportunities for women in commerce, but in most places men took the lead in the import-export business and women engaged in petty retailing or local commerce. Colonial governments ignored or failed to see women's political roles and undermined their political influence. . . . Christianity and Western education spread ideologies that undermined women's autonomy and economic independence."[7]

As housewives and mothers, the loss of economic autonomy in the initial stages of the colonial transition forced elite women across Africa to campaign for vocational education. Igbo women's economic welfare and that of their children depended for the most part on proceeds from farming and trading. Access to farmlands was linked to women's relationship to men as daughters, sisters, and wives. In Igboland at the time, women's farming activities revolved around the production of family staples, such as cassava and vegetables, while men, were responsible for status crops, notably yam.[8] As Ifeyinwa Iweriabor explains, "It was through the effort of their [women's] labour that they . . . supported the man [husband] and themselves. It was the fruit of the sweat of their labour that constituted the surplus out of which the man paid them back by 'providing' shelter and maintenance. It was also the only way for women (with the exception of a few eccentrics or beloved daughters of son-less fathers) to have access to shelter and a means of livelihood since carefully designed, revered and guarded inheritance laws dispossessed females of land."[9] Although the division of labor came with strict conditions for women, it provided both economic support and a measure of bargaining power for them. Elite Igbo women's new status as housewives within elite circles made them full economic dependents to male breadwinners with little or no option of acquiring income and managing their own money.

Another major change that significantly affected elite women's lives was the clear urban-rural separation. Life in the townships kept women away from and greatly weakened the already established social network of extended families that served as a crucial support base. Even though this social network presented its own challenges, the Igbo wife was expected to anticipate and prepare herself for the role into which she was stepping. The husband's extended family, in particular, potentially presented threats that any Igbo wife had to respond to with wisdom and skill developed over time. While the separation by distance, in a sense, protects the elite wife from some of these threats, she still needed some bargaining chips to negotiate her place within the nuclear unit. The rural–urban divide, in addition, made the village forums for women's associations inaccessible to elite women. Not only were they separated by distance from groups that had, in the past, provided crucial support but their concerns also became largely irrelevant to the challenges that village women faced. Over time, elite women were forced to develop their own advocacy forums in order to survive in a new environment.

Changes in the marriage institution itself constitute one of the most important elements of the colonial transition.[10] Whether polygamous or monogamous, marriage in precolonial Igboland, and to a large extent in contemporary society, was not designed to be a nuclear affair. Despite the tensions that came with this relationship between nuclear and extended families, married couples were expected to draw from many sources of love and support. The Western nuclear model circumvented these sources to establish a firm entity built mainly on the commitment of a married couple. Monogamy in elite circles created a dilemma for couples whose signatures on dotted lines upheld a biblical affirmation they could not uphold: "a man will leave his father and mother and be united to his wife and they will become one flesh."[11] In the African sense, it seemed to read a little differently: "A man and woman, their extended families, and possibly a cowife or more, if the occasion warrants, must unite and mobilize their efforts and resources to contain the support and conflicts this union embraces." Married couples were expected to establish a nuclear unit with certain ties to the extended family they were expected to nurture.

The hybridization of two social orders allowed the incursion of different versions of marital partnership, none of which improved women's status as partners. Even as Christian missionaries persistently showcased "Western" monogamy as the superior model, polygamy also remained widely accepted. Although many elite men shunned traditional polygamy, they tended to be attracted to its pervasive incursions into the newly hybridized social order, which defied both missionary and colonial assaults. The successive legal ordinances introduced to regulate the practice failed to produce any remarkable results in women's favor.[12] The courts since the colonial era have had to contend with the challenges of reconciling English law with customary law within ethnic groups. Court officials were directed to "recognize native law and custom when not repugnant to natural justice and humanity or incompatible with any ordinance, especially in matters relating to marriage."[13] But without any clear guidelines for such interpretations, legal amendments were often applied in an ad hoc manner. The different marriage customs of the various ethnic groups in Nigeria made even more difficult any attempts to find a set of common legal codes. More important, the imposition of Western legal dictates over indigenous law, a relationship that was hardly symmetric but in many ways symbiotic, made it possible for the ruling class to inscribe patriarchal continuities that served men's interest without any of the indigenous checks and balances that protected women. For instance, the first ordinance, enacted in 1863, endorsed Christian marriage but made no provisions for women's inheritance rights and strict monogamy between the parties. Marriage under this ordinance placed elite women in what seemed, to their counterparts outside the circles, an enviable status but provided little if any security for women in cases of divorce, separation, or the death of a spouse. This ordinance was replaced by the marriage act of 1884, which was in large part a response to early Christian missionaries' opposition to polygamy and child marriage.[14] In principle the ordinance strengthened the legal status of elite wives by enshrining strict monogamy with provisions for divorce and inheritance. But many elite men evaded monogamous commitments. They found sufficient loopholes in the double standard of customary law and Victorian attitudes to marriage, especially where both systems affirmed women's subordinate status in marriage and their moral responsibility to society. Strict monogamy remained a dream partly because it was difficult to reconcile ordinance provisions with a multiplicity of customary laws from the many ethnic groups. Moreover, the ad hoc manner in which cases were settled established very little precedence for any subsequent critical reviews.[15]

What emerged in the postcolonial setting was a variety of male-female relationships with both traditional and modern features. These varied configurations can be seen as a response to the challenges of an emerging social order that demanded the coexistence of old and new cultural values. Like other African cultures, the Igbos practiced both polygamy and monogamy. But marriage in whatever form was not simply an individual decision but invited other forms of association, which served as support bases for couples. Not only did men and women, married or single, find significant support within the extended family, but other associations based on gender, age, and, in many cases, economic cooperation equally offered crucial support in an environment where individuality provided little basis for communal life. Community members invested their time and resources in these other forms of association, expanding their social worth and sphere of operation beyond marriage. In contrast, the colonial model distanced monogamy from its indigenous cultural roots and support bases, and it was therefore practiced with considerable modifications to suit local conditions. Individuals and groups responded to these challenges depending on their specific circumstances. For instance, while in the Islamic north both culture and religion reinforced polygamy, the Christian south proved a little more receptive to monogamous unions in new elite circles. Both groups practiced monogamy, but not strictly according to Western prescriptions. These prescriptions were accepted only in cases where it remained compatible with social norms that legitimized men's privileges over women's. Many felt, for instance, that polygamy could provide a ready solution for childless monogamy. Moreover, the need for a male heir to carry on the family lineage was seen to justify the need to take another wife.[16] The social trends of the time also helped to promote polygamy in the new elite circles. Most important among these trends was the emergence of a wealthy group of male elites who had the financial means to acquire more wives.

Evidently, the introduction of Western monogamy greatly weakened the checks and balances embedded in indigenous models. Historical evidence clearly showed that most female elites found strict monogamy to be a better alternative to both traditional polygamy and marriage in hybridized forms. They criticized the perverse reproductions of both indigenous and Western dictates that govern marriage in elite circles. Their statutory claims on divorce as elite wives, for instance, had little cultural backing where women were expected to guard their own separate means of generating income. Moreover, legal provisions for widows were left at men's discretion since statutory law upheld a widow's rights to one third of her husband's estate and the rest to her children, only if the husband died without making any provisions for the management of his estate. Where a widow had no support from her children or natal family for intervention, these provisions could be successfully contested by her husband's people.

Similarly, statutory law granted custody to the spouse better placed to care for the children, but most Nigerian cultures usually allowed men to decide who their children should live with (e.g., parents, sisters, aunties) and where. Since these cultures were predominantly patrilineal, the weight of tradition as reconstituted in a colonial setting often overruled the dictates of statutory law, shifting the verdict in men's favor.[17] This was also in an era when very few Nigerian women could muster the political and economic savvy to confront the status quo.

It is important to note, however, that for elite women the possibility of ending up in polygamous unions was not particularly a looming threat. These women faced the more common and pervasive threat of *polygamous incursions*. Polygamous incursions are men's extramarital relationships that do not constitute legitimate unions. These relationships can range from one-night stands to an affair with a much younger woman to a steady relationship with a mature mistress. Such relationships were certainly not peculiar to African cultures. But the strong presence of polygamy, a legitimate cultural institution, allowed them to flourish unchecked. Society treated men's extramarital affairs with much complacency, and women were forced to accept them as part of the African man's excesses, which Christianity and Western influence could not eradicate. Existing studies on polygamy appear to ignore the myriad of male-female relationships that polygamy as an institution tends to reinforce. These studies tend to focus mainly on the polygamous marriage unions.[18]

Extended family ties also greatly influenced the gender relations of power within elite households. The common pattern of women's absorption into a husband's extended family persisted even as the traditional bases they previously drew upon were increasingly being eroded. In customary terms, the elite wife was still considered a wife to all members of her husband's (immediate and extended) family, whose loyalty goes first to the daughters in their lineage. As in most of Africa, married women in Nigerian ethnic groups maintained very strong links with their natal family. Although such ties did not necessarily challenge established gender hierarchies and privileges, they provided some checks and balances that reduced women's vulnerability in marriage.[19] On the whole, marriage ordinances promulgated since colonial times significantly weakened the status of customary marriage without establishing any firm conditions for women's recognition and security in statutory marriage. Subsequent changes in family law, while safeguarding a women's right to be provided for, did not particularly strengthen their property rights in marriage as wives. The 1965 Estate Law, for instance, stipulates, "If the court on an application by or on behalf of a dependant is of the opinion that the disposition of the deceased's estate affected by his will or the law relating to intestacy is not such as to make reasonable provision for the maintenance of that dependant, the court may order that such reasonable provisions as the court thinks fit be paid out of the deceased's estate."[20]

This provision certainly lent more weight to the cultural view of family property ownership and widened the range of dependents who can claim "family" membership. Research shows that even when the will is in her favor, a widow may lose most of her inheritance to her husband's relatives. Often, the ordeal of going through the courts compels less resilient women to seek settlement through the usual extended family channels.[21] In the end, marriage and family life in elite circles incorporated an assortment of indigenous and foreign features, creating patriarchal continuities and contradictions. Despite the modifications introduced, English law remained poorly equipped to either replace or find a common ground with customary law.[22]

The experiences of Igbo career women in this book show that the hybridized social order in specific African settings continues to present hard choices for women. Women retain their subordinate status without the indigenous balance that accommodated their engagement in economic activities. The social stigma attached to being single continues to heighten the pressure to obtain the social credential of the title Mrs. Marriage and procreation still constitute the major basis for social organization and interaction, and both men and women are expected to fit into their assigned roles. But for women the premium placed on getting married virtually precluded other forms of social success. This premium rose as a woman got older. When it came to procreation, it did not matter what kind of union a woman found herself in. Her assumed inability to bear children could readily jeopardize her marital status and even material well-being. Thus, many elite women placed marriage at the top of their priority list, with hopes of strengthening it with children. Those who planned to pursue careers struggled to balance new aspirations with the rigid responsibilities inscribed into their primary roles as housewives, mothers, and companions.[23]

Nevertheless, women made choices depending on their personal circumstances. In the Nigerian case, the majority of elite women made considerable adjustments in their career to accommodate their domestic obligations. But archival records document many cases of women in colonial Lagos who were well established in their career before marriage.[24] Obviously, what became the status quo across the continent embedded both patriarchal continuities and contradictions. The 1947 memorandum on education in Africa, for instance, observed "a well marked tendency on the part of . . . [African women] who have passed through secondary school and . . . [seen] the prospects of a career to defer marriage and flout parental and family wishes on the subject."[25] Again, archival records reveal similar moves by Nigerian women since the colonial era.[26] Even in contemporary society they continue to wrestle with the challenges of juggling marriage and career demands.

The hybridized social order also reconfigured society's construction of morality, especially for women. On the one hand, elite Nigerian women were expected to embrace Western notions of good homemaking and sound morals, many of which found a perverse harmony with indigenous values. On the other hand, intractable myths and expectations associated with tradition often forced women to comply with the status quo. In the end, the hybridized order narrowed elite Nigerian women's opportunities for social mobility. In a new social arrangement where success hinged on male-female competition rather than cooperation, the dictates of culture, especially with respect to female chastity and fertility, kept many ambitious women from competing with their male counterparts. The impression was soon created that educated women might not easily defer to their husbands. There was also the popular belief that women who postponed marriage in order to further their education were prone to sexual immorality. Although they were never formally expressed, these beliefs gained considerable currency in elite social circles. They also discouraged many parents outside the elite circles from sending their female children to school. Apparently, the emerging ruling class was not to welcome a group of educational professionals that threatened their dominant position.[27] It found a solid base of patriarchal continuities to anchor newly revised gender expectations for women in the elite society. In many cases, Nigerian men advocated new cultural standards that also found a close ally in the Victorian ideals of womanhood promoted by the missions. For instance, Okechukwu Ikejiani, a leading national figure in the years after independence, criticizes what he sees as misplaced ambition by Nigerian women:

A Nigerian housewife who cannot bake a light loaf of bread or prepare a good dish or soup that is tasty, or happily employ her odd moments with a needle, or darn the stockings of her husband, and who relies on servants and cooks to carry out all the routine of the house, may be a very charming lady; she may keep her husband and friends posted about the new novels and new articles in the [newspapers]; she may try to make up for her serious shortcomings by teaching in a school or being a nursing-sister or secretary-typist; she may be a good writer in the columns of our papers and participate actively in many of the social and political courses of the day, but she is an inefficient housewife and home-maker, and today in Nigeria it is not given to many to make up for that. The lack of efficient housewives is as serious as the dearth of efficient mechanics.[28]

In cursory terms, Ikejiani's claims did not seem to find much resonance in a cultural setting where women have always engaged in economic activities to support the family. Moreover, the domestic "obligations" on which he based his assessment of Nigerian women's efficiency as housewives and homemakers also appeared to be far removed from indigenous specifications. But in critical terms, Ikejiani's arguments could be justified in terms of the broad social expectations of marriage and motherhood crucial to the very survival and growth of African societies. Indeed, these expectations often embraced the totality of women's visions in the sense that there was little demarcation between the domestic and public spheres in the indigenous setting to create conflicting extradomestic ambitions. As noted earlier, even the seemingly extradomestic roles in Igboland, such as chief priestess or herbalist, helped to nurture the social organization of community life. For Igbo women, the new elite arrangement neither accommodated the indigenous constructions of their domestic roles nor provided a good support base for the new gender roles it created.

Ikejiani's criticisms, however, should be directed not at Nigerian women but at the patriarchal continuities and contradictions of a hybridized social order that presented more dilemmas for women than men. In the Igbo context, for instance, the model of marriage and family life Ikejiani promoted certainly broke ranks with Igbo culture and traditions at various junctures. For example, it left women in a vulnerable economic status without any legitimate base to question their dependency on the male breadwinner. Evidently, elite men, such as Ikejiani, forcefully espoused those patriarchal ideals (such as women's limited access to the public sphere and status as companions to male elites) that legitimized their claims to a dominant status within and outside the home. They conveniently left behind certain aspects of indigenous culture that could question this dominance.

Obviously, elite women were well aware of the contradictions of the legal dictates they lived under and in many cases found themselves in circumstances that necessitated similar moves. In the early stages of colonial rule many of them promoted some aspects of the hybridized social arrangement that favored them.[29] For instance, many leading society ladies of the Lagos colony strongly opposed the recognition of marriage under native law and custom in colonial circles because they felt that elite men could easily exploit the potential liberty to marry more wives. The hybridized legal system, they recognized, placed more weight on statutory rather than customary marriage. But this was only in principle. In a social order where the cultural safeguards that demanded some degree of accountability from both partners were quickly eroding, they repeatedly made a case for tightening the loose ends already appearing in the new system. While customary law under the new social arrangement retained women's freedom to walk out of an unsatisfactory marriage, there was still virtually no security in terms of widely established legal procedures for settlement with regard to divorce, separation, or death of a male spouse, or for child custody. These guarantees could only be sought (and might not necessarily be obtained) under British legal statutes. Hence, society ladies, especially those who studied abroad, advocated the "pure" Western model rather than the colonial hybrid, which they felt took root on indigenous soil in a form they did not desire.[30] Their stance was certainly not a rejection of an indigenous alternative. It was rather a clear recognition of and response to its weak base in a hybridized social order that did not confer any appreciable status on women.

Based on the experiences of Nigerian and Igbo women, it is safe to argue that with respect to marriage and family life, both indigenous and Western values and dictates helped to further marginalize women's status. Indeed, the robust germination of British sexist values on indigenous African soil was hardly an accident, given the huge insertions of alleged indigenous patterns. The crystallization of female elite with clearly defined features in colonies, such as Nigeria, was not entirely a British creation but one that in many ways was nurtured by an already existing indigenous social arrangement. Cultural practices and norms of the indigenous ruling class came to reinforce (or, in some cases, alter) Western racism and sexism. Colonization may have introduced gender stereotypes foreign to the local cultures, but they found a fertile ground to flourish well beyond the colonial era. These hybridizations of indigenous and Western cultural dictates cannot be simplistically viewed as mere collusions between two male ruling classes to set the boundaries of operation for an emerging female "class." The patriarchal continuities and contradictions of the newly hybridized social order must also be analyzed as contestations of power among social groups that produced their own contradictions as dynamic responses to the challenges of social transformation. The contemporary relations of gender, as portrayed in literature, as well in the stories Igbo career women tell, portray vivid glimpses of an ongoing struggle.

Elite Igbo Women in Contemporary Society

Elite women in Nigeria have come a long way since the colonial era, when their social prospects precariously hung on their relationships with men. But as the voices we hear in this book suggest, elite women's lives continue to revolve around a number of major features of social organization. In a sense, these features control the pulse of gender relations. They include marriage and family, procreation and son preference, polygamous incursions, and extended family ties.

Marriage and Family

Elite Igbo women's marital status is still perceived as the major determinant for their acceptance as adults. Their primary roles as wives, mothers, and companions to men therefore command the highest social regard. Since higher education confers, in principle, a prestigious extradomestic status on women, women must ensure that their career ambitions do not upset their primary roles. Many forms of formal training below the tertiary level can provide paid jobs for women, at a level that does not threaten the domestic balance of power. Access to higher education for women may not only upset this gender hierarchy in the family but may also overturn the larger social arrangement that restricts women's entrance into adulthood and citizenship mainly through marriage. Thus, Igbo women must carefully negotiate their options and the possible social threats as they tread the career path. Women who plan to pursue a professional career are often expected to carefully keep such aspirations within the confines of their marital obligations. This dilemma, Christie Achebe points outs, is shared by all Nigerian women: "[Contemporary] Nigerian society has prescribed to the woman the narrow role[s] of helpmate and mother. . . . Note that this restriction is for all women, whether educated or not. I say this because even for the educated woman, whose aspirations and awareness have been raised (whatever demands her newly acquired status make on her), society persists in the expectation that she give her traditional role primary focus. In fact, where she plays a role outside the family, the double message is 'go ahead, provided that you do all the cooking, look after the children and carry out all your traditional duties creditably.'"[31]

Certainly the general subordination of women by men and their confinement to the domestic sphere are not unique to Igboland or Nigeria. Women the world over experience the pressure to embrace socially prescribed roles. But the specific characteristics of those roles differ across space and time. Igbo culture places great import on marital and familial identities in very unique terms. Often, unmarried women remain excluded from many adult roles and their attendant privileges. Igbo families diligently groom their younger women to gain social acceptance as potential brides. Given the urgent demands of procreation for women, many of them consider finding a husband the major prerequisite to other forms of social recognition. Marriage is equally viewed as the natural and proper status for adult men, but they are not as urgently beckoned to procreation demands as women. In any case, men are not held to similar standards of social recognition as women. Women who seek to improve their social status cannot afford to ignore the Igbo adage "di bu ndo" (a husband is a shelter) since other avenues of social mobility do not make up for marriage and procreation. Safiya Muhammed endorses the strong assertion voiced by women in this volume. The burden of sustaining the marital union, she argues, falls more on women than men: "Nigerian society sees to it that marriage is much more of a commitment for women than it is for men. Our society does not only tell a woman that she is a failure if she fails to lure a male into marriage, it also cuts off most lines of escape from that inevitable path by barring her from other forms of social success."[32]

The social pressure on Igbo women to get married can be seen as part of society's effort to sustain the very foundations of social organization. The Igbo woman's life should revolve around her husband and children. In order to ensure that she is well on track, both immediate and extended families often make it their business to improve and protect a girl's marriage prospects. They monitor her life, applying pressure at crucial intervals to propel her into that socially acceptable sphere that, in their view, is the main prerequisite for pursuing any other aspirations in life. For contemporary female elites, marriage is still the supreme goal most of them are drawn to for both personal and social satisfaction. Indeed, virtually all the single women in this book expressed their ultimate desire to marry and bear children. They are, however, reluctant to embrace the rigid specifications that come with marriage.

As single women get older with no suitors in sight, age can become the all-important issue around which these pressures are directed. Igbo families are well aware that as their unmarried daughters advance in years, society becomes increasingly doubtful of their procreative ability. Their presence can become an embarrassment to the family. This is especially the case for the *ada* (eldest daughter), who may be blamed for blocking the way for her younger sisters.[33] Moreover, single women who have not attained this expected status may even invite the dubious impression that there must be something wrong somewhere. Although beauty and mutual attraction play an important part in choosing a bride or attracting the right suitor, any one or more of these labels—wrong social background, morally irresponsible, too old, or simply unlucky—can spell far more trouble for women than men. For instance, certain families and clans in Igboland historically bore social stigmas as osu or in their social conduct as men and women (see chapter 1). Although the significance of this cultural "mutation" has diminished to some extent, its impact on the marital decisions of Igbo men and women in contemporary society is still considerable. One would think that in the twenty-first century cultural stigmas like the osu label should not even receive mention in elite Igbo circles, where education, economic status, and political influence have become the crucial determinants of social prestige. Yet among the contemporary elites, osus continue to be discriminated against when it comes to marriage, leadership positions, and the conferment of cultural titles. The religious clergy, who could have played a significant role in aborting its progress, has not taken a firm stance against the osu dynasty in Christian circles. Hence, among practicing Christians parents maintain this cultural segregation by their intervention in the marriage decisions of their children, even those living abroad.[34] Besides the impact of cultural stigma, a woman's social reputation can ruin her marriage prospects. It is not uncommon for a community to destroy a young woman's reputation, especially where hearsay becomes the basis for assessing moral standards. The "well-brought-up" girl must watch what she wears, where she goes and who she is seen with in her careful attempts to tread the path of social acceptance.[35]

Since this social pressure does not weigh as much on men, male suitors hardly come under society's watchful eye. But this is not to suggest that young men are free to make their own decisions about marriage. Obviously, an Igbo man well into his thirties in Igboland would be expected to marry and settle down soon. For an adult male to remain single well after his peers are married may even be looked on as a mark of irresponsibility. This is because, unlike the spinster in a similar position, all he needs is to find the potential bride and make the move. Family members and friends (depending on how close the relationship) equally seek out subtle and bold means of getting such men to "wake up." It is very common for those close to him to arrange either planned or "chance" meetings in order to introduce him to potential brides in the hope that one will catch his fancy. For both the elite male and female, the crucial difference lies with the timing and intensity of pressure applied. Unlike the woman, the pressure to marry exerted on the Igbo man is mainly a way of ensuring that he enters adulthood and takes his place beside the elders—as soon as possible.

Procreation and Son Preference

Marriage in itself, especially for women, does not provide complete relief from all social pressures. As the experiences of Igbo career women vividly portray, married women also face their own set of challenges. For both men and women socialization in large part includes preparation for marriage since the marital status helps to cement an adult's sense of belonging to the community. As adults, marriage confers on them the acceptable status society requires of them for contribution to community life. But establishing the proper marital status marks only the first step in climbing the ladder of social expectations for women. Motherhood and producing a son, in that order, are the preconditions for marital stability.[36] As do most African societies, Igbo culture celebrates motherhood in folklore and with rituals, songs, and girls' names.[37] Despite the previous attempts of state and federal governments at curbing the long-existing trend of early marriage for girls, especially among the Muslims in northern Nigeria, their schooling often gets interrupted. The social and economic benefits of large families may have greatly diminished in today's society, but a childless marriage is still doomed from the start.[38] In most parts of Nigeria, women's sexuality is strongly tied to reproduction, and discussions of sexual relations are often restricted to adult private forums. It is therefore not surprising that sex education has received little support within and outside the Nigerian school system. The importance attached to procreation is reflected in social attitudes toward modern contraceptive methods. Elite women's use of modern contraceptives is often perceived as an attempt to control their sexuality and thus a threat to their chastity. As socially acceptable forms of birth control, Igbo culture encourages abstinence or prolonged breast-feeding for specified periods in between births. Moreover, abortion is illegal in all states of the federation, except in cases where the life of the mother is threatened. Family planning agencies, such as the Planned Parenthood Federation of Nigeria, operate under strict guidelines. They often target married women, whose access to the services provided must be granted by their husbands.[39] They are well aware that husbands are likely to be the ones to make decisions about family size and the use of birth control.[40]

Again, one must point out that the dilemma over procreation is one faced by both men and women, although the pressure might be felt more by women. Indeed, the rigid social stance on son preference complicates the dilemma for any couple. Male heirs are important to men, not only for the continuation of their lineage, but also as proof of their manhood. The affective but biased impressions conveyed by names given to Igbo children at birth strongly portray the value placed on sons. Names given to boys—such as Obiora ("everyone's hope"), Obiajulu ("the mind is pacified"), or Amaechina ("may the lineage never become extinct")—find close parallels with those of girls—such as Ndidi ("patience") or Nkechinyere ("what God has given"). The desire to produce male children compels many women to keep trying regardless of how many daughters they already have. Couples who desire a small family may therefore end up having more children than originally intended.[41] The man who has no children cannot really lay claim to a male identity in society, and the man who produces only female children is simply not man enough. Besides the demonstration of manhood, male heirs have, in customary terms, more direct access to ancestral economic resources, especially land. This direct access is tied to their expected familial obligations as future heads of households. Male heirs still command a high currency in a culture where the rites and ceremonies that accompany birth, marriage, and death are largely dictated by men.[42] Thus, even though formal education and paid work can substantially narrow the gap in the economic value of male versus female children, son preference continues to exert significant influence on elite marriages. It is therefore no surprise that many Igbo men would go to great lengths to find a male heir. Women, however, often bear more of the blame for either a childless marriage or one that has not produced male heirs. When she fails to produce a son, the Igbo wife's failure is widely lamented, and when she is successful, the joy is widely celebrated. For instance, *ewu umuito* (lit., goat for three children), the celebration of three consecutive male children, is still practiced in many parts of Igboland.

According to the women I interviewed, adoption, an option that did not exist in the past, seems to be gradually gaining acceptance in elite circles. Adoption, however, comes head-to-head with various other mechanisms within Igbo culture for addressing the problem of childlessness, especially the need for a male heir. When the Igbos talk about a person's father they are not necessarily referring to a direct biological tie. The Igbo culture, in a number of instances, confers paternity on individuals based on socially prescribed rules, which differ across Igboland. For instance, the child of an unmarried daughter may establish paternity with the biological father, a stepfather, or the mother's family. Similarly, a man separated but not divorced from his wife may inherit all her children, including those born outside his home. Moreover, families without male heirs can appoint male daughters or female husbands as alternative routes to continuing the family line.[43] Usually people in the community know about such children but do not openly discuss issues related to their biological identity. Often some of these instances provide for the continuation of the patrilineal lineage. They can also present an opportunity for women to redeem themselves. Since there is often more than one party involved, each instance is rarely decided on by the biological couple.

Indeed, the extended family system in its role as a general manager, overseeing the welfare of its members, shares the burdens of raising children. It redistributes the responsibility of child rearing to ensure that the haves lift up the have-nots. It is therefore very common to find younger relatives living with their elite uncles and aunties in the cities. These relatives are often expected to help out with domestic work and, as the stories of women in this book reveal, many of them are reduced to maids in the household. As child dependents, these relatives may attend school or learn a trade and eventually attain a better social status, at least compared to their parents. But who their fathers and mothers are and where their first loyalty lies is usually never in question.

In contrast, modern adoption introduces a complete stranger into an existing bloodline. But it has one unique advantage. Adoption provides elite couples and female elites with children outside their bloodline that they can raise as their own. Modern adoption in elite circles also circumvents almost all the parties that, in any traditional alternative, must be consulted, by placing the decision largely in the hands of individuals and couples. As an alternative to meeting procreation requirements, the practice is still confined to the upper echelons of the elite circle. Women in this study pointed out that modern adoption by Igbo elite couples, unlike that in Western countries, is often carried out with great secrecy. Obviously, most married couples who take this route guard their decision to adopt children in order to circumvent questions about bloodlines. In order to affirm a husband's manhood, a wife must keep such questions at bay. According to the women, even in cases where the adoption of a child is publicly known, the personal details often remain confidential. When handled properly, therefore, adoption can provide an alternative route for contemporary elites for addressing childlessness and son preference. For instance, an adopted son can restore the much-needed affirmation of manhood a man craves, if not in his home, then in the larger society. This alternative can also reduce the pressure faced by elite women in monogamous unions.

According to Igbo career women, the decision to adopt may be easier for the economically secure unattached woman. It also seems that regardless of who takes the adoption route, the female adoptee is likely to gain more acceptance in society than will her male counterparts. The little girl, my informants explained, would have fewer problems locating her family roots since she potentially belongs to another social lineage by marriage. Nevertheless, the practice, at present, remains a thorny issue within the larger society because of the cultural emphasis on bloodlines.

Polygamy and Polygamous Incursions

The persistence of polygamy as a social institution has defied modernization theorists who predicted a departure toward conjugal unions in postcolonial societies. It could be argued that the control and management of communal landholdings, the demand for farm labor, and the need to legitimize paternity, among other factors, encouraged polygamous marriages in precolonial societies. In Africa and a few parts of Asia, polygamy's resistance to the forces of social transformation is often linked to its economic advantage to men. A 1963 United Nations report notes that "one of the strongest appeals of polygamous marriage to men in Africa is precisely its economic aspect, for a man with several wives commands more land, can produce more food . . . and can achieve a high status due to the wealth which he can command."[44] But these rationales do not hold in contemporary elite circles, where women and children no longer constitute economic assets in the traditional sense. Children no longer represent additional farmhands. Instead, their preparation for adult life through schooling constitutes a major financial responsibility to the household. In any case, polygamy as a practice that bestows certain advantages to African men today requires a substantial financial outlay. Research shows that the worsening economic situation across Africa has significantly reduced the incidence of polygamy. Fewer elite men, these findings note, can afford the luxury of basking in the attention of two or more wives.[45]

Obviously a childless marriage or, in many cases, one without a male child, are strong invitations for men to initiate polygamous marriages. Such marriages still present opportunities for the man to try his luck. This may go anywhere from the bold introduction of a new, often younger, partner into a long-standing monogamous marriage to keeping the affair a secret (usually only from the wife, who is often the last to know) until the desired results are produced. But many elite men are attracted to polygamous incursions whether or not their marriages have produced children, including male heirs. They would often declare a monogamous marital status even as they engage in extramarital relationships as part of their macho African identity.

Social and academic discourses on the institution of polygamy in Africa raise very few questions about women's views and experiences of polygamy, especially within elite circles, where monogamy is perceived as the norm. Obviously, most elite Igbo women would view polygamy as a social institution that privileges men. It is certainly not an element of culture that any group of African women, given better options, would embrace. Buchi Emecheta, in *The Joys of Motherhood*, a novel set in colonial Nigeria, relates the silent agony endured by young Nnu Ego, whose husband takes a second wife. In her gloomy one-room lodging in a colonial city, "Nnu Ego fought back tears as she prepared her own bed for Nnaife and Adaku [his new wife]. It was a good thing she was determined to play the role of the mature senior wife; she was not going to give herself any heartache when the time came for Adaku to sleep on that bed. She must stuff her ears with cloth and make sure she also stuffed her nipple into the mouth of her young son Adim, when they all lay down to sleep."[46]

Emecheta captures the dynamics of Igbo marriage in transformation, a process that has introduced its own continuities and contradictions. Social relations in urban elite circles cannot afford the traditional "separation of sex from gender that gives women . . . space and power, . . . manifested in the valuing of children and the support of communal mothering."[47] In the traditional setting wives had their own huts, and these separate living arrangements gave them a reasonable degree of autonomy and privacy. In contrast, the crowding of urban life, for most city dwellers, forces women like Nnu Ego to suffer the humiliation of sharing a room with her husband and new cowife. In this urban context, it is not simply sharing a man that causes the pain but also the humiliation it brings into a personal space that Igbo tradition formally reserves for women.

It seems that the hybridized structure of gender relations helps, in various ways, to keep alive cultural facets deployed for the reassertion at every juncture of polygamy as a social institution. This structure maintains the institution of polygamy today as a weapon to subjugate women. For elite women, however, it is polygamous incursions that pose an ever-present threat. While none of the women who participated in this study is involved in a polygamous relationship, each is clearly aware of the various polygamous incursions that could threaten her marriage at any time. In fact, a good number of the married women would not completely vouch for their husbands' innocence of extramarital affairs. But they do not torture themselves with thoughts of what their husbands might be doing with other women. These women are preoccupied with meeting procreation requirements, the cornerstone of their marriages, which could justify their husbands' exercising of traditional prerogative.

However, women have adjusted to polygamy and in some cases have even exploited it to their advantage. Wambui Wa Karanja describes the case of "inside" and "outside" wives: instead of settling for undesirable monogamous unions, some elite women choose to establish a separate marital home with a married man well-established in society.[48] The latter maintains two or more marital homes and shares his time between the wives. As Karanja observes, the highly educated woman who accepts this arrangement not only meets the social expectations of today but also guarantees herself the freedom to pursue a career and live her outside life away from her husband's direct control. Marriage to a much older man with older children, including male heirs, also removes the pressure for procreation and son preference. Where procreation is not the primary reason for the union, the outside wife does not have to deal with the anxiety that age and childbearing requirements present. She may also enjoy greater access to wealth and freedom from regular domestic schedules.

It could then be argued that polygamous incursions would thrive in African elite circles as long as the following conditions hold: marriage continues to be viewed as a rite of passage to adulthood, the legitimacy of both monogamy and polygamy that is deeply ingrained in the hybridized social order remains unquestioned, procreation and male preference continue to be viewed as the central elements in African marriage, getting married and having children are seen as women's primary achievements in life, and the economic differential between male and female remains highly significant.

The persistence of these conditions, however, does not leave Igbo and other African elite women completely helpless. Compared to Igbo women's traditional bases, such as farming and trading, higher education confers upon elite women some degree of economic autonomy not directly tied to family subsistence. It can therefore offset the social pressure to pursue marriage at all costs, expanding women's range of options. Moreover, growing urbanization, which is fast producing urban melting pots, may increasingly weaken the younger generation's attachment to specific cultural strictures, such as whom and when to marry. In addition, women's access to wealth, particularly landed property in the cities (a home away from home for men and women alike), has increased. These developments may have significant salutary effects on Nigerian elite women's struggle for emancipation. But at present Nigerian women still confront many challenges. The contemporary hybridized social order in Igboland continues to endorse procreation and son preference even as it fiercely opposes women's access to ancestral land and the marital rights conferred by the modern legal system.

It is important to recognize that, on the whole, the institution of polygamy, especially as practiced in current elite circles, has undergone significant modifications. Traditional Igbo societies practiced both polygamy and monogamy. Both kinds of marital unions allowed men some degree of freedom to engage in various forms of extramarital relations, including the acquisition of concubines. The institution has emerged today in many pervasive forms, some of which rest partly on Western notions of male sexuality. Thus, the fact that these reconfigurations thrive in contemporary society can also be attributed to the fertile ground provided by the hybridized social order.

Extended Family Ties

Extended family ties also present a crucial challenge to contemporary elite marriage. As noted earlier, Nigerian families, regardless of the ethnic group, often maintain very strong ties with the extended family. The strength of an elite marriage is in many ways determined by its linkages with the extended family. In the search for domestic hands to help out in the elite household, for example, family relatives are often sought out first. The elite wife or husband can also find some support among family members in dealing, for instance, with the tensions of a childless or sonless marriage. The strength of established links may weaken in the younger generations, but is rarely completely severed. Sheila Ekong notes that contrary to theoretical expectations, "the continued existence of attachment to wide kin groups among Africans generally and Nigerians in particular" continues to perplex scholars.[49] A new wife is usually absorbed into her husband's family and considered a wife to all the members. In many respects, her husband's relatives are considered an extension of the conjugal family. Men tend to direct their loyalty first to the women in their lineage and second to their wives. On their part, women maintain very strong links with their natal family after marriage. But again whatever influence the Nigerian woman garners from these support networks depends on her relationships with male members of the family. In many cases, the control that comes with this influence may only be exercised over women who are not similarly situated. In effect, Ogundipe-Leslie argues, a woman can exercise some influence over wives in her natal family, but she remains a subordinate in her husband's family: "This situation [only] gives emotional power to women. Thus women take consolation from this fact and help oppress other women who come into their own lineages as wives. It is generally known that women in their own lineages form the emotional support of the men to the extent that the men cannot function without them. Yet such men will express in words the most blatant of male dominance. Such emotional power often satisfies women to the point of preventing them from wanting to take more public actions or resist the subordination they suffer within their own marriages."[50] It is therefore obvious that for the elite wife and her household extended family ties are at one level complementary in terms of the support networks they provide. At another level, they tend to introduce conflicts that can weaken the nuclear tie that holds elite couples together.[51]

Extended family ties are further complicated by the fact that married couples do not pool resources. Thus, a wife's economic security rests on both the fruit of her labor and her husband's loyalty. The Igbo female wage earner's financial autonomy is constrained by the dividing loyalties harbored by the elite household. The stability and survival of the elite household are tied to its relationship with the larger extended families on both sides. This relationship often places the former at the giving end and the latter at the receiving end, financially. Hence, for both the elite wife and husband, making ends meet also encompasses balancing the established loyalties on both sides with those of the immediate household. Women who share their stories in subsequent chapters point out that female wage earners use their financial resources and social influence to nurture ties with both their natal and marital extended families. But the women also admit that their bargaining power in this case largely rests on the intensity of a husband's loyalty to his own extended family. Thus, pressures exerted on the nuclear family by in-laws on both sides remain a major source of conflict with which spouses must wrestle.

Of course, a female wage earner's direct control of her money does not necessarily translate into total independence. Her financial autonomy is mostly tied to her direct responsibility for children. Hence, for the professional female elite the strongest financial loyalty shared with the husband is to their children. Children constitute not only the major basis for building marriage and family but also a mother's most important economic investment for the future. Although the importance of this investment for career women is mediated by their position in paid work, children remain the strongest allies in marriage, an asset they would go to great lengths to protect and nurture. Regardless of her contributions to the family's capital base, financial and otherwise, the elite wife's inheritance rights in marriage are still weak. The rights to landed property and financial investments are not automatically shared with the husband. In fact, polygamous and extended family incursions can undermine her marital status, and, therefore, weaken these rights further. Thus, the female wage earner's investment in her children comes first, after which other possible means of capital accumulation may be considered. As the women who share their views in this book explain, the motivation to raise her children and offer them the social opportunities that will transform them into productive adults is perhaps the strongest force that keeps the Nigerian mother at work despite the daily frustrations she goes through in a dismal economy.

Between Household and Career

The manner in which private and public spheres are carved out in contemporary Nigeria, especially within the elite circle, makes it very difficult for the professional woman to deal with all her responsibilities. The nuclear family in elite Nigerian circles places the burden of managing the home on the "woman of the house," regardless of whether or not she works outside the home. Her domestic obligations trail along, whether she stays at home or engages in paid work. How she balances her domestic duties with her career is her personal challenge. For the career Igbo wife, therefore, access to paid work is largely dependent on the extent to which she can find a replacement at home that is financially worth the cost of her exit. This double burden carried by female wage earners is a global phenomenon, although much of the debate it has attracted has focused on the lives of Western women. Igbo career women's experiences of managing the home and family clearly suggest the need to tease out the peculiarities of the double burden of specific groups of women.[52] The organization of domestic work in Nigerian elite households reflects, in contrast, both British and indigenous patterns.

Domestic work within the indigenous cultures is certainly a women's affair. But the public-private divide is hardly distinct and women's traditional economic activities often blend with the rest of women's reproductive work. Indeed, there is virtually no distinction between productive and reproductive work. Moreover, the social construction of maternity nurtures a network of both friend- and kin-based relations that provides, among other things, domestic labor.[53] Domestic labor in elite households reflects both the existing gendered organization of family life and the conditions of colonial settlement. Colonization instituted a culture of house-helps (houseboys and housemaids), a labor pool which is affordable mainly to those in the higher echelons of society. The fringe benefits of high-level employment for the colonial elite included domestic servants, a demand initially met by a large pool of male labor. Men assumed the role of domestic servants in the early stages of colonization for a number of reasons. Foremost, the initial restrictions to women's entrance into modern society created a scarcity of employable female city dwellers. Moreover, for the white colonial elite, who started this trend and many of whom left their families in Europe, the dictates of both Western and traditional morality made men better candidates than women. Besides, the abundance of untrained labor provided a large pool of men to draw from. Nigerian women who were married to highly placed men in the elite circles also took their cues from the wives of colonial officials and brought in paid domestic hands. This privilege was in many instances contested by their spouses, who tried in various ways to curb the potential freedom this arrangement provided.[54] But the rising status of Nigerian men in the formal employment sector also meant they could afford domestic servants. For many highly placed elite men the benefits of private- or public-sector employment came with hired help (cleaners, cooks, gardeners, and driver). But most elite families depended on a pool of young relatives, who offered their services in exchange for food, board, and, in many cases, vocational training.[55]

As Nigerian men increasingly moved into formal employment, domestic work quickly became a female preserve, an arrangement between the madam of the house and her female servants.[56] But increased public assess to schooling, among other factors, has over time dried up the pool of available hands. In search of domestic labor, elite households are increasingly seeking out less privileged groups outside the network of extended family relatives.

Igbo career women's descriptions of who does what and why reveal some peculiar patterns. As Bridget Anderson asserts in the Western case, it is important to expose "other kinds of power [relationships]—not just patriarchal [ones] . . . reproduced" by the distinct public-private divide.[57] With its cultural and colonial antecedents, the social reproduction of domestic labor in elite Nigerian households is in many ways problematic. The definition of domestic work in elite Igbo circles, the status of domestic hands (paid and unpaid), and the conditions of work have all created a complex set of relations with blurred boundaries that the simple analysis of a double burden does not capture. As I will argue in chapter 7, the term house-help captures the diversity of workers within this domestic pool. The relations of power are better examined in terms of the principal subjects involved in the process today—the woman of the house and her female house-helps. The latter, as will become clear in the voice chapters, do not easily fit into the Western definition of a housemaid, an employee who maintains a distinct relationship with the madam and her household. But, as the experiences of working mothers in this book suggest, this pool of domestic hands makes it possible for female wage earners to hang on to paid work but not necessarily to exit from domestic labor.

3

From Housewives to Career Women

Women and Formal Education in Nigeria

Colonization and capitalist expansion presented formidable challenges for women in various parts of Africa. But it is also clear that women sought ways to either resist or negotiate their position. Igbo women and their counterparts in other Nigerian ethnic groups managed to contest social expectations and expand the limitations set by society. Placed in a weak bargaining position, elite Nigerian women used every available avenue to negotiate the restrictions of their new social status.

Women's Entrance into Formal Education in Nigeria

Before the advent of European formal education in Nigeria, young children were prepared for their adult roles according to the cultural dictates of particular ethnic groups. While the specific roles allocated to men and women varied, the organization of daily life maintained a clear gender division. Of the more than two hundred and fifty ethnically diverse groups in Nigeria there are three major groups. The Hausa-Fulanis constitute the majority in the north while the Yorubas and Igbos dominate the south. Among the Muslim majority in Hausaland, women of the higher classes were destined for married life spent in seclusion, often with other cowives, while men dominated the public spheres of commerce, religion, and government. But in rural Hausa communities, Muslim men and women engaged in farming, with tasks divided along gender lines. Yoruba women in western Nigeria were highly regarded for their prowess in petty trade, although those who lived in agrarian communities engaged in some form of subsistence farming. In Igboland young boys followed their fathers to hunt and farm while young girls helped their mothers in cooking, looking after younger siblings, farming (food crops), and petty trade.

European education made its debut in Nigeria with the establishment of the first primary school in Badagry by Christian missionaries in 1842. Western schooling was much better received in the south than the north, which already had an established Islamic educational system. By the end of the nineteenth century the missions had introduced Western schooling to other towns in southern Nigeria such as Abeokuta, Calabar, Lagos, and Onitsha. But the colonial authorities soon consolidated their presence and began to regulate educational policies, including the provision of grants for the administration and further expansion of the new system. The primary agenda of the missions was to evangelize Nigerians, train the indigenous clergy, and, later, provide the colonial administration with a band of junior personnel to serve as caretakers.[1] Although the missionaries encouraged the enrollment of both male and female children, training for females was primarily meant to prepare them to be housewives to the growing number of male elite.

Like their counterparts in other African countries, elite women in southern Nigeria found themselves in a precarious situation. Membership in the new elite society confined them to a marriage where they were expected to simply cater to the demands of husbands and children. Women's place in the new elite circles was a major concern to emerging female organizations. Indeed, it was largely elite women's weak socioeconomic status as full-time housewives that motivated these organizations to boldly advocate for women's vocational training. As Kristin Mann explains, "Elite women embraced Christian marriage for two reasons: because upholding civilized values had become part of their special responsibility as women, and because making a good Christian marriage to an elite man provided their only means of sustaining membership in the elite. . . . And yet Christian marriage confronted elite women with a dilemma. . . . [They] had become dependent on elite men, but elite men failed to fulfil their expectations. After years of disappointment and marital strife, influential women began to rethink aspects of Christian marriage."[2]

As the vulnerability of their status became more evident, Igbo women joined forces with the rest of the elite female minority and began to push for training that would take them beyond domestic service.[3] With time, some of the girls' schools began to operate two streams. The regular program provided the needed prerequisites for those who wished to train as teachers, secretaries, and nurses. The second stream included a short course for girls who were being prepared primarily for marriage. Most were already betrothed to men who wanted them to receive some instruction in the usual school subjects as well as considerable training in the care of the home, gardening, and service to their home communities.[4] Although women's job prospects were largely limited to pink-collar occupations such as teaching, secretarial work, and nursing, elite women's organizations in Nigeria fought for more openings for women in the school system and in paid work. They lobbied Christian missions and colonial authorities to respond to women's gross underrepresentation in schools, especially in northern Nigeria, where Islam posed a formidable barrier against the expansion of formal education.

In general, Christian missionaries were far ahead of the colonial administration in Nigeria in expanding school facilities. Hence, women's enrollment tended to fare much better in schools managed by missionaries and other voluntary agencies. Even though subsequent colonial interventions through financial grants made room for some progress, the emerging pattern of gendered access and segregation could not be reversed. Table 3.1 shows the growth of primary education from the early stages of Nigeria's colonization.

Although the colonial administration's increased involvement in school expansion improved school enrollment for girls, especially in Lagos colony, the gender inequality continued well into the twentieth century. The remarkable gains women made at the primary level with the addition of government schools did not eliminate the marked gender gap in total enrollment. At the dawn of Nigeria's independence in 1960, female enrollment at the primary level still trailed far behind that of males, especially in northern Nigeria. Only in Lagos, the nation's former capital, did male and female enrollments approach anywhere near parity (table 3.2). The gender inequality in enrollment at the secondary school level in the precolonial era also reflected an established pattern that was only more pronounced. The gross underrepresentation of girls in secondary schools was equally well in place by the time Nigeria gained political independence. Again, the

Table 3.1. Growth in Primary School Enrollment, 1912–47

Region	Year	Government and Native Administration				Voluntary Agency (Assisted)				Voluntary Agency (Unassisted)			
		No. of Schools	Avg. Attendance			No. of Schools	Avg. Attendance			No. of Schools	Avg. Attendance		
			Boys	Girls	Total		Boys	Girls	Total		Boys	Girls	Total
Southern provinces and Lagos and colony	1912	59	3,873	111	3,984	91	9,673	2,059	11,732	(a)	(a)	(a)	20,100
	1926	58	8,800	575	9,375	192	28,229	7,046	35,275	3,578	(a)	(a)	96,600
	1930	64	9,599	1,061	10,660	275	37,885	10,534	48,419	2,387	72,951	9,403	82,354
	1937	108	10,667	1,516	12,183	339	52,803	16,661	69,464	3,086	116,819	28,144	144,963
	1947(c)	183	21,604	4,436	26,040(c)	473	114,935	38,824	153,759(c)	4,328	294,322	64,270	358,592(d)
Northern provinces	1912	5	(a)	(a)	350	—	—	—	—	29	(a)	(a)	(a)
	1926	68	(a)	(a)	2,207	1	(a)	(a)	(a)	56	(a)	(a)	3,003
	1937	195	(a)	(a)	9,130	22	2,623	807	3,430	322	5,909	806	6,715
	1947(c)	400(b)	19,551	5,571	25,122(c)	167	15,804	5,584	21,388(c)	543	18,107	6,045	24,152

(a) Figure not known.

(b) Includes twelve middle schools giving a five-year course subsequent to a four-year junior primary course.

(c) The figures for 1947 are of enrollment, average attendance figures not being available, and are from returns made in respect of the year 1946.

(d) In addition, there was, in returns for the year 1946, record of 23,873 boys and 6,161 girls in private venture schools in the southern provinces.

Source: Annual Report of the Education Department of Northern Nigeria, 1954–55. In Albert F. Ogunsola, Legislation and Education in Northern Nigeria (Oxford: Oxford University Press, 1974), 27.

Table 3.2. Primary School Enrollment by Sex, 1955–60 (%)

Year	Northern province M	F	Eastern province M	F	Western province M	F	Lagos (capital) M	F	All Nigeria M	F
1955	77	23	73	27	66	34	58	42	70	30
1956	76	25[a]	68	32	64	36	57	43	67	33
1957	75	25	66	34	63	37	55	45	65	35
1958	75	25	65	35	62	38	54	46	64	36
1959	74	26	63	37	62	38	53	47	63	37
1960	73	27	63	37	61	39	53	47	63	37

[a] Due to rounding, percentages do not total 100%.
Source: Compiled from Nigeria, *Annual Digest of Educational Statistics* 2, no. 1 (Lagos: Federal Ministry of Education, 1962); Nigeria, *Annual Abstract of Statistics* (Lagos, 1962).

Table 3.3. Secondary School Enrollment by Sex, 1955–60 (%)

Year	Northern province M	F	Eastern province M	F	Western province M	F	Lagos (capital) M	F	All Nigeria M	F
1955	91	9	89	11	87	13	78	22	87	13
1956	90	10	88	12	82	18	75	25	84	16
1957	91	9	90	10	80	20	72	28	82	18
1958	90	10	89	11	78	22	70	30	80	20
1959	90	10	89	11	78	22	69	31	80	20
1960	91	9	88	12	77	23	56	44	79	21

Source: Compiled from Nigeria, *Annual Digest of Educational Statistics* 2, no. 1 (Lagos: Federal Ministry of Education, 1962); Nigeria, *Annual Abstract of Statistics* (Lagos, 1962).

southern provinces maintained their lead over the northern (table 3.3).

Higher-education statistics for the colonial period are scanty, but the available data clearly indicate, as would be expected, that women were hardly represented. The first postsecondary educational institution in the country, Yaba Higher College, was established in 1932 and by 1960 had 83 female students out of a total enrollment of 1,150.[5] In 1960 the University of Ibadan, established in 1948, had a total student enrollment of 1,116, with 79 female students, most of whom majored in the arts.[6] It seemed that higher education for Nigerian women was established, at the onset, with clear boundaries that were to govern their access to paid employment.

Paid Work and the Prospects of Women's Schooling in Colonial Nigeria

LaRay Denzer traces Nigerian women's entrance into paid work to 1885, when Hannah Cole, a "native of West Africa," was hired as a nurse in the colonial civil service.[7] This was long after a generation of men had served in the public sector. Although the number of female employees increased in the 1920s and 1930s, their representation compared to males remained quite low. In fact, until the 1950s the annual national labor reports revealed dismal levels of female participation in paid work, despite steady pressure from elite women's organizations.[8] Although a few women found themselves competing for the higher-paying jobs in male preserves, most female wage earners congregated at the lower ranks of formal employment.[9] Most women in paid work were clerks, telephone operators, and shop assistants.[10] With limited career opportunities, even women who climbed higher up the educational ladder, especially those who were privileged to study abroad, ended up in the two most popular pink-collar professions—teaching and nursing. The solid pattern of gross female underrepresentation in formal employment was already in place before Nigeria gained political independence in 1960 (table 3.4).

Low enrollment, high dropout rates at the primary level, and a shortage of facilities are often cited by school authorities and education boards as the main reasons for Nigerian girls' historically poor access to formal education.[11] But women's low enrollment and high dropout rates, especially at the primary level, were mostly a response to the school system's initial reluctance to absorb girls and provide them with opportunities similar to those offered to boys. Neither the

Table 3.4. Distribution in Paid Employment by Sex, 1956–60

Year	Women	Men
1956	9,625	437,747
1957	10,537	485,039
1958	12,580	465,764
1959	17,287	416,070
1960	25,423	474,526

Source: Nigeria, *Annual Report of the Federal Ministry of Labor, 1960–1961* (Lagos: Nigerian National Press, 1961), 41.

missions nor the colonial authorities were ever comfortable with giving Nigerian women professional training. It was generally assumed that girls were either not suited for or could not stand the stress of the kind of educational training available to boys. Indeed, the limited educational facilities provided for girls placed a benchmark on how far girls could stretch their ambitions. In assessing Nigerian women's overall progress in schooling and paid work, one cannot, therefore, easily dismiss this blatant discrimination in the early stages of the country's development. Obviously, the uncertainty surrounding Nigerian women's social status since colonial days rested on both local and foreign biases. Girls found little support in the school system to forge ahead and faced a myriad of indigenous gender dictates outside of school that raised suspicions about their training.

Apparently, Nigerian families found it difficult to balance this new asset with young girls' much-needed labor and the social demands tied to marriage and procreation. This dilemma made paid work in the future a far-fetched possibility which, even if it materialized, could seriously threaten important requirements society expected them to meet. In contrast, society provided Nigerian men with better justifications and more attractive prospects. They had access to the expanding opportunities in public service, political forums, and paid employment in the private sector, a strong socioeconomic presence that strengthened their dominant status in the elite circles. There was no indication, at least in the initial stages, of any official efforts by colonial authorities to encourage women's participation in higher education and their representation in paid work.[12] Instead, the historical transition progressed with the bid for power between an emerging male ruling class and the colonial incumbents. In the end, colonization introduced new patterns of gender discrimination that shaped women's opportunities in the civil service, private-sector employment, formal politics, and modern commerce in postcolonial Nigeria. These patterns have been reproduced in various forms in contemporary Nigeria, despite the significant strides women have made in the school system.

Women's Progress in Postcolonial Nigeria: The Boom Years and Beyond

In 1960, Nigerians ushered in an indigenous regime that made the development of human capital for nation building one of its top priorities. But it was not until the 1970s that the country launched its most massive expansion of the school system. The oil boom of the early 1970s made way for the inception of the Universal Primary Education (UPE) scheme in 1976. Apart from boosting overall school employment, the UPE was also meant to eliminate regional imbalances in access to schooling, and therefore it especially benefited girls in northern Nigeria. After a decade of UPE, women's representation at the primary and secondary levels has stayed above 40 percent of total enrollment. The gender imbalance, especially in the south, has narrowed considerably, with primary and secondary school enrollments in 1996 increasing markedly to 44.3 and 49 percent, respectively. Female representation at the postsecondary level has also improved greatly, although men still maintain their lead in total enrollment (table 3.5).

Women's increased access to schooling in the postcolonial era, especially at the tertiary level, was strongly tied to changes in the nation's oil fortunes. Nigeria's oil wealth expanded public subsidies and made it much easier for parents to send both male and female children to school. But the prospects of formal education for boys and girls increasingly differed as they advanced through the school system. The few women who made it beyond the secondary level had access to tertiary training not as a target group but as a minority that could be only grudgingly accepted. In a sense, the discrimination Nigerian women faced in the school system paved the way for their entrance into a formal employment setting in which the seeds of foreign gender segregation were already growing. University education was largely geared to intellectual rather than vocational training, and the civil service had from the colonial period drawn its middle- and senior-level staff from the pool of university graduates. But gender segregation kept men and women in two different competing groups as they entered the civil service. In addition, job descriptions included salary

Table 3.5. National Postprimary Enrollment by Sex, 1992–96

Year	Males	Females	Total
1992	1,979,045	1,621,575	3,600,620
1993	2,182,034	1,850,049	4,032,083
1994	2,419,782	2,031,547	4,451,329
1995	2,354,713	2,049,278	4,448,991
1996	2,229,527	1,971,804	4,201,331

Source: Compiled from Federal Ministry of Education Annual Statistics, 1992–1997. In *Annual Abstract of Statistics* (Abuja: Federal Office of Statistics, 1998), 191.

scales designed to reward men as family breadwinners. Hence women were already disadvantaged as job seekers before they entered the labor market.

Women were also not as well positioned as men to take advantage of the employment prospects that came with Nigeria's oil boom. Men's exclusive access to the science and technology disciplines enabled them to move into far better jobs created by the oil boom, in the more lucrative and rapidly expanding private sector. Women's domestic obligations in elite households further curtailed their options in both the civil service and the private sector. In most cases, Nigerian women with tertiary education credentials were forced to stay in the civil service, which provided more flexibility for juggling domestic and paid work.

The oil glut at the close of the 1970s, with its waves of economic depression, only worsened the employment prospects of male and female graduates, eroding some of the gains made by Nigerian women in previous decades. The oil glut, coupled with endemic political instabilities, marked the beginning of Nigeria's economic collapse. The country's mounting foreign debt led to the introduction of a series of World Bank structural adjustment programs (SAPs) in the 1980s. SAPs forced a downscaling of the public sector and also brought economic activities to a halt. The government, with its buoyant resources during the oil boom, could at least stem the surge in unemployment among tertiary educated graduates. But since the 1980s unemployment rates have escalated and with a shrinking public service the government has no way of absorbing the huge numbers of graduates churned out annually by the school system.[13]

The mid-1980s also witnessed a growing economic gap between public- and private-sector workers, and women seem to be increasingly ghettoized in the former.[14] Inflationary pressures following the economic crisis have also depressed real wages. The brunt of the decline in real earnings is borne by the public sector, where proportionally more women than men end up. As shown in table 3.6, the public service witnessed in the early 1990s a mass exodus of male workers in search of better opportunities. Between 1990 and 1991, for instance, more than one hundred thousand men left the service, resulting in a 9 percent increase in women's representation. Although the total number of female workers actually decreased over this period, this shift in gender representation suggests that male workers were much more anxious to leave the civil service. It was suggested in the early stages that this brain drain benefited women, who were left behind to fill the

Table 3.6. Established Federal Civil Service Staff by Sex,
1990–93

Year	Female	%	Male	%	Total
1990	44,872	15.6	242,661	84.4	287,533
1991	44,768	24.4	138,486	75.6	183,254
1992	45,881	24.0	145,448	76.0	191,329
1993	47,426	24.1	149,645	75.9	197,071

Source: Compiled from Federal Civil Service Statistics. In *Annual Abstract of Statistics* (Abuja: Federal Office of Statistics, 1998), 248–49.

gaps.[15] But as the "advantage" stretched into the next decade, its quali-fied nature became evident. In the first quarter of 1992, for instance, three thousand disgruntled professionals (mostly men) left public ser-vice. These workers "did not rate their chances of advancement in the professional civil service" high enough to stay behind.[16] Many of them opted, instead, for private business ventures. But even with their increasing representation in public service, women have yet to claim their share of that workforce (see table 3.6).

In addition to women's poor representation in public service, the distribution of Nigeria's civil servants into specific ministries and departments also confirms a sharp gender segregation. Women tend to concentrate in Education, Health, Information, and Cultural Affairs, while men remain overrepresented in Justice, Transport, and Aviation.[17]

The private sector evidences a similar, but stronger, discriminatory pattern. Both the financial boom that came with the SAPs and the sub-sequent deregulation of Nigeria's currency benefited men more than women. For instance, between 1986 and 1991 the total number of commercial and merchant banks in Nigeria rose from 41 to 120,[18] and the boost in employment benefited mostly men, who were more likely to possess the required credentials. Compared to their male counter-parts, many female job seekers not only lacked the required educa-tional prerequisites but also faced additional barriers in private-sector employment. These obstacles are traceable to gender biases in work settings, job structures that favor men, and the social restrictions placed on women's job options that employers often consider.

The experiences of women in this book show that social percep-tions of appropriate jobs for women as well as the social expectations about their current and prospective roles as wives and mothers play into employers' decisions about hiring women. The crisis in the labor market has heightened a resort to unofficial channels, encouraged by corrupt networks endemic to the rank and file of the formal sector. Men and women alike are aware of the informal shortcuts for survival in paid work. However, the average educated Nigerian man, compared to his female counterparts, is better placed in terms of competition for available job opportunities, access to further training, and business incentives in the private sector. Obviously, the diminishing prospect of formal education does not help the situation. But men still have a wider range of career options, even beyond paid work. It is therefore not surprising that their dominant status at the tertiary level has not as yet been seriously challenged by women.[19]

Igbo women's experiences of formal education and paid employment continue to be strongly mediated by the patriarchal continuities and contradictions ushered into contemporary Nigeria. The policies of Christian missionaries and the colonial administration, on the one hand, and the response of the indigenous ruling class, armed with its selective sociocultural expectations imposed on women, on the other, were crucial to the creation of a hybridized social order and the legitimization of patriarchal continuities and contradictions that define women's place in contemporary Nigeria.

Schooling and Paid Work: "The Good News in Colonial Specifications"

Missionary education made its debut on Nigerian soil with its own sexist and class-based norms, offering male children far more extensive prospects than female children. Many of the missions who lobbied for more girls' schools with improved facilities were initially reluctant to support their training beyond the primary level. In fact, the subsequent resolve of the missions to make higher education accessible to Nigerian women was mainly a response to pressures from elite parents, who gradually came to grips with their daughters' vulnerable position in elite circles.[20]

It must be conceded, however, that the missions' attitude to Nigerian women's education reflected, in part, the prevailing situation in England. The British educational system at the time encouraged public schooling for the masses and private institutions for the privileged classes. Both the public and private streams tended to promote literary more than technical skills. Public schools, in particular, opened their doors to more boys than girls, restricting the latter to domestic education. Unequally shared public grants ensured a wide variation in the nature and quality of instruction received by male and female children of various classes. Before its advent in Nigeria and other African countries, this pattern had already been repeated in older British colonies, such as Canada and countries of the Caribbean.[21]

Entering the scene long after the missions had consolidated their position, the colonial regime did not introduce any radical departures from the prevailing trend. This was hardly surprising considering the very purposes for which formal education was carried to the colonies.[22] As in the other colonies, formal education in Nigeria was primarily meant to serve an imperialist agenda. The colonial administration was not prepared to risk the emergence of an educated class that might jeopardize its interest in the long run. It therefore tailored the system to its local employment demands. As Uduaroh Okeke notes, "no serious attempt was made to train Nigerians in higher skills. So the Europeans were the skilled technicians and administrators, and Nigerians were happy to be clerks and laborers doing what they were told."[23] When the Christian missions, for instance, joined the local outcry for tertiary institutions on Nigerian soil, the colonial administration was reluctant to pursue the project. When it eventually acceded to the demand, a statement by Sir Hugh Clifford made clear the extent of the administration's support: "It can only be described as farcical to suppose that . . . continental Nigeria can be represented by a handful of gentlemen drawn from a dozen coastal tribes—men born and bred in British administered towns situated on the seashore—who in the safety of British protection have peacefully pursued their studies under British teachers."[24]

This attitude influenced the nature of most tertiary institutions established during the colonial era. The first such institution, Yaba Higher College, was designed to train assistant officers in the medical and technical departments within the civil service. The underlying emphasis of the college's mission did not escape Nigerian social commentators of the time. According to Okechukwu Ikejiani and J. O. Anowi, "The operative word here is 'Assistant.' There was no intention . . . to give the Nigerian an education that would make him an authority in his field and one that would give him poise and dignity in the presence of his fellows. His duty, as a colonial, was to assist his imperial masters, not to supplant them."[25] In fact, the patterns of men and women's introduction to paid work within and outside the family fitted neatly into the imperialist agenda. Obviously, the patterns, inconsistent as they were, and blatant contraventions models inherited from England can be explained only in terms of the advantages accruing to colonial authorities. As Ifeyinwa Iweriabor puts it, "Being short of human power, and essentially exploitative in nature, the Colonial Government could not afford the luxury of the sort of rabid discrimination against women that it operated within domestic borders. . . . The Nigerian family in practice retained its productive role in the sense that urbanization did not necessarily confine women to the home. Women's contribution to the national economy . . . ranged from labouring on construction sites (where they are paid less than men), nursing, teaching. . . . [T]hey are also dominant in trading and catering services, and of course, remain the prop of Nigerian agriculture."[26]

Of course, the colonial administration was very mindful of the conflict that could result from pitting Nigerian women against their male counterparts, and it saved its "rabid discrimination" for the higher ranks of formal employment. This discomfort is evident in the following colonial directive to the secretary of state for the colonies in 1950, regarding the promotion of female nurses: "The idea of a comparatively young African female nurse being placed in a position of authority over African male nurses where she will be required not only to control them but to teach them is still strange in Nigeria. There is considerable difficulty in filling positions of responsibility, and it is essential that their [women's] capacity to occupy such positions should be thoroughly tested locally before they are promoted."[27]

Colonial authorities virtually kept women out of the middle and higher ranks of civil service not by officially denying them access to tertiary training but by substantially lowering their chances of acquiring and utilizing their credentials. Where a diluted form of advanced training was reluctantly offered to Nigerian men, the case for women's access to this training could not have garnered much public support, especially since there was initially no intention to employ them in the civil service. The colonial administration's refusal to employ women in many of its establishments until almost a century after its inception certainly discouraged ambitious Nigerian women. As Denzer notes in her review of Nigerian women's employment in the civil service, "British officials were quite explicit in their reasoning—they did not want to risk unsettling male civil servants who might resent female competition. On this point British male chauvinism coincided with African male chauvinism to limit opportunities for women."[28]

Obviously, colonial patterns of occupational gender segregation in Nigeria's formal sector also reflected, in part, the uneven duplication of capitalist models outside the West. Western stereotypes of female jobs became more defined as more Nigerian women entered formal employment and began to move up the formal employment ladder. Interestingly, these stereotypes survived the era and presently coexist with other patterns not common to the West. These stereotypes have created new identities and roles that do not necessarily fit into indigenous forms. As Janet Bujra explains it, "Establishing foreign stereotypes entails definitive cultural re-socialization, not simply in the skills of the job, but in terms of what it is to be a woman. Such women are forced to create a model of womanhood which has no precedents in African society. . . . On the one hand, men are here found doing work which in Europe is thought of as 'women's work.' . . . On the other hand, where women are in occupations which in Europe are thought of as 'naturally' female, they are not in practice building on existing cultural stereotypes of women, but creating new ones."[29]

Nigerian women certainly welcomed formal education and paid work as important assets in a new social era, but they were aware that these assets could take them only so far. Sexist restrictions in paid work kept most educated Nigerian women in occupations considered suitable for women by British standards and in positions where men would not be under their supervision. Female workers were placed in separate ranks with less attractive working conditions compared to the men.[30] Coupled with their limited access to schooling, Nigerian women stood on vulnerable ground as they struggled to find their place in colonial Nigeria.

Blame It on the White Man:
Our Governments, Our People

Critics who blame colonization for African women's marginalization solely on the actions of Christian missionaries and colonial authorities must also recognize that women's restricted access to formal education was highly instrumental to the consolidation of elite male ruling classes in most of Africa.[31] In the case of Nigeria, the reluctance of several postcolonial regimes to reverse the trend and improve women's access to social opportunities largely exonerates the colonial masters from charges that have been made in the past.[32] Katherine Mamuddu strongly decries the apathy of African universities over the issue of gender equity in admission and points to a prevailing lack of recognition of the importance of equal participation and full use of resources in the development process.[33]

The attitude of Nigerian governments toward women's education was closely aligned to the dictates of our indigenous social orders. Nigerian society in the colonial era and beyond in many ways supported the policies and programs of indigenous governments. Poor female enrollment, especially in the colonial era, for example, was also in part a result of society's reluctance to loosen its grip on women's lives. The free labor women provided within the household, among other factors, tightened this grip. Apparently, access to schooling came to depend in part on whose labor the family could do without. Victorian values of female domesticity certainly found a close alliance with the primary dictate of early marriage for girls among Nigerian ethnic groups, further legitimizing men's status as family breadwinners in elite circles. Many Nigerian parents of the colonial era, especially the "illiterates" outside elite circles, considered schooling a disruption of girls' preparation for marriage, an irrelevant sidetrack that added little to their future domestic role. For many of these parents, formal education neither fit into the women's traditional roles nor made any economic provisions for them outside marriage. Even the expansion of women's career prospects did not easily change this attitude. This was partly because early marriage increasingly presented a faster and more reliable financial payoff for fathers, into whose coffers the bride wealth went. The transition into a cash economy, Eunice Okeke explains, gave new meaning to what was originally an exchange of gifts and goodwill from the bridegroom's family to the bride's. "Marrying daughters off to men with ready cash became a source of income for parents. Allowing a girl to go to school or remain in school would therefore delay the income or cause the parents to miss the chance of having a wealthy son-in-law. When the parents did not have enough money to pay the school fees of all their children, it was the girls who were withdrawn from school to get married. The bride price realized was used to pay school fees for sons. Consequently, the dropout rate of girls was excessively higher than that of boys. Theoretically, the school doors were open to both boys and girls, but the nation's societal/cultural values and practices interfered greatly with women's education."[34]

Although the custom of bridal payment became a growing concern for colonial authorities, their numerous attempts to regulate the practice proved unsuccessful. Parents could easily carry out the necessary private negotiations away from the watchful eyes of government officials.[35] In addition to the attraction of ready cash, many parents, especially in eastern Nigeria, where the Igbos constitute the majority, also had mixed feelings about the prospects of higher education for girls. Although educated women were increasingly attracting better suitors, it was important that women did not exceed the proper level beyond which their chances of "marrying well" could fall. Igbo parents feared that with such advanced credentials their daughters could price themselves out of the marriage market. As the 1947 memorandum on African schooling indicated, educated male elites often preferred educated spouses but were not likely to marry older or more educated women, a situation that left unmarried educated women with some hard choices.[36] Women's access to schooling, as a social right, therefore found little support among Nigerian parents. Parents who sent their daughters to school were essentially building up a resource base for another man and his extended family. A stronger argument for women's education rested on the concern over their vulnerable status in the elite circles. The challenge for elite women became one of finding the right balance between marriage and career prospects.

Nigerian women's experience in formal employment reflects similar patterns. Gender segregation in paid work was perceived as a foreign invention, but it certainly found support in an already existing gender hierarchy, which the colonial administration, loaded with its own foreign biases, was not prepared to confront. In fact, the relations of gender within elite families helped in great measure to sustain what was seen as a foreign influence. Nigerian male elites, Awe reveals in his historical review of Nigerian women's progress since the colonial era, treated their wives' careers as jobs that could easily be dispensed with when the occasion warranted. Female nurses and teachers, for instance, often resigned from their jobs to follow their husbands to new locations that might not hold similar employment opportunities for them. Some of these women even had to resign in deference to their spouses' high positions in government.[37]

Obviously, colonial power was not exerted on any African society outside its cultural medium. Much caution went into the implanting of foreign patterns to ensure the proper cultural fit for achieving the desired results. The cautious approach to tertiary training for Nigerians also portrayed a good understanding by colonial authorities of an already established patriarchal order they could tamper with only at certain junctures. It is therefore not surprising that these biased patterns survived well after the colonial authorities officially left Nigerian shores.[38] On the whole, in tracing both colonial and indigenous imprints, "gender, more than class," was and still remains responsible for women's access to formal education as well as the career choices they make.[39] This is clearly shown in the profiles of career women explored in subsequent chapters.

The Structure and Organization of Formal Employment in Contemporary Nigeria

In general, the structure and organization of formal employment in Nigeria reflect many typical features found in anglophone Africa. The public bureaucracy and modern economy nurtured by colonization strongly shaped the system of formal education that emerged in contemporary Africa. The formal education system supplies most of the workers in paid employment. In Nigeria this workforce can be collapsed into four major categories: the bottom rank of unskilled workers such as cleaners, janitors, and gardeners; the junior rank, including messengers and clerical staff; the middle rank, from supervisors to junior professionals; and the management and board of directors. Even most of the workers in the bottom rank are usually expected to have at least a sixth grade education. Until the mid-1970s, workers often rose through the ranks, but the expansion of public schooling, especially at the tertiary level, in the past three decades has catapulted many university graduates into the middle-level and senior positions.

Hiring procedures depend on the nature and level of available positions. Individual departments could fill available vacancies in the two lower ranks. For the middle-level staff, the federal and state civil services usually conduct mass recruitment exercises once every few years to fill departmental vacancies, but with the public service cuts that came with the SAPs such exercises have become less regular. The higher echelons are usually filled through individual staff promotions or political appointments. Whether civilian or military, incumbent regimes often register their strong presence, especially in sensitive areas such as the president's cabinet and the diplomatic missions. Until the onset of the economic decline in the 1980s, civil servants, especially teachers, were usually promoted en masse every three years. Currently, promotion exercises are less comprehensive and more haphazard. In contrast, the private sector recruits workers continuously, depending on the existing vacancies in particular establishments. Given the competition for fewer but better-paying positions, the private-sector recruitment process is more rigorous. Advancement in the private sector also involves stricter evaluation for individual workers.[40]

Job structures in the public and private sectors are generally derived from colonial models and therefore do not differ remarkably from each other. In both sectors there are wide gaps in remuneration packages between the lower and higher job ranks. This pattern is traceable in part to racial inequalities that were embedded in the colonial civil service. These inequalities also reinforced gender segregation, with women at the bottom rungs and in sex-typed positions. As Bujra points out, men in most African countries benefited from this colonial legacy: "The perpetuation, in many areas of Africa, of colonial salary scales based originally on racial privilege, has meant that inequalities of reward between workers at various levels in the occupational hierarchy are more marked than in developed capitalist societies. These patterns of inequality have been reinforced in the postcolonial period by a[n initial] general shortage of personnel with even minimal educational qualifications—and especially [of qualified] women."[41]

Nor have work structures and conditions of service departed significantly from the colonial arrangement. Most positions are full time, and except in the case of shift workers, there are essentially no adjustments in the established daily working schedule. Public servants usually work eight hours a day, starting at 7:30 in the morning. For schoolteachers the workday ends at about 2:30 in the afternoon, although slight variations exist across the country. Private-sector employees usually work longer hours, but many firms maintain a nine-to-five schedule. A number of policy changes in the postindependence era have remedied the gross discrimination in women's employment. For instance, the colonial salary differentials between male and female workers of similar ranks have long been equalized.[42] Expectant mothers are entitled to a three-month maternity leave with full salary. However, many private firms pay half the basic salary, allowing only major benefits, such as the housing allowance. Policies about nursing mothers remain unclear outside the civil service, where a one-hour break is allowed each day for the first six months of the postnatal period.[43] These provisions notwithstanding, women experience overt discrimination across the rank and file of formal employment. Married women, especially working mothers, appear to bear most of the brunt of discriminatory practices. For instance, they pay proportionally more tax than their male counterparts because only working fathers receive a child benefit. Moreover, female civil servants whose husbands occupy government subsidized housing automatically forfeit the substantial rent subsidy all civil servants receive. Until 1992 male civil servants also received a "wife allowance."[44] Such discriminatory treatments have their roots in colonial administrative policies, which were built around the male breadwinner and his dependent wife and children. Women's traditional responsibilities and entitlements were overlooked in those areas where colonization and the emergence of a male ruling class created new privileges for men. This ideology persists despite its inherent contradiction to women's direct responsibility for children as well their increasing economic contributions to family upkeep.[45] This legacy has all but disappeared in many Western countries, where mothers—paid workers and homemakers included— are now direct recipients of a child benefit paid by the government.

Besides these overt forms of discrimination, Nigerian women must deal with the subtle and more pervasive patterns that are intricately woven into the structure of the labor market. Some of these inequities can be traced to women's earlier exclusion from economically viable training opportunities, the reluctant admittance of women into the civil service, and their segregation into sex-typed jobs with less attractive working conditions than the male preserves. As more recent statistics show, these gendered patterns have not changed significantly and their implications for Nigerian women's prospects in the modern wage economy are more far reaching than often assumed.

The average work setting in formal employment is not originally designed to welcome women. Even single women, without the conflicting obligations of marriage, are barely accommodated in such an environment. The relatively lucrative areas in public service are mainly male preserves. Indeed, the skepticism of men at the top and the generally hostile response to women in these perceived male preserves may speak more to their historical evolution than to any doubts surrounding the competence of prospective female applicants. Many work settings are structured with certain "unofficial" expectations tied to job descriptions that keep qualified women away. The technical job structure and expectations, in this case, may not be gender specific, but the dynamics of male bonding in place may not accommodate female colleagues. These ingrained biases sustain gendered representations across departments, placing men and women in noncompeting pools when it comes to advancement within the rank and file.

It could be argued, however, that these formal work settings, which call for some degree of close interaction with the opposite sex outside the culturally allowed spaces, present their own challenges for both elite men and women. Based on the views of women who share their stories in this book, some of the discomforts are shared by both men and women. In many cases, they must relate to each other outside culturally defined spaces, in positions that stand on no indigenously recognized tenet, yet crossing boundaries that may be disapproved of socially. Where they have to work with men, paid work in general—and the colonial models on which work settings are modeled in particular—deny women a social space outside men's direct gaze. Yet for men the world of paid work increasingly entails a redefinition of elite women's primary roles as wives, mothers, and companions to elite men.

The SAP Era and Beyond:
Women, Paid Work, and the Home Front

Women across Africa in many ways share the struggle to survive in a dismal economic climate. Until in recent times intellectual debates have, for very good reasons, focused on the experiences of the huge majority in the informal sector of African economies. In many parts of sub-Saharan Africa today, women battle the impact of the SAPs. Whether as market traders in Accra, Ghana, fish sellers in Zairian villages, food farmers in the rural areas of Malawi and Cameroon, women struggle under the increased burden of family subsistence as their men's economic opportunities dwindle in both the informal and formal sectors.[46] Kept for the most part outside the formal sectors of African countries, women are forced to employ both traditional and new survival strategies to feed their family or generate income. These strategies include petty trading, food farming and processing, sewing, soap making, illegal brewing of beer and alcohol, fabric dyeing, and prostitution.[47]

The experiences of the tiny but important female minority in paid work have not received much attention in social debates and deserve to be investigated. In Nigeria, for instance, the economic downturn since the late 1970s has made it impossible for most Nigerian elite households to live on one income. Whether as self-employed or paid workers in the modern economy, men now struggle not only to boost their contributions to family upkeep but also to help stabilize monthly budgets. Beyond the widespread waves of economic inflation they created, the SAPs have scaled down social support. The unprecedented cuts in public funding have seriously affected social programs, especially in education and healthcare. Although the impact varies across social classes, the emerging gendered pattern is reflected among the female minority in elite circles. As Eunice Okeke, one of the early observers of this trend, points out, paid work for elite Nigerian women has become increasingly important both for their own economic security and for family subsistence: "Work for a wage, even if the work is not at a status equal to that of men's, enhances a woman's prestige and provides her with economic independence from both her parents and her husband. Today, men prefer marrying women who are in the paid labor force. Women's income supplements the men's income and enhances male prestige. It is now common in Nigeria to find married women returning to school after years of absence . . . at their husband's urging."[48]

Given the dismal economic situation, many Nigerian female wage earners would go to great lengths to protect their jobs, despite the challenges of juggling the responsibilities of domestic and paid work. Even the few who by privilege or tradition remain in the household as housewives are increasingly awakening to the uncertain future forecast by present economy trends. The wage earners must continue to negotiate the tensions of meeting obligations in two virtually incompatible spheres. Although Nigerian women's representation in formal education and paid work has greatly improved since the colonial era, social emphasis on their primary roles remains quite strong. Women's overall share in childcare and housework has not declined enough to reflect their progress in schooling and paid work.

Getting into Paid Work and Surviving the Challenges: The Nigerian Way?

Both male and female wage earners in contemporary Nigeria confront the challenges of getting into and surviving in formal employment. These challenges are further complicated by the fact that most formal channels of facilitating the organization of work settings are simply not effective. Changing economic, political, and social trends have created an atmosphere where bribery and corruption thrive as viable assets for getting ahead. Every Nigerian ethnic group has its own slang that captures the strong presence of corruption in the distribution of social resources. In the Igbo metropolis, especially within elite circles, one hears the term IM, which stands for *ima mmadu*, a popular Igbo expression that literally means "knowing someone." IM points to one's proximity to highly placed persons in society who can use their influence to obtain favors for others. As one local commentator puts it, in Nigeria "opportunities for competition are circumscribed by unfavourable social and economic development" and for many people, the resort to unofficial channels is almost inevitable.[49] The sharing of employment opportunities along ethnic and religious lines further complicates the politics of gender and class in paid work.

In addition to IM, a specific politics of gender called *bottom power* is also blamed for making things worse. Women are often accused of using bottom power, their sexual attraction, to exert some influence on those in formal authority. Commenting on the collision of IM and bottom power in the rank and file of formal employment, Zahra Nwabara remarks, "'Long legs' and nepotism are very common in Nigeria and the majority of people, men and women, suffer from these practices, because the[y] . . . come from the 'wrong' class . . . ; they are not rich, they do not have rich and influential friends. However, it should be mentioned that . . . women's [appointment] in senior positions are due to these practices, unfortunately. But then, it is almost impossible [for women] to get senior appointments in any other way."[50]

Agbese and Nwabara, among other critics, point to the exacerbation of an age-old problem. The politics of favoritism, which breeds these corruptive practices, has very deep roots in Nigeria. The Nigerian state, they claim, even in the very early stages of its formation was riddled with ethnic rivalries that drew clear lines of loyalty in politics and social governance. Even the common interests of class and national progress shared by the elite were often expressed along those lines. In the early years after independence, a number of social critics were quick to identify the persistence of culturally reinforced nepotism and called for drastic policies to arrest the trend. As one notable critic, J. W. Hanson, argued, "There is needed a whole series of new functional attitudes towards efficiency, hiring and promotion. Functional competence, not family or town or clan loyalties must become the criterion used when filling niches in a modern industrial society. The task of changing such attitudes is formidable."[51] At a time when formal employment was virtually the exclusive preserve of men, Hanson was speaking to a male audience. But as Agbese and Nwabara point out, both men and women are now well woven into the myths and realities of this historical trend. Indeed, the stories of Igbo career women in subsequent chapters lend credence to Agbese and Nwabara's concerns. Their stories provide vivid examples of IM and bottom power in their workplaces.

Despite the social barriers to and the limitations of schooling and paid work as viable assets for social mobility, Igbo women hold tenaciously to them for many reasons. The career women in this book are aware of the social expectations they must meet, and they accept, to some extent, their limited capacity to embrace paid labor. As they point out, an increasing number of highly educated women are entering the labor market, many of them establishing a career before getting married. Such women value the financial independence their jobs provide as well as the potential boost to family income, which is attractive to men given the present economic times. But beyond the economic status attained by this group of highly educated female wage earners, the desire to fulfill themselves professionally also ranks high among their reasons for engaging in paid work. Formal employment for these women provides emotional fulfillment and a healthy departure from full-time domestic life.

The experiences of women who share their stories here show that it is not formal education and paid employment per se that determine women's social advancement. Rather, it is the manner in which these assets have evolved both as avenues for social mobility and as vehicles for perpetrating cultural and foreign forms of gender subjugation. These women's stories also demonstrate the various ways in which the larger female collective contest their subordinate status. In their struggles to move ahead as career women, Igbo women negotiate the barriers posed by patriarchal continuities and exploit the cracks provided by patriarchal contradictions to advance their claims to power and social resources. These women are aware that, despite their declining economic prospects, education and formal employment remain the crucial assets to social mobility in Nigeria. Their stories clearly portray their high level of sensitivity to the social expectations and boundaries that shape their lives. Their comments reveal a keen awareness of the social pressures and problems they are barraged with. But the decisions they have made about family, schooling, and work strongly point to their own personal convictions as to how far society should shape their destiny. If the experiences of these career women are any indication of progress made, one can safely argue that a significant number of African women today are taking a slightly different route: redefining the relations of gender to upset an established status quo. Both their actions in some instances and silence in others question the specific paths to social recognition that society insists they must carefully tread.

As was mentioned in chapter 1, the material in the chapters that follow comes from a series of interviews conducted between August 1991 and March 1992. Note that the ages of participants have not been adjusted to reflect the time that elapsed between the interviews and publication.

4

Your Life Is Not Entirely Your Business

Marriage and Social Status

Initially people ask, Who is the father of this girl? But after
some time they begin to ask, Who is the husband?

—*Erimma*

If the children are all girls, it is naturally the woman's fault.

—*Chika*

We [African women] do not accept polygamy by nature. Like
the white woman, we are also jealous.

—*Rose*

As far as they [in-laws] are concerned, the wife is a visitor in
the house. So they are free to do as they please.

—*Ifeyinwa*

As was the case in many African societies, the Igbos carefully stipu-
lated rules and regulations for the process of socialization that guided
men and women into adulthood. Marriage was the primary rite of
passage into adulthood. But attaining the status of married person
was only the beginning (see chapter 2). Individuals, male and female
alike, were expected to conduct themselves in certain ways within
marriage or face serious social and personal consequences.

The nature of marriage and family life, the gendered expectations
surrounding them, and the social boundaries placed by Igbo society
have over time also yielded in some ways to social transformation. For
instance, within and outside marriage the indigenous avenues of social recognition, economic autonomy, and political voice were significantly weakened by the introduction of formal education, commerce,
law, and employment (see chapter 2). In a hybridized social order where

foreign and indigenous cultural features struggle to take root, both the taken-for-granted privileges of tradition and new assets introduced through colonization were contested by social actors with various degrees of intensity. In a continuous struggle that presented many challenges, Igbo women contested their place in society. But as the experiences of women in this book vividly portray, individual women's responses to these challenges vary depending on social location and personal circumstances.

Evaluating Choices and Making the Decision

Erimma emphasizes the importance of marriage as the one and only marker that signifies a woman's entrance into adulthood. She is thirty-five years old, single, and teaches chemistry in a secondary school. At her age and surrounded by schoolchildren, Erimma understands first-hand the way society looks at not-so-young single women like her. She captures this social mood in an Igbo adage: "In Igbo culture every woman must marry. *Must* [is emphasized] because, as the Igbos say, initially people ask, Who is the father of this girl? But after some time they begin to ask, Who is the husband? If you allow them to keep asking who your father is, then you have not arrived." Erimma lives in Enugu, a major city in the Igbo heartland. Enugu is an old metropolis that draws job seekers from various parts of Igboland. Igbo women who venture into formal employment, even in the private sector, might for social reasons prefer Enugu to bigger cities like Lagos and Port Harcourt, which offer far more lucrative opportunities. Enugu is closer to home, and for a single Igbo woman like Erimma, the choice to stay in Enugu is prompted more by the fact that she is still unattached than by any yearning to preserve a sense of belonging. Erimma struggles to contain the increasing urgency with which society, in subtle and covert terms, reminds unmarried women like her of the passage of time. Leaving her rural community of extended relatives probably reduced the degree to which she is nagged about her "problem." But residing among people of different social backgrounds in a city like Enugu does not completely remove unmarried women from the social glare. Individuals regularly find themselves among groups of people during events, such as funeral ceremonies, weddings, meetings hosted by town unions, and professional gatherings. Although age still commands considerable respect among elites, a woman's marital status strongly affects how she is treated in any social circle.

Erimma is well aware that Igbo women who pursue other ambitions without meeting this primary requirement may have to contend with a society unappreciative of their achievements. Since marriage is expected to crown other aspirations outside the domestic sphere, Erimma's status is at best incomplete. In contrast to her married female colleagues, Erimma remains vulnerable to social scrutiny. Nnenna, thirty-four, a legal manager in a commercial bank, is married with two young children. Although she married early enough and has no first-hand experience of the problems women like Erimma experience, she can well empathize with them. She recounts the painful experience of a close friend who "is about thirty-five years old and not married. When she tells you about her experiences you pity her. Wherever we go, people would like to attend to me first, as a Madam, before listening to her, a Miss. Of course, I can only qualify [in many cases] as a Madam if I'm wearing two wrappers.[1] . . . The office is also a problem. The men are bound to make sexual advances. Our people do not have respect for women who are single and past their prime, regardless of their educational attainments."

Ifeyinwa, thirty-eight, a married civil servant with five young children, takes issue with this social logic, insisting that what is seen as a rite of passage cannot straighten anyone out: "Society sees the unmarried adults, especially the females, as being irresponsible. Even if you're married and for one reason or the other you opt out of that marriage, leaving your children behind, you're also considered an irresponsible person. . . . I don't really believe that marriage makes one responsible. There are also many married men who are irresponsible." Elite women, such as Ifeyinwa, can voice their disapproval at what they see as society's misdirected, unjust treatment. But no woman would want to make herself a target for social disapproval or ridicule. Igbo culture, Chika explains, makes no accommodation for spinsterhood. The unmarried woman is regularly reminded of her problem and may not find close allies to support her even in elite circles. As an unmarried female teacher several years ago, Chika recalls, "You find that at the end of each working day, there is no one to visit because all the girls are married and busy with their families, some with one or two children already." Chika's clique of old friends had all gotten married and gave her the cold shoulder every time she visited. She knew she was no longer welcome in that circle.

Some single women who find themselves in a similar situation might simply shun the married circle and seek out birds of the same feather. Others go to great lengths to nurture the old ties, remaining at the margins of the new clique. Each woman, Chika explains, responds to the pressure in her own way, given her personal circumstances, weighing options and possible tradeoffs. But ultimately, that pull to attain the rites of passage keeps every head turned in a similar direction. Ogechi, thirty-six and single, a vice-principal in a coed secondary school, admits, "The ultimate ambition for any woman is to get married at some point in her life. . . . No matter how hard you work, no matter how forward-looking, how upwardly mobile, if you're not married, [people] still look down on you. Even if it is your choice to remain single they will think there is something very bad about you, which prevents men from coming for your hand. That is the Nigerian reality. I don't think any Nigerian woman can escape that except if she decides to live abroad or join a religious order."

Interestingly, neither Erimma nor Ogechi is prepared to accept society's dictate at the expense of personal values and priorities. Even though they went to great lengths to explain the premium society places on marriage and why, their responses clearly show that they are prepared to push the boundaries of social expectations. Of course, their social locations could well dictate the intensity with which Erimma and Ogechi could resist or capitulate to the pressure, since the decision is not entirely theirs to make. Uzoamaka, for instance, has had to deal with pressures subtly exerted over the past two years by relatives beyond her immediate family. She is thirty-five, a schoolteacher, and lives with her parents. Her father retired a few years ago from the middle ranks of the civil service. Her mother is a housewife and barely literate. The family has maintained very close links with many relatives in the rural areas, some of whom have consistently voiced their concerns about Uzoamaka's single status. Against her initial convictions, Uzoamaka gradually began to entertain the concerns of family members. "I came to realize," she calmly states, "that if you really want to be a part of this society you have to consider marriage. I mean, your life is not yours. In family circles you used to move freely; people will now draw you aside and ask what the problem is. They are so bothered about your single state that you wonder if it is really your business or theirs."

For single women such as Erimma, Uzoamaka, and Ogechi, who are well over thirty, age often becomes the all-important factor around which these pressures to marry revolve. Igbo families are well aware that as their unmarried daughters advance in years, society becomes increasingly doubtful of their procreative ability (chapter 2). Erimma, Uzoamaka, and Ogechi also face additional pressures because they are first daughters. As the ada among her siblings, each woman's "refusal" to marry might affect the marriage prospects of younger sisters. Despite their academic and professional achievements, these career women's marital status conveys to society an "adamant stance" against a very important cultural injunction. Such a stance can also hurt younger sisters' chances. Such unmarried women might even be perceived as being unfair to younger sisters who may not be prepared to tread a similar path.

In contrast to her single counterparts, Ngozi has been spared not only the social pressure from society to marry but also much of the usual prodding that comes from well-meaning parents. She is thirty and a senior accountant in a commercial bank. Her father, now deceased, was for many years a permanent secretary in the state civil service. Her mother is a successful businesswoman and one of the first Nigerian female university graduates. Ngozi and her three siblings studied in Britain. She finished her university degree two years ago and returned to Nigeria. For much of her adult life Ngozi's parents did not interfere in the details of her personal life. Hence, the pressure exerted by people outside her immediate family is a new experience for her. "The problem . . . is that your life is not yours. Here, people have not learned to mind their own business. I'm not personally worried about being single . . . , but people around here will make sure that they continually remind you about the passage of time. . . . I try not to worry because it is better to wait for the right person than to rush into a marriage that won't last."

Ngozi's relatives in the village may not understand her desire for a better world. In their eyes she is probably not too old for marriage. But she is certainly not getting any younger. Many of them would be disturbed by the fact that Ngozi, at her age, does not seem to be perturbed by the social discomfort regarding her situation. Some may even find it difficult to understand her reluctance to take this next logical step. Those relatives back in the village are worried by the fact that she keeps postponing the joy of being under a man's roof and bearing his children. In the normal course of life, Ngozi's life should by now be revolving around the responsibilities of her marital household. Although Ngozi has a friendly but certainly distanced relationship with her relatives, they still have their own subtle ways of conveying disapproval. "Even though I do help some of them out financially," she explains, "that does not stop them from urging me to get married. . . . Even in their squalor, their thinking, especially the women, is that you're nothing without a husband and kids."

Economic decline has created a greater financial burden for those in elite circles who were often considered far more privileged than their poor village relatives. Before the advent of the SAPs and other economic upheavals that followed, pressures for financial assistance were often directed at the nuclear family and men in particular. Except in families where women's economic or marital status gave them far more privilege than others, relatives were more likely to approach men. But with many elite families struggling to survive and fewer capable elite men to fall back on, the question is not who should help but who has the means to help.

However, some of the concerns shared by Erimma and Ogechi are somewhat remote in Ngozi's life. Given her social background, Ngozi's immediate family has conveniently placed some degree of 'social' distance between themselves and her relatives. Her schooling experience appears to have stretched this distance further. Ngozi's mother was one of the early graduates of higher education in Nigeria. She excelled far above her male and female peers and therefore appreciates the leverage formal education and employment offer women. According to Ngozi, her mother took her time in deciding whom and when to marry. By the standards of her time, she married late. Ngozi's mother went to great lengths to encourage both her male and female children to work hard in order to fully tap the opportunities formal education offered. In Ngozi's view women should not rush into marriage simply to please family and friends: "Once you're exposed, you realize that there is a better world out there and you want it for yourself." Her appreciation for this better world, Ngozi explains, has long been nurtured by her own mother's experience. She is happy to point out to anyone who cares that her mom "is not particularly worried, maybe because she herself didn't get married early."

Each of the single career women who shares her views here recognizes that, despite her professional status, she must also grapple with the choice of whom to marry. She must decide when to signal her readiness to her immediate family and her extended family, whose support would be readily given. Anything that may be seen either as her inability to attract a suitor or as an arrogant stance that drives potential suitors away is deeply felt within this network of immediate and extended families, who make it their business to see an end to the situation. But as career women these women do not see marriage as something one should do to escape the wrath of family and friends or a step they must take to feel complete as adults. They are clearly concerned about the *kind* of union it is going to be. These women are not likely to embrace marriage primarily for economic security. For women in their position, any potential marital union is not about what a man can do for them but primarily for the emotional fulfillment they could share with a partner. Their defiant stance is not really against marriage. It is instead against a system that exploits every agency and nuance of society to force them into marriage at all costs. They see this system as discordant with present realities. They question the rigid definition of marriage that forces them to mortgage their lives.

Nevertheless, they do not have their heads in the clouds. They realize that society has its own weapons and penalties used in shepherding its flock. These women have to weigh their options and know when they have negotiated their best option. In their view, women do not simply bow to social pressure and accept marriage. The decision to eventually accept a suitor's hand is in many cases the result of a careful and protracted evaluation of pros and cons (see chapter 5). Their views and actions signify a redefinition of marriage; they place it among other aspirations they are not willing to completely surrender.

After Marriage, What? Procreation and Son Preference

The greatest challenge any married Igbo woman can face is the inability to bear children for her husband. Since children are central to the survival of Igbo marriage, when couples marry the assumption is that they are ready to raise a family. In the Igbo context, couples are expected to put procreation at the center of their plans, building other dreams around it. Giving one's marriage a few years to mature, taking the time to prepare for children, or waiting until a reasonable degree of financial stability has been reached are not considered valid reasons to postpone starting a family. Since children are the bedrock of the union, it is around them that other aspects of married life are expected to revolve. When children do not arrive after a few years, the union is already standing on shaky ground. Mma, a lawyer who runs the legal department of a commercial bank, captures the plight of the childless Igbo woman in her own experience: "You know what they do to us [women] in Igboland? Without children they don't think there is any hope for the marriage. I went to various hospitals, and the medical reports showed that there was nothing wrong with me. Of course, it is often assumed that the fault is with the woman. I can't remember my husband going for any medical tests. I was the one who was worried. He didn't appear disturbed."

Mma's painful marriage lasted only three years. She and her husband, a medical doctor, were married in 1978, a year after they graduated from the university. They left the next year for further studies in Britain. When the marriage failed to produce any offspring by the end of the second year, her husband's family became impatient. "We didn't plan to return to Nigeria when we did, but the pressure from his family was relentless. The letters kept coming, as well as phone calls from his sisters. My husband just woke up one morning and told me we were leaving. He didn't even complete his specialist course. Luckily, I had finished mine. . . . We came home . . . and the mother, sisters, and brothers continued to harass us. . . . With time he changed sides and . . . eventually I had to leave."

As Mma's story reveals, it is usually the women who bear the blame for childless marriages and those that have not produced male heirs. The possibility that a couple's inability to bear children could be the husband's "fault" is never entertained. Even in contemporary elite circles, where education and science should correct any cultural myths about procreation, the woman is still held responsible for the sex of the offspring.[2] While elite women are often prepared to undergo medical exams and treatments to improve their chances, many elite men would not even entertain any suggestions that could point to a verdict they are not prepared to accept. After the separation, Mma stayed with her parents for a few years before she could pull herself together to step back into the professional world. As a staunch Catholic, she explained, she did not even consider remarrying. Even though she desperately wanted to have her own child, Mma also refused to try her luck in less formal relationships with men, an option some women in her situation might consider. She instead opted for what she considered a more acceptable alternative for a woman of her social background and currently lives with her adopted four-year-old daughter, Aneta. By adopting a child without any blood ties to her natal family, Mma clearly stepped out of the established cultural boundaries in Igboland. Mma's decision to adopt a girl was quite deliberate. According to her, adopting a son would raise the question of identity, which could undermine any legitimate claims to inheritance as well as his sense of belonging with male relatives in the future. For her little daughter, Mma reasoned, marriage into another family would take care of these potential questions. It is evident, however, that Mma, given her religious background, needed the support of immediate family in taking on the challenge to adopt Aneta (see chapter 2 on adoption as a relatively recent option in elite circles).

Except for the two young mothers, Chika and Nnenna, all the married women who share their views here have one or more male children. Chika, the schoolteacher with three little girls, decries the hefty blame she has to carry as the one responsible for this family problem. Although she is not overly concerned about not having a son at present, she also recognizes that her husband could still exercise the option that could change everything. She acknowledges,

> Even the men know that it is not the woman's fault. The Igbo man would push all that behind to enable him to shift the blame. . . . So if the children are all girls, it is naturally the woman's fault. . . . The woman is the one mostly derided and the man just sits back and watches her take the blame. My husband is educated. He knows the score too. . . . That, however, does not rule out the fact that he, like most Igbo men, believes that it is my fault. . . . If he didn't, why look for a second or third wife?

Chika is precariously hanging on to the hope that she will one day provide her husband with at least one male child. But in her view, the threat of "full blown" polygamy (i.e., having a cowife imposed on her) is still remote. Nnenna, the bank manager with two female children, is in a similar position. According to her, women in her position may not feel much compulsion to keep trying for a male child, but she has to consider her husband's feelings:

> If I were to have my way I'll stop at two [children] because these girls give me so much joy. . . . They are very intelligent. . . . But with this Nigerian male thing . . . the man would like to have a male heir even if he [the son] is a thief or a tout. . . . I am going to try . . . for my husband's sake. . . . You see, because I care for him, I would like to have a male child for him since I know that he would prefer to stay married to one woman. . . . At the moment, they [husband's family] probably think that the marriage is still too young to start pestering us. . . . I know my husband and I are very close, but . . . this is Nigeria. There is always a brother or sister or parent [in-laws] to do the prodding.

Both Chika and, more so, Nnenna argue that their socioeconomic status provides a strong bargaining position, especially in the worsening economic climate. But for now they prefer to sit tight and nurture their marriages even as they try to avoid underestimating whatever threats may lie ahead. Each woman intends to build her security around other sources of strength. As Chika maintains, "I know that as long as I give these girls the best I can afford, a good education, they would grow up to assume all those [financial] responsibilities that are normally expected of men. If my husband decides at any time that the marriage has to end simply because I could not give him a male child, . . . that is fine by me. . . . I know I can take care of myself." Nnenna agrees with Chika: "Even if he decides to take another wife . . . , I wouldn't care . . . because I can fend for myself and my children."

Son preference is fairly common among other Nigerian ethnic groups as well. This might be due to the fact that gender remains central to social organization in certain ways that remain unique to African cultures. Son preference continues to exert considerable influence on gender relations in these cultures because it feeds on other established institutions, especially its companion, polygamy.

Of Polygamy and Its Incursions

The challenges of meeting procreation requirements in Igboland certainly open up a legitimate window for polygamous marriage and polygamous incursions to flourish in elite circles. As Chika explains, not having a male child leaves an obvious cultural challenge Igbo elites are not yet ready to handle: "You cannot begin to think outside the village context. You have to consider what happens in the place where your roots are . . . in the village there are certain issues women are not allowed to handle or discuss. . . . If there is no male child in the family, who protects the [widowed] woman when such issues arise? For instance, if I end up without a male child, when the girls are getting married and their father is not there, who would handle the issues involved?" Even though Chika lives permanently in the city and visits the village only on occasion, her life is still rooted in the dynamics of kinship relations outside the domain of her everyday life. Her statement below captures the vulnerable position of an elite wife who has not established the very traditional roots that would protect her and her children: "When there is a son he naturally takes charge and decides who will have the last say. Without him the uncles will take control. You know how some of them pretend to be on your side only to go behind [your back] and plot against you. . . . Before you know it, the girls have all married and the uncles are fighting over their father's estate and there is no one to stop them."

The threat of polygamy distorts the picture further by shifting the responsibility to the woman. As Ifeyinwa, the civil servant with five children—a boy and four girls—remarks, "It is common to see a woman, in the attempt to have a male child, bear as many as ten children, and some even die in the process." Men can turn to polygamy to enhance their chances of bearing children (see chapter 2). Women have few alternatives since adoption is yet to receive the much-needed cultural acceptance. The married Igbo women in this book agree that the Igbo wife may be more inclined to persevere than to seek a divorce. This is because the decision to leave could be much costlier for her than for her husband. For instance, even the Igbo woman armed with a career knows that she is not automatically guaranteed child custody if she chooses to leave her husband. The law grants custody to the spouse it deems to be in a better position to protect the interest of the child. In principle this provision gives women an edge over their spouses, but in many cases men exploit their traditional privilege with little or no social resistance.[3] For women, divorce may therefore not be a wise decision. Interestingly, the older respondents appear to be more tolerant of this cultural requirement than the younger women. These older women seem to accept any predicament procreation puts a couple in as part of the challenges culture presents. They are concerned mainly about how women can manage the situation to lessen the impact. Mary, fifty-five, a schoolteacher with four grown children, insists, "It depends on the confidence you have in your husband. If you're really close, . . . he should be able to convince you about the need for a male child. You wouldn't want to make him a laughingstock among his mates, especially in the company of their own sons. You would feel that it is unfair not to give him another chance, even though there is no guarantee of having a son. . . . Some men would even ask their wives to select a woman of their choice. When he is very gentle about it, you cannot but give in."

Christie, forty-nine, an assistant director in a government department, accepts polygamy as a culturally legitimate option that elite women must come to terms with. What she feels should be addressed are the hateful antagonisms between cowives that this type of union can, if unchecked, create. In her view,

It is un-African for a woman to leave her husband because he took another wife. It's not proper. The problem, however, is that usually when the second wife arrives, she is labeled "the one that will have a male child" and the first wife "the one that didn't have a male child." There is, therefore, the tendency for the man to discriminate in favor of the second wife. . . . Ordinarily, the fact that your husband wants to marry a second wife should not cause trouble. If he is a good husband, he seeks your consent. . . . The problem is that many [elite] men don't approach it this way. [Nevertheless], if the [woman] leaves merely because her husband is getting a second wife, people will blame her. So for that reason alone, she might stay whether she likes it or not.

Rose is fifty-eight and an assistant director in a civil service department. Her inherent acceptance of polygamy as a legitimate cultural institution is rooted in her strong belief that most African cultures and the men they breed are different. "Some of our men," she points out, "have also experienced the evils of polygamy." But for some innate reason, African men seem unable to resist the urge to indulge in this practice. Both polygamous marriage and polygamous incursions into monogamous marriage are, she admits, bitter pills for women, especially elite wives, to swallow. No African woman would voluntarily embrace polygamy. But every victim must accept this painful reality. Rose argues her point: "The [romantic] love we read about in literature, which should be the ideal, is unknown to the Nigerian—or the African—man. I will say this many times over. The white woman does not love any more than we do. It is not that we do not know how to love. The problem is that the Nigerian man does not appreciate your giving your whole self to him. He can fling it away at any point."

The African woman, Rose advises, must find ways to gird her loins, to prepare for the shock any time, and to find ways to lessen the pain if that reality visits her. It does not help the Igbo woman who faces sharing her man with a cowife to sit and moan. Speaking from the experiences of women friends, she warns any prospective victim, "You can break down mentally . . . such a pain can kill. . . . So you restrict the relationship to material things. We [African women] do not accept polygamy by nature. Like the white woman, we are also jealous. . . . [Polygamy] breeds suspicion."

The younger career women, in contrast, totally reject these views. They categorically reject that part of tradition that reinforces polygamy through son preference. Son preference, they insist, demands a woman's acceptance of polygamous ties in order to further her husband's patriarchal sphere of privilege. These younger women unanimously castigate polygamy in all its forms—from sharing one's husband with unknown partners to leaving the marital home for a cowife. Both the married ones, like Chika and Nnenna, and the unmarried ones, like Ogechi and Erimma, refuse to buy into any cultural justification that supports polygamy in contemporary society. The young mothers without male children recognize the threat of polygamous incursions, but would never give their approval to a second wife. All of them recognize, however, that each woman's personal circumstance could reinforce either her resistance to or her accommodation of the unpleasant situation. Indeed, the personal responses of the married women here reflect their relative bargaining power. Chika, the school teacher married to an architect, admits that it would not be easy making it on her own, "[provided] he is able to take good care of us. I would move to a part of the house with my children and give them [husband and new wife] space to enjoy themselves . . . [laughter] . . . or try their luck at producing a male child. The problem would start when he says he doesn't have money to pay my children's school fees. Of course, he has to have money because training the child is his responsibility. . . . As long as they [husband and new wife] don't step on my toes, he is free to do what he wants."

Nnenna, the bank manager married to a university professor, agrees with Chika. The only difference in her case, she explains, is her economic status. If the unavoidable happens, she states, "I wouldn't stand in his way because I have my own personal pride. . . . There is nothing I can do if I am unfortunate enough not to have a son. . . . I'm not God, but the day he decides to go ahead [and marry another woman], that is the day I will move out of this house. I wouldn't stay to get the crumbs. In any case, I would've gotten the best of him." Interestingly, the differing views expressed by these Igbo career women convey different levels of acceptance. The older women legitimize polygamy for procreation requirements. They also accept their men's extramarital escapades as merely part and parcel of their polygamous privilege that women must live with. All the younger married women reject polygamy on any grounds. But the older ones seem prepared to accommodate a husband's extramarital affairs under certain conditions. It really boils down to how vulnerable a woman's situation is; how the pros of her decision weigh against the cons. Chika points out,

Whether he has a girlfriend at all is not in question because most men, even the ones you think are very poor, do it. That some [married] men are not well off does not stop them from keeping a lover. They must have a girl outside. It is like one of the norms in society, something you have to live with. Normally, a woman would not frown on it as long as the man doesn't overdo it. . . . As long as I don't find out, I would like to convince myself that he doesn't have any other woman. . . . As long as he keeps his tracks covered the burden is much lighter to bear.

Despite the different vulnerable locations where a woman in either group could find herself, the young women, more than their older counterparts, strongly decry elite society's inherent acceptance of polygamy, which has created an atmosphere in which men are free to roam about and exercise their sexual privilege unquestioned. Elite women find themselves in circles where they battle with other women in order to attract or keep male partners. As Nnenna exclaims, such a battle may be brooding in one's own home, with little or no support from those you most expect it from. She cites one common threat many Igbo elite women dread: "Can you imagine divorcing your husband because he is seeing another woman? You go to your mother and she says, 'Eh? Go back to him. Go and stay with him!' [Even] if . . . my husband is sleeping with the maid, she'll likely ask me to send the maid away and forget it. My own mother!"

Obviously the legitimacy that a culture confers on polygamous unions and incursions still has significant weight, even in elite circles. Igbo women's economic advantage can go only so far to challenge an established order. If women like Nnenna, a bank manager, would consider such traditional strictures before making a move, Chika, a mere teacher, is even in a more vulnerable position. She admits just how far she can go:

What can you do? You don't have a choice in matters such as this. The way I look at it is that as long as I am getting what I think is my fair share from the man, and as long as he doesn't overdo it, then. . . . By overdoing it I mean, for instance, either bringing his girlfriend home or if we are going to a party, the girl comes too; if I ask him for money or a set of handbag and shoes, he tells me that he can't afford it, when I know his girlfriend and she dresses well, yet he wants me to look like a house girl. That is where the trouble will start.

Of the three groups, the single women are the most overt in their rejection of polygamy, both in its traditional and modified forms.

Ogechi, the vice-principal, says, "I know that if it's just getting married, the suitors are readily available . . . , [but] I think there are a few things you must feel comfortable with. Nobody wants the perfect man, [but marriage] is not something that can be forced on somebody. . . . I might consider marrying a widower, . . . but if marriage means having a cowife, I will never agree to that. . . . I think women should learn from the experience of others. There is no need to walk into a ditch someone has fallen into previously."

Ngozi, the banker who studied in Britain, agrees: "With my present job, I can give myself more, materially, than most men can give me. Why settle for less? Besides, Mr. Right is going to come. Until then, I can't allow myself to be pushed into what I don't want. . . . I know there are more women than men and some girls will tell you, 'I don't mind being number seven or ten as long as the man has money.' Of course, you get the money, but not the companionship." Despite the different views shared, all the women equally decry the contempt and division polygamous marriages and incursions breed among women. Pushed into a vulnerable position, they all agree, women often resort to fighting one another. Ngozi describes the acrimonious atmosphere in her workplace:

> I think any single girl poses a threat to [married women] because we tend to look trimmer and dress better, and maybe because we don't have to deal with family problems. They feel that getting closer to us single girls may jeopardize their marriage. . . . You'd be surprised how many women think like that. Of course, we do get on very well in the office. We crack jokes and all . . . , but these pleasantries never extend beyond the office. . . . I'm not interested, whoever their husbands may be, but I can understand their predicament. We all know just how far the Nigerian man can go. Even if married women trust their single female friends, they may worry about their husbands making fools of themselves and humiliating them. Where some men end up marrying their maids or their sisters-in-law, what won't they do?

Unattached career women are seen as a potential threat to the marriages of stay-at-home wives or those whose status keeps them well out of these professional circles. These career women could easily attract their husbands—a dangerous diversion for a married man. For the elite wife, extramarital relations pose a serious threat to her marriage, both emotionally and financially. After all, the man is expected to shower the mistress with money, gifts, and attention. Cast in the position of potential "other woman," single women in formal work settings try to maintain a professional distance from their male colleagues in order to avoid any amorous advances. Mma, forty, the legal adviser for a bank, has worked hard, with her own clique of divorced and separated women, to build the necessary support for survival. Since her separation from her husband nine years ago, she has increasingly sought out women who can relate to her life experience. "Most of my friends," she acknowledges, "are . . . separated, you know, . . . single mothers. . . . Many of them are people I used to know . . . , some from my university days. It so happens that we have found ourselves in the same boat. I can think of at least five of such friends. . . . You know what happens in Nigeria. At least in our circle, there won't be any talk about stealing somebody's husband or misguiding somebody's wife. And you can bet we are under no illusion as to what marriage itself can offer us."

Outside formal work settings, friendship between married and unmarried women may also arouse suspicion. The married woman who does not trust her husband with women must carefully watch his relationship with unattached female friends. Single women are then faced with the challenge of keeping their relationship with both spouses above suspicion. They could easily be accused of stealing a friend's husband or misguiding someone's wife. The resulting tension discourages many elite women from sustaining close ties with female friends. Mma and her friends have mobilized themselves to build a support base against the usual social onslaught on their marital status. In a culture where there is always a waiting list for a husband, these women who have made at least the first round and in society's eyes *failed* may be expected to walk with drooping shoulders. But Mma and her friends can certainly manage on their own. With children to raise, in most cases, and a profession to deal with, they have more than enough on their plates. In any case, their economic status increasingly places these women in the position of benefactors to less privileged male relatives and friends. Under "normal" circumstances, a good number of such men would have had a thing or two to say about these unattached women's lifestyles. But as grateful recipients, they readily swallow such reservations.

On the whole, all the Igbo career women who share their views here, agree that both spouses have much to lose in a union they have heavily invested in. An elite husband, the younger career women point out, must weigh the spousal support he enjoys, and his children's welfare, against any rationale for indulging in extramarital relations. They feel that with the increasing need for two incomes, men are more cautious than before about such dangerous attractions. They believe that unlike the majority of Igbo women, their social status not only strengthens their bargaining power within the nuclear household but also provides them with a few options. They can either exit the union entirely or simply distance themselves as much as possible from an ugly situation.

Of course, most of the married women, especially the younger ones, remain suspicious about their husbands' lives outside the household. Most admit, however, that there are no obvious signs of infidelity at this point. But the differing responses to polygamy between older and younger women are indicative of both individual circumstances and, more important, a changing social arrangement. While older married women like Mary endorse polygamy with necessary revisions, the younger married ones are unimpressed about all that those they consider cultural apologists have to say and overtly express their disgust for polygamy in any form.

Situating the Nuclear Unit within the Extended Family

Igbo career women accept that the relationship between the nuclear and extended family could seriously affect their marriage. Again, the degree of impact depends on each woman's personal circumstances. Relatives from either side of an extended family consider elite spouses as part of a larger group whose members carry one another's burdens. But a husband's relatives, more than the wife's, are more likely to exert their influence as legitimate members of the household. More often than not, the elite wife's relatives see themselves as guests and therefore might not directly assert their views. The women in this book, who speak from their own experience and that of others, agree that there are no well-established rules for the elite wife. She must feel her way and use diplomacy as situations present themselves. Since she lives in the city, away from the close scrutiny of most of her husband's relatives, the elite wife is protected from the daily wars within her husband's family.

Apart from spreading the nuclear family's benevolence as much as she can, the elite wife, in her visits to the village, should try to present herself as a good mixer. According to Chidimma, a thirty-one-year-old schoolteacher and mother of five, it is crucial that the elite wife avoid any wrong that advertises her privileged status. Married to a medical doctor with strong extended-family ties, Chidimma describes some of her own tactics: "Once you go into the village, you have to shed your education and any airs you have because they will be quick to say, 'Eh, the acada[4] woman is here.' You may have to play and dance [socialize] with women you have little in common with. In fact, some of the relations, including the women, would insist that I kneel to greet them and call them 'my husband.'[5] You try your best to avoid incurring their wrath in any way."

For many elite wives, any tensions associated with such visits could be contained, given the short time they usually spend with their husband's family. As career women who speak out here explain, husbands' relatives who live within the nuclear household could pose more of a threat than those in the village. Relatives who reside with elite couples could very easily become the village dwellers' conduit for monitoring what goes on in the city. Their crucial location then allows extended family influences to filter through the barriers of distance and familiarity. But according to Ifeyinwa, a thirty-eight-year-old civil servant and mother of five, how an elite couple relate to one another is also a good indication to a man's relatives as to how strongly they can assert their rights in elite households. Drawing from her own personal experience, she believes that "a lot depends on the man you married because most of his relatives might come with the impression that the house belongs to [him as] their brother, cousin, or uncle. In fact, as far as they are concerned, the wife is a visitor in the house. So they are free to do as they please." Ifeyinwa's husband has given her the run of the household and this has enabled her to maintain her stance. She insists, "I will not give them a free hand to behave any way they like in my house. If you want to eat, you can't just go to my pot and help yourself. If you want anything in this house, you must seek my permission; otherwise you're in trouble. You can't do whatever you like because [you think] it's your uncle's house. The house . . . belongs to both of us." But Ifeyinwa is quick to admit that without her husband's support his relatives may flout her orders, knowing that the man of the house would very likely come to their defense. In her view, a lot depends on where a husband's loyalty stands. In order to improve her vulnerable status and protect her children, the elite wife has to negotiate any loyalties established before she came into the picture.

The potential for conflict between an elite wife and her husband may be heightened when he has to cater to a good number of his relatives, especially siblings. Chidimma's husband, a physician, has both his parents and siblings to look after. Many of his siblings are still in school. Her husband prefers to handle this responsibility on his own. According to Chidimma, "They [husband and his siblings] normally keep me out of such discussions. When his brothers visit, they hold private discussions with him. I would know if he has given them money, but not the exact amount or what it's for. He would not, for instance, tell me that he has given them school fees or pocket money." Chidimma exercises diplomacy in this case, with a keen awareness of how far she can go. She feels she is not an equal partner, comfortably enough placed to share her views. But she has her ways of keeping abreast of what is happening. From time to time, she notes, "I do come across their letters to my husband. Then, I have an idea of what is going on. Normally, I won't make any noise about it. Once you start complaining, he becomes more secretive about his financial dealings with other people and begins to confide even less in you." Chidimma does not want to jeopardize any trust they have established as a couple. She knows that, in her husband's handling of extended-family affairs, she can come in only as an invited guest.

Older wives may be in a position to exert more authority than younger ones, having acquired the status of a mother and, sometimes, grandmother within the extended family. Alice was a teacher when she met her husband in the 1960s. Later she went back to the university and studied law. She describes the remarkable change in her relationship with her in-laws over time. This change, she believes, has more to do with age than professional status. "As a young wife they expected me to join the rest of the wives in communal chores like cooking during the Christmas season. When I didn't show up it was seen as pride on my part, as an acada woman. Now, they wouldn't expect me to be there. I'm not a young wife any more and they can't impose sanctions on me." Obviously, Alice's age, in addition to her professional status, has given her an edge over the younger wives within the extended family. Age is still highly revered in most African cultures and a woman's status within the extended family, and the larger society, appreciates as she gets older.[6]

All the women who share their views and life stories here agree that an elite wife's relationship with parents-in-law receives top priority. The elite wife, they point out, must be careful to maintain a decent relationship with her parents-in-law, especially the mother-in-law. Depending on her relationship with her son, a mother-in-law's wrath could become a nightmare for the elite wife. According to Chika, the inherent conflict in the relationship between wife and mother-in-law lies in the fact that "the average Igbo woman sees her daughter-in-law as a threat—somebody who has come to take her son away from her. . . . Being human, she is likely to exhibit some hostility to her son's wife. That tendency will always be there." Rose's experience as a new wife illustrates one aspect of this inherent conflict. Rose is fifty-seven, the mother of three grown children, and a top executive of a school board. Rose shares an experience in the early years of her marriage:

> During the [Nigerian civil] war when my husband was away in the army, I had to stay with his family in the village. I was accused of all sorts of crimes, like not fetching water or firewood or pounding yam for his mother. I had never done any of these chores before. My mother-in-law was not happy about my having a kitchen separate from hers and wanted us instead to share as was traditionally done. I stood my ground and her reaction was, "Are you more beautiful than my own daughter?" The daughter was illiterate and married to a senior civil servant. To my mother-in-law, there was no equal to her daughter. So, when I told her that I'm better than her daughter, she lodged a report with her as the ada and hell was let loose. Luckily, they sent for their son and son-in-law, who was also a [university] graduate. In their view, they felt that my response was justified and so their intervention saved my neck. Their son-in-law also told them that I was not supposed to do all those chores for their mother and that her daughter had not been subjected to the same treatment in his own family.

One of the basic ways parents, especially mothers, think they can express the bond they have with their sons is in the choice of whom they marry. Many parents would want to have a say in how this decision is made. Unlike daughters who marry into another family, sons bring their wives into the family. Parents know full well that this young woman coming into their son's life will become a part of the family, a change that will dramatically reshape relations with their son. Igbo parents often express great concern over the marriage of both male and female children. For instance, they often want their children to marry as close as possible to home. But their worries about a son's prospective partner differ a little from that of a daughter's. Chidimma, for example, is from another part of Igboland and her marriage did not receive her mother-in-law's blessing. The mother-in-law had wanted her son to marry a young woman whose close roots would have provided the crucial element for building a relationship between daughter and mother-in-law. Chidimma recounts how she has little or no control over what has remained a thorn in her side: "After her visits, she would go back and make all kinds of complaints against me to her younger children, who in turn passed them on to my husband, and he would eventually confront me. She wouldn't even give me the slightest impression that I had wronged her. . . . In any case, I was not their choice for a daughter-in-law. [She] says often that I don't understand their culture. . . . It's not easy to change a mother's mind in such matters. Once she decides she doesn't like you, she sticks to her opinion . . . however hard you try to please her." The stories of these Igbo career women also show that elite men are not immune to the hazards of the conflict between nuclear and extended families. They experience considerable tension as they struggle to protect the nuclear family while maintaining close ties with relatives. As Rose's experience suggests, one way elites deal with this tension is to establish their own priority scale. Those who place the nuclear family at the top of this scale go to great lengths to protect their wives and children, despite the disapproval of family members.

On the whole, the comments of Igbo career women in this volume suggest that distance still plays a key role in reducing the possibility for conflict. Elite women are spared much of the friction that could escalate with closer and more contact association. Moreover, they can use their economic resources to dilute the competition for a man's loyalty by pampering in-laws—especially a mother-in-law who remains an irregular visitor—with gifts and personal attention. Certainly, the level of support, material and otherwise, demanded by the man's relatives plays a crucial role in terms of how the relationship between wife and in-laws is constructed in practice. This is not to underestimate the pressure, financial and otherwise, that the wife's side of the family could exert.

Old Wine in New Gourds: Contending with the Relations of Gender in the Contemporary Hybridized Social Order

The experiences and viewpoints of Igbo career women shared here clearly reveal the patriarchal continuities and contradictions embedded in contemporary structure of gender relations. Like their counterparts across Nigerian ethnic groups and the continent, the subordinate position of elite Igbo women is ideologically constructed on a number of levels, the important elements of which are inextricably interrelated. Their experiences vividly portray the dialectics of traditional and foreign ideologies played out in everyday life. Thus, the challenge for these career women lies in navigating the layered facets of this hybridized culture in various contexts. Even the interpretations of Igbo culture by these career women reflect the tensions experienced by men and women as they strive to find stability in a changing social order. In accommodating son preference and to some extent polygamy, for instance, the older women are not necessarily endorsing basic patriarchal dictates that reinforce women's oppression. These women do not embrace the double standard created and are thankful that fate has spared them the pain that could have arisen from such an arrangement.

But the differing views of older and younger women clearly show that things are changing. The more dramatic break from tradition observed among the younger female generation suggests a greater independence and personal autonomy in asserting their views. Indeed, the actions of the younger women, especially the unmarried professionals, raise some interesting questions: How are they able to resist the strong social forces that force many women to accept unattractive cultural dictates, especially the pressure to settle for a traditional marriage? How are they able to negotiate the double standards that society maintains? If being single carries such a heavy social price for women in general, why do the unmarried women refuse marriage? Why would these women live under such enormous societal pressure to maintain a socially unacceptable marital status and lifestyle? What keeps them going despite the limited options they are left with? Their individual assessments of the situation clearly show that these women are well aware of the threats society holds out. It seems that despite the stigma their marital status may create, these young professional women can rest their radical stance on a strong economic status and sphere of influence outside the domestic sphere.

Although every one of these career women stresses the importance of marriage and family to them as individuals, the conception of marriage, especially among the younger ones, deviates significantly from what society offers. In fact, their continual reference to "what they are expected to do" points to a clear distinction between social expectations and their own personal convictions. It is obvious that the younger women have come to redefine existing social expectations with values and normative patterns very different from the existing standard. The single women, such as Uzoamaka, Ogechi, and Erimma, appear to have a pretty good idea of what they want in a husband and would not simply accept any suitor in response to existing social dictates. Such resistance may well threaten the existing social order. The young women's views about polygamy may indicate a new trend. Married or single, the younger Igbo career women who express their views and stances here strongly oppose the practice, dismissing the traditional views of their older sisters. But it is also interesting that while they would not personally embrace an outside wife, none of the women interviewed is critical of other professional women who accept this option.

These younger career women are definitely breaking ranks with the norms of social behavior that militate against their progress in the contemporary society. The steps they are prepared to take, subtle in many instances, brave and almost confrontational in others, are certainly cushioned by their social position. As highly educated female wage earners, their status has given them more options than the less privileged majority. It has provided them with a few more choices that other women can only dream of. The younger women are increasingly pushing the boundaries of normative gender behavior, renegotiating the gender relations of power and at every stage. Their stories go to show that regardless of their inherent limitations for women, higher education and paid labor continue to provide a crucial power base on which women could rally forces in the struggle to take control of their lives. Patriarchal continuities and contradictions continue to exert considerable influence on the utility of formal education and employment for women. But the leverage that education and employment provide, especially for those in the socially valued professions, still makes these assets the most viable weapons for negotiating patriarchal continuities and contradictions in contemporary society.

5

Gendered Lives, Gendered Aspirations

Igbo Women and the Marriage-Career Conflict

> If I was to do it all over again I would first of all go to the university . . . finish my education, and then find a job before getting married.
>
> —*Alice*

> It wasn't a time to stand up to your parents. . . . I did complain . . . but my father said, "No, teaching is good for women."
>
> —*Uzoamaka*

> You need a man [husband] as a sponsor since a lot of us did not come from well-to-do families.
>
> —*Chika*

> [Some of my colleagues] were scared of furthering their education because . . . they thought they'd be branded acada.
>
> —*Uchenna*

For any group of African women, the decision to move up the educational ladder in the hopes of getting a paid job that would improve one's standard of living is neither a simple nor straightforward plan. Obviously, various forms of formal training and the paid positions they attract do not hold exactly the same prospects the world over. These assets take on their meanings and values within particular social contexts, which determine their utility for both women and men. Young schoolgirls in Igboland may not be critically aware of social boundaries, which could curtail their career aspiration. But as they move through the grades they begin to identify and respond to acceptable social options.

The life profiles of four elite women reveal the challenges many Igbo women must deal with as they cautiously pursue academic and career ambitions,[1] as well as their struggles to balance married life with a full career. Alice, a lawyer, runs her own firm. Uzoamaka teaches economics in a secondary school. Chika recently left a twelve-year teaching career for a managerial position on the state education board, and Uchenna is a senior accountant with a commercial bank. These profiles were carefully chosen to represent both the major eras in Nigeria's history as well as the usual career patterns associated with these eras. Every story, upon close examination, highlights some of the commonalities shared by women of similar social status in Nigeria and across Africa. At home, in school, and in the workplace, these women's experiences bring to light the interaction between their personal circumstances and the typical challenges common to elite Igbo women. After the personal profiles of each woman are presented, we examine the career choices they have made as well as the social boundaries and trends that shaped their options.

Personal Profiles

Alice

Alice, forty-eight, is a lawyer and is married with five grown children. Over the past fifteen years, she has managed to establish a small but reputable private practice. Although the law profession in Nigeria is still dominated by men, women's representation in law school is on the rise.[2] Until the mid-1980s, when the private sector began its rapid expansion with the influx of financial institutions ushered in by the SAPs, most female lawyers sought employment in public service. Alice is one of the few women with an established private practice. For a woman of her time and social background this is a rare achievement. The following account of her life from the early years shows a woman whose achievements to date set her apart from her peers within and outside the legal profession.

Alice's father was a primary school teacher. Her mother, a housewife, had no formal education. Alice started out as a secondary school teacher, a modest achievement by today's standards but one that placed her well above her peers in the 1950s and 1960s. Reflecting on her childhood years, Alice remarks, "Maybe this has to do with my nature, but I was not interested in getting married. . . . When one got married in those days, the doors to further training were practically shut. I was bent on improving myself." She attributes her success in school to the support of a doting father and an enlightened husband, both ahead of their time. Alice's father stirred in her the initial aspirations that prodded her at every stage. She was the youngest of six children and he wanted things to be different for her. "In those days," she explains, "We didn't have boyfriends. Your parents would tell you the man they approved of among your suitors. . . . My two elder sisters got married without even completing secondary school. They had to depend on their husbands. . . . You know what that means . . . my father encouraged me [to take a different path]. . . . He did not want me to be like them."

Early marriage interrupted her sisters' education, ending any career plans they might have had. Without an alternative source of income, they became fully dependent on their husbands, who, according to Alice, treated them badly. There was little Alice's family could do. Her father was in no position to support his daughters and their children. He was determined, however, that things would be different for Alice. As he declared to her on many occasions in her early school years, "You will be better prepared." He made it clear that no suitors would be considered until she completed secondary school. She graduated at sixteen and started her teaching career in 1960.[3]

For Alice, who by now had set her sights on obtaining a teaching diploma from the university, this was only a starting point. Once she secured a teaching position, Alice began to study for the university entrance examinations. She knew that her family would now welcome interested suitors and so could not afford any delays. In 1963, Alice gained admission into the University of Ibadan, the country's premier university, for a two-year teaching diploma. This was her first contact with women from western Nigeria.[4] As Alice explains, the University of Ibadan opened up a whole new world: "when one got married in those days, the doors to further training were practically shut, [but] I was bent on improving myself and . . . when I got to the University of Ibadan, I found that I was behind time. . . . I saw so many [Yoruba] women . . . who had advanced even further. It was then that I decided [after graduation] to prepare for [the entrance exam] into a full degree program."

Alice completed her training and resumed her teaching career shortly, but she could not resist the pull to return to Ibadan and pursue a full degree program. Quietly she started making plans for the next stage of her educational career. At the age of twenty-two she was offered admission into the program and with her father's approval she got ready to return to Ibadan. But in the last few months before she left for the university, a very attractive suitor showed up, her present husband. It was clear to Alice that the family would not support her plans, at least not at this time. She also knew that she would have to do more than get married. Acknowledging the expectations of society, she notes, "It's not the Igbo way . . . you know . . . getting married and not starting to have children immediately. It's not our custom." Desmond, her fiancé, seemed like a nice man, a good choice. He was Igbo and from a good family. He graduated from a college abroad with a social science degree and was working overseas as a diplomat. Once the traditional marriage ceremonies were completed Alice left Nigeria to join her husband at his foreign mission. Alice accepted the constraints marriage posed and postponed her plans for further training until her domestic responsibilities eased up. But in the wake of the 1967–70 civil war, Nigeria recalled many of its foreign diplomats and Alice's husband brought his young family home. Once again, she had to put her plans for further studies on hold.

As Alice gradually settled down in Nigeria, she quietly explored the possibilities of reentering the educational track at some point in the future. In the period that her career ambitions were on hold, she had begun to rethink her initial plan to continue with teaching. She discussed the matter with her husband a number of times and with his support decided instead to go for a law degree. She took on the challenge of acquiring the necessary prerequisite qualifications for the entrance examinations to law school. In 1972, after six years of marriage, Alice gained admission into the law school at a nearby campus of the state's only university. As she explained, her change in plans was for the most part the result of her husband's advice and encouragement. Although Alice's earlier aspirations were geared toward furthering her teaching career, her husband suggested law, an opportunity he had missed because he had no one to sponsor him. Alice points out that unlike many elite men of his time her husband did not dismiss her educational ambitions. He not only allowed her the freedom to further her educational aspirations but also wanted her to pursue a fulfilling career.

But she also points out that his support came with the usual strings attached. Alice knew early on that she would still have to wrestle with a dilemma elite women like her, especially those with high professional aspirations, faced. She admitted that his support did not necessarily mean his taking on her domestic chores. In juggling household responsibilities and schoolwork, Alice was expected to maintain a balance her husband and children could live with. Hence, she carefully planned her daily schedule to ensure that the household schedule was not unduly disrupted. The fact that the campus was only a short distance away from their residence was helpful. But with her youngest child only six weeks old at the time she started classes, the entire arrangement, Alice recalls, still proved to be a trying experience. In retrospect, she points out, "If I was to do it all over again, I would first of all go to the university . . . no disturbance from marriage and all, finish my education, and then find a job before getting married. I would not be studying and rearing children at the same time. I really found it very difficult."

After graduation from law school, Alice took her time exploring career options with her husband. She could either enter public service or establish a small private practice. These options, she felt, would enable her to conveniently combine family life and a career. But after a series of discussions with her husband, who gave his support, Alice finally settled on private practice. Again, her husband stepped in and suggested that she join an already established private firm in order to gain experience. He made the necessary arrangements with a reputable firm, where she spent nine years. During this period she had her last two children. Finally, in 1986, with her husband's financial support and all her children in school, Alice opened her own private firm and gradually began to build her legal practice. Since then she has maintained a modest practice, holding off any plans for expansion at present despite very tempting opportunities. She explains, "I can't combine all that work with a family to look after. . . . It's easier for a [male colleague]. He comes home and everything is ready for him. He is waited upon [hand and foot] by his wife, the maid, and the children. After relaxing, he goes back to chambers to work. For me, I have to combine legal practice and family chores." For now Alice is content with keeping her practice at its present scale. In her view, this is one way she can skillfully manage her "briefs" at home and at work.

Uzoamaka

Uzoamaka, an economics teacher in a secondary school at Enugu, is thirty-five years old and engaged to be married in a few months. The glimpses of her views and responses to social expectations point to a long battle to wrest her destiny from the hands of both her family and society. Over the past ten years she has taught in a number of secondary schools within the city. Uzoamaka laments the fact that she could not really embrace her own desires because of the society she found herself in. She insisted, "I never really wanted to marry. In fact, I used to think I could remain single if I choose to. After all, it's not every woman that is cut out for marriage. I felt that there is so much hassle with marriage. Besides, the examples around me were hardly encouraging."

She started her educational training without any clear directions about a future career. She had a love of the sciences and went about her schooling, especially at the secondary level, hoping to get into either medical or pharmacy school. But the prospects of pursuing either of these prospects died even before she finished secondary school. Her inability to fulfill her ambitions, according to Uzoamaka, was largely because of her social background. Neither Uzoamaka's father, who was a junior staff in the state civil service, nor her mother, a petty trader with no formal education, seemed well informed enough to provide the necessary guidance. But even without their active involvement Uzoamaka worked hard at her studies, setting her sights on a university education. She considered herself brilliant among her peers, excelling in both the arts and the sciences, but knew very little about the subject combinations required for either of the careers she aspired to. In her view, she did not receive any counseling about future careers from any of her teachers in secondary school. By the time she got to her senior year in the secondary school, Uzoamaka realized she had made a grievous mistake. Looking back, she admits, "I selected the subjects taught by the teachers I liked. I hated the physics teacher and so I dropped physics. I skipped literature because the teacher scolded students at the least opportunity. In the end, I collected a random assortment of arts and science subjects."

As a result, Uzoamaka did not meet the admission requirements for either medicine or pharmacy. Nor did the subjects she had studied add up to the prerequisites for other options she could have considered. She was greatly disappointed. Although her high grades guaranteed her a place in the school of education, this was a career path she had little enthusiasm to pursue. But as Uzoamaka noted, getting admitted into any of the universities was considered a great achievement, especially for a young woman with her family background. She was, however, very hesitant about entering the teaching profession. Since medicine and other professional careers in the sciences were no longer possible, she decided in the end to try for professions like business administration and accounting. But the opportunity to spend an extra year to prepare for entrance applications also seemed out of the question. Her father insisted that she continue with the opportunity at hand: a teaching career. Recalling her feelings at the time, she remarks, "Even at the time I got the admission letter, I knew I was heading in the wrong direction and was intent on effecting a change once I got in. . . . My elder brother was already in the same university studying medicine. Given my level of exposure and position in the family, I had to listen to my father. It wasn't a time to stand up to your parents. . . . I did complain, however, midway into my first year, opting for a bachelor's degree in economics . . . but my father said, 'No, teaching is good for women.'"

Uzoamaka went on to complete her degree in education. She accepted a teaching position shortly after graduation and lived with her parents. For obvious reasons she did not consider looking for jobs outside Enugu. As a spinster, she was not expected to take charge of her life and head in any direction she chose. In her situation such decisions would not be left entirely in her hands. She notes, "I didn't even know I had other options. As you know, teaching was a job you could get any day just by applying and attending the interview, at least, as of then. . . . Looking back now I realize that if I had bolted and refused to train as a teacher . . . if I had not listened to him [my father] and just left for Lagos [after I graduated] . . . , I would have advanced further, possible branched away from education, and actually gone for something that would have given me more satisfaction than my present job."

By the end of her first year of living at home, Uzoamaka began to feel the pressure. It was as if everyone was waiting for her to do something now that she was done with schooling. The fact that suitors were coming meant that she had little or no excuse to give for her parents and her overinquisitive relatives. As she remarked, "In the past three years I came to realize that if you really want to be a part of this society you have to consider marriage. I mean, your life is not yours. In family circles you used to move freely; people will now draw you aside and ask what the problem is."

To Uzoamaka, the pressure was misdirected and the impressions of her situation held by people around her were simply overwhelming. She just could not reconcile herself with their worries. "They are so bothered about your single status that you wonder if it is really your business or theirs. [For example], my aunties would visit and stay overnight so as to have a heart-to-heart talk with me and to find out whether there is something wrong with me or it's a problem of suitors not coming at all." According to her, many young women would eventually give in to the pressure to marry, especially when they were not shielded by distance away from home. Over the months that her present fiancé was making his presence felt among family members, she knew she had to make a decision. "After some time I realized that, like Igbo people would say, there is actually an age you get to in this society when you have to get married. Otherwise, they will think that you're wasting yourself. As the pressures mounted, I realized that it was not just my problem. Other people have to be considered. So I started to feel the way they felt. At least, I had to do something to assure them that I'm normal."

But even before she met her fiancé, Uzoamaka was already getting tired of teaching. She could no longer ignore the general dissatisfaction among teachers in public schools and the deteriorating working conditions. The SAPs introduced a host of economic policies that shrank the formal employment sector, especially public service. The latter suffered a major decline in unemployment, worsened working conditions, and the mass exodus of workers (mostly males) to the private sector. Since the emergence of the SAPs the teaching profession seemed to attract mostly those who had no other options elsewhere. A good number of disgruntled teachers accepted what at the time offered at least a meal ticket. Uzoamaka could not see herself simply marking time in a career that offered neither career satisfaction nor advancement. But any career moves at the time, she told herself, presented their dilemmas. She knew, for instance, that she would not be offered a study leave to train for a career outside the civil service. But resigning from her job would not only mean paying her way through school but also losing her source of income. She also had to contend with pressures from her parents to find a suitable partner and get married. In the end, she settled for a part-time program to earn a master's degree in education, referred to as the Sandwich program. The program is usually offered over the summer holiday. It therefore tends to attract female teachers, especially married ones. But for single female teachers like Uzoamaka, opting for the Sandwich only guarantees that they keep their livelihood. Yet many of them flock to the Sandwich program as their only choice in the interim. For Uzoamaka, "This was something I did because I wanted to keep myself busy. I was not getting anywhere in this job and many of my colleagues were getting their master's through the Sandwich program. . . . I didn't have the courage to bolt from my job and pursue a full-time professional course. I would've gone for an MBA rather than the Sandwich. I just did it to tell myself that I'm not decaying in this place."

Predictably, the program did not make any difference to Uzoamaka's quest for a career change. She knew she had to get out of teaching. But the pressure to get married mounted as she desperately explored her career options. The pressure came not only from her parents but also from her extended family and friends. Fortunately, the inception of a part-time business degree program at a nearby university campus eliminated her career dilemma. She promptly applied and was admitted. But by the end of the program's first year she could no longer keep away the stream of suitors seeking her hand in marriage. By the time her present husband showed up she was tired of being hounded by family and friends. The young man, in any case, seemed likeable, presenting an aura of charm, gentleness, and respectability. Unlike previous suitors, she quickly took to him and in a few months felt it was time to take the leap. She eventually accepted his proposal and with the support of both families began making plans with her fiancé to get married. After two years in the business program she left her teaching job to join her husband in Lagos. When we last corresponded she was pregnant and had put all career plans on hold until after the birth of her baby.

Chika

Chika is thirty-eight years old, a biology teacher with eleven years' experience, and the mother of three girls between the ages of three and one. She completed her secondary school education in 1973, amid the unsettling atmosphere of postwar Nigeria. Her childhood ambition was to become a medical doctor, but as she claims, "Nobody was there to advise us and we just picked subjects at random." She admits that since both parents had minimal formal training they had no specific aspirations for her other than ensuring that she got some education before marriage. Residential single-sex schools were the norm in her time and she attended one. The female teachers, especially those who taught science, did not help much. They did not encourage students to embrace the sciences. Chika received little or no advice from her teachers about subject choices and career prospects. In her view, the school authorities, especially her teachers, destroyed her chances of getting into a career she really loved. Chika wanted to be a medical doctor and regrets especially her decision to drop physics, which was a major prerequisite for entrance into the medical school. None of her teachers impressed upon her the future consequences of her decision. Without physics, she could not even apply to the medical school. That she did not go into the medical profession, Chika laments, was "not because I could not have made it but because I was not properly advised. If I were to go back in time I would definitely select the relevant subjects."

Stressing the importance of "getting it right the first time," Chika points out that women like her from humble origins cannot easily change such career decisions. With very little resources to educate their other children, her parents could not afford to give her a second chance. She could pursue careers after marriage but only with a husband's support—if he should choose to give it. "You need a man [husband] as a sponsor since a lot of us did not come from well-to-do families," she points out. "With marriage, the responsibility shifts to your husband." Chika's family had other siblings to care for and the boys were especially important.

Having lost all hopes of making it to medical school, Chika settled for a bachelor's degree in zoology. She planned to work with either the state's Ministry of Agriculture or the Forestry Department. But after her graduation in 1978, Chika could not secure employment in either of these establishments. Like many university graduates entering the shrinking job market at the close of the oil boom, Chika had only a few options and teaching presented a ready alternative. Unlike some of her male colleagues who moved to bigger cities to widen their job search, she had to live close to her parents:

> You know how the family is here [Igboland]. My parents had so much control over us. . . . If I had suggested moving to Lagos to look for work, they would have asked who I was going to stay with. Until I started working, I can't remember ever going out of town on my own. My parents planned my movement, when to visit this auntie or that uncle and how long. . . . They just wouldn't trust that I could take care of myself if I was left without some kind of supervision. One ends up not getting the kind of exposure required in order to strike out successfully into life. I still regret not striking out on my own, not moving to Lagos.

With the SAPs and the subsequent expansion of private investment, especially in the banking sector, the past two decades have witnessed an influx of young professional women from various parts of the country into the commercial centers, particularly Lagos. While some single women now brave the risks of such a move, most feel compelled to stay close to home in order to improve their chances of getting married. Most parents prefer that their children find marriage partners from the same ethnic group. The personal ambition and independence expressed by the single professional woman, who sets her sights on the bigger metropolis, might not work in her favor when it comes to attracting marriage suitors. Living in a city far from home, outside the watchful gaze of her family, would attract negative moral overtones. In fact, Igbo men in large cities may not even consider her marriageable since many head home when it is time to find a bride. Moreover, Chika would most likely be attractive to prospective Igbo suitors, including those coming from the cities, as a "homegrown girl." Igbo parents, she points out, would not easily embrace a nonnative as their son-in-law.

Hence, Chika stayed at Enugu and soon accepted a job she had never considered making a career out of. She was not even swayed by the financial incentives the government offered to keep those already in the system and attract new ones.[5] To make matters worse, the usual pressures to marry began to mount. Throughout her three years of teaching, her parents kept dropping hints. In her view, "Marriage [is] primarily . . . a restriction to the usual carefree life one lived as a spinster. The moment you get into marriage there are things you must not do and things you must do. But on getting into my third year of teaching I realized it was time, because most of my friends were getting married. You find that at the end of each working day there was no one to visit because all the girls were married and busy with their family, some with one or two children."

Chika got married in 1982 and two years later gave birth to twin girls. She went back to work after the usual three months of maternity leave. In the subsequent months she came to the conclusion that teaching was not for her and soon resumed efforts to change her career. The decline in employment opportunities from the 1980s was doubly frustrating for married women, who often had far fewer options for retraining or transfer. She could not afford to leave her job since her income was needed to keep the family afloat. Her husband, an architect, had gone into private practice, running his own little firm. The business seemed to be doing fairly well, but in the unstable economic climate Chika could not count on a regular household allowance from him.

As she weighed the options open to her, Chika concluded that she would have to work out her exit from the public service in stages. Like Uzoamaka, she realized she would have to keep her job until the career move was completed. After several attempts, she was transferred in 1991 to a desk job at the state's education commission. In her new job she is responsible for hiring, placement, transfer, and promotion of teachers. The flexible schedule has made it possible for her to enroll in the evening law program at the same university where Alice received her law degree. Chika appears quite excited about the program but hates the increased responsibilities she must shoulder. Like Alice, Chika has her husband's support in principle, but she is responsible for the practical exigencies of balancing paid work, schooling, and managing the home. "In this environment," she points out, "the man does not want to know how you cope or what you are going through in order to ensure that you run the home smoothly. All he cares is that he gets his meals on time. He doesn't care if you have to wake up at 2 A.M. to [ensure that things get done]." With three female children and no male child in sight, Chika still maintains her decisive stance against polygamy as a possible option for solving the "problem." Her husband might consider this option at any time (see chapter 4), but for her the challenge is to work toward a secure economic future for herself and her children.

Chika was in her second year in the law program the last time we corresponded.

Uchenna

Uchenna is thirty-four, single, and a senior accountant in a commercial bank. She holds a bachelor's degree in accounting and a master's degree in business administration, both of which she earned in the United States. The opportunity to study overseas was, for Uchenna, the fulfillment of a childhood dream. From the time she was little, she had often dreamed of going to Europe or North America to study. But this dream was shattered by her father's death during the Nigerian civil war. He was a primary school teacher and the main breadwinner in the family. His death transferred the responsibility for the family's well-being to Uchenna and her mother:

> As the oldest child, the only option was to finish secondary school and assist our mother in raising my five younger brothers. The suitors came, but I had made up my mind to work to support my family. I refused

their offers in order to ensure that my brothers made it through school. I know the Igbo culture expects the husband to shoulder some of his wife's responsibilities, but I had a lot! . . . I had to take up the challenge to become the father when our father died. To the extended family it seemed all hope was gone for our progress. . . . I went through a lot to help my brothers.

Soon after completing secondary school, Uchenna found a job as a bank clerk and for the next few years concentrated on training her brothers. As she made plans for her younger siblings, she also explored career options for herself. Her mother's experience, she points out, provided a good lesson in planning her own future. Widowed with six children and no formal training, her mother was in no way prepared to step into her husband's shoes. To Uchenna this was a sad and constant reminder that kept her dream alive. She was further motivated to earn a university degree because many female university graduates were recruited into supervisory positions above her over the five years she worked at the bank. "It's possible," she admits, "that the men who wanted to marry me . . . could have provided for my brothers as well. However, I knew it would be very difficult to go back to school after having kids. Most Igbo men would tell you, 'You have all these kids, why are you bothering yourself? Sit down and look after them.' I wanted to be educated."

Uchenna worked hard to keep her siblings at school until she was twenty-four, when two of the boys graduated from secondary school. She started making plans for further studies in the United States. Her mother was greatly disturbed by her plans. Uchenna's boss, a father figure in her life, also disapproved of such a move. He had no problems with Uchenna furthering her education but felt that marriage should come first. Her female colleagues equally tried to discourage her, pointing out that she was taking a risk leaving the country unmarried. Uchenna's dilemma was heightened even more when a few months before her departure to the United States, in 1982, she was promoted to the rank of supervisor in her bank. She agonized for weeks over her plans but finally left Nigeria.

Uchenna finished her studies in 1987 and rejoined the bank as a senior accountant. Her success, she argues, has made up for all her efforts. Those female colleagues who tried to discourage her, she notes, have not done so well themselves. In fact, "Some of them may be around my age or older, but they were scared of furthering their education because . . . they thought they'd be branded *acada*. If you're *acada*, they teased, nobody would want to marry you. Well, most of them are still not married, and without the education too!"

With her studies completed and the opportunity to pursue a professional career realized, Uchenna now wants to find the right man for marriage. As she puts it, she has not quite arrived. She wants to get married as soon as possible and is getting increasingly concerned because she finds that she is too "qualified" for the few suitors who have made tentative gestures so far. She has made a conscious decision to stay in Enugu rather than move to Lagos.[6] Among other reasons, Uchenna feels that "it is not easy to just move to Lagos or up north as a single girl. It's like you don't have anybody to look after you. You can easily be drawn into city life. You don't have to comport yourself as properly as you would be made to around here. . . . Of course, some of those women who work in Enugu do whatever they like, but then, you can't ignore tradition, can you?" Obviously, social impressions, for Uchenna, take priority above professional ambitions and her own confidence in how she comports herself. She is adamant about staying close to home for now:

> Going to Lagos to look for a job is ruled out. Who will I stay with and what will people think of me? If, for instance, I get a job in a merchant bank, I could move, but I would have to deal with being branded "one of the girls." You know, some will even say, "How come she has been in Lagos all this time and no man has talked to her?" I would like to marry someone I want, not someone people feel I deserve because they think I'm loose. . . . You know, it's like my going abroad and coming back still unmarried. The general feeling is often, "Hmm, . . . after all, she has been abroad, she flew in the air, she went underground, yet . . . nobody showed any interest in her. Are you the one to be saddled with this reject?"

Uchenna, in a sense, is treading a familiar path. Many young Igbo women can relate to her story. She is struggling to maintain a protective distance from relatives and putting her career plans on hold while she explores her options for marriage.

Gendered Lives, Gendered Aspirations?

Certainly, other equally important factors, such as ethnicity, class, and religion, also affect these profiles, although I do not focus on them here. Nevertheless, these personal profiles offer many useful insights into the gendered norms that currently mold elite Igbo women's lives, educational aspirations, and career paths. Each life story is also to some extent a response to the social, economic, and political trends of the time. As their experiences demonstrate, these women have not simply accepted the dictates of society at the expense of their own personal development. While each woman's struggle is deeply located in the specific circumstances of her life, every one of them has shown varying degrees of resistance, both overt and covert, to the social pressures they experienced. Most important, their stories point to a looming reality: contemporary society, particularly in elite circles, is in a state of flux. The social, political, and economic trends of the last three decades have increased the fluidity of many social dictates. There is a clear separation between what appears to be socially approved of and what individuals feel is reasonably acceptable. This is partly because these social norms seem to have also been changing over time. Thus, Alice and the three younger women make reference to even the recent past, when certain social norms commanded much more currency than now. The historical pattern deduced from these life stories suggests that the fluidity of social relations over time could provide spaces for groups and individuals to contest the cultural status quo and redefine their stance. These elite Igbo women contest in both overt and covert terms some of what may be seen as established social norms and expectations in the hybridized social order. The younger women, especially, are at a crossroads, questioning existing social norms, yet keenly aware of the risks of defiance at every level.

These personal profiles also highlight some recurring themes in elite Nigerian women's experiences from the colonial into the postcolonial eras. Each of the profiles presented in this chapter has been shaped by the prevailing social conditions of their era. As a young girl, Alice did not nurture any aspirations of joining the legal profession. As a profession, law was not in the basket of choices suitable for Nigerian ladies in the 1960s. Alice accepted her place in the male-dominated social order and the limitations it imposed on her. Although her educational aspirations as a spinster were well beyond the reach of many Igbo women of her time, they remained within the confines of existing social opportunities at every stage.[7] She equally admits the influence of male authorities in her life, which enabled her to circumvent society's tight hold. The pressure to marry daughters off at a handsome price must have been weakened somewhat by the 1960s as the myth of blissful domesticity created by colonialism and Christian education wore thin.[8] Decades of colonial rule produced an elite female group whose lives presented a crucial lesson on women's survival in an emerging society forged by patriarchal continuities and contradictions. Many parents encouraged their daughters' educational aspirations merely out of concern for their economic survival in a new social arrangement.[9] Alice's father wanted his daughter to attend school, not as a goal in itself but for the security it would give her in marriage. In his view, marriage was the ultimate goal and must not be threatened by extradomestic ambitions.

As an elite wife, it is very likely that Alice's resort to further training, especially before the advent of the SAPs' harsh economic climate, must have presented some concerns to her husband. For one thing, elite men of her husband's status often assumed they could comfortably carry the family's financial burden without their wives' help. For another, such highly placed men would have had strong reservations about "upsetting" the household routine and the children's schedule. In fact, a lot of Igbo men in this situation would also be wary of career quests that could reduce the personal attention they received from their wives. There is, indeed, a general impression that postsecondary education for women, especially in the male preserves, such as law, medicine, and engineering, could threaten a husband's dominant position at home. It is one thing to send a woman to school to enhance her status as an elite wife and mother. It is another thing to promote her eventual acquisition of a new status that could overshadow her husband's. Even the prospects of having the family adjust to the hectic demands of certain career paths might discourage the financially comfortable elite husband from providing the necessary support. In other words, a woman's pursuit of further training simply out of a desire to achieve had a social ceiling beyond which it might become awkward either for tentative suitors or the bewildered husband.

Although Alice hoped to complete her education as a married woman and mother someday, she was aware that fulfilling this ambition depended greatly on her husband's cooperation. That support came much more easily than would be expected for a number of reasons. Finance, for instance, was not a major problem for two main reasons. First, during the oil boom the cost of education was heavily subsidized by public funding. Second, an elite family with a breadwinner of her husband's stature could easily shoulder the additional financial burden. Having a lawyer for a wife is something Alice's husband can boast about with great pride. He does not have to feel threatened since he already occupies a higher social status compared to Alice. As a wealthy businessman, he is highly regarded in various social circles. As the Igbos say, "Mma nwoke bu ego" (a man's beauty is in his wealth)—Alice's husband can relax and enjoy his wife's accomplishments. In any case, Alice, like any smart professional wife, accepts her subordinate status at home and has packaged her career ambitions accordingly. She seems to understand the conditions of the unwritten contract: her husband's support and approval in exchange for a career that must not impinge on domestic responsibilities (for instance, she has restricted her work schedule to the standard hours). Ready access to a nearby university may also have helped her case. Alice's reliable presence at home was crucial to easing any inconveniences her studies may have imposed on the family. Her prudent management of her career has also dispelled any threats to her husband's position as the husband, breadwinner, and head of the household. While the economic rewards that would accrue to the family may not have presented a strong incentive at the time Alice undertook her career, the present economic climate has made it all the more a wise investment.

Despite the male support in Alice's favor, one cannot ignore her own resilience in stretching the boundaries of that support, making room for new opportunities while carrying the heavy burden of domestic responsibilities. Alice's story deviates somewhat from the experiences of many ambitious elite women of the 1960s. In an era when most women married early, with few making it to the university, she could not afford to wait for too long. The myths surrounding acada, women's morals, their submissiveness in marriage, and their procreative ability must have carried more weight in her time than today.[10] For Alice, higher education presented a world of opportunities she very much wanted to be a part of. But she was prepared to do whatever it took to reconcile the world of social expectations with that world of opportunities. Despite the crucial support provided by the two important male figures in her life, she would still be considered highly ambitious by the standards of her day. At a time when many Nigerian women rarely made it to secondary school, it was unusual for a village girl to set her sights on tertiary training. As vague as they were at the beginning, Alice's ambitions were sustained and brought into fruition by her own tenacity. And the professional part-time programs that catapulted women like Alice into traditional male preserves were not established primarily for women. These programs were more affordable to young, upwardly mobile males struggling to establish their careers and to older men with money in their pockets who needed a professional degree to crown their life achievements. Yet elite women increasingly seized such opportunities for their personal advancement, despite the social constraints they wrestled with. Given their experiences and the strides they have made, women like Alice have much wisdom to offer the younger female generation as role models.

Chika, Uzoamaka, and Uchenna belong to a different era than Alice. Although society still felt discomfort about where women were headed and how far they were prepared to go, higher education with career prospects had become widely acceptable by the time Chika, Uzoamaka, and Uchenna started school. Since the public bore a substantial part of the financial burden for education, the implication was that anyone could aspire to any level. But in reality, individuals still needed a private financial outlay as well as their families' support in order to make it through higher education. With their families' support, financial and otherwise, university education was accessible to Chika and Uzoamaka. Of course, society endorsed their access to tertiary training only as an asset that could strengthen their vulnerable status. In this sense, the primary emphasis in Chika and Uzoamaka's training did not seem to deviate much from the prevailing social expectation. Like many Igbo women today, they confronted a rigid hierarchy of gender relations. Not surprisingly, the translation of their personal ambitions into concrete academic and professional achievements presented challenges they were unprepared for.

Uzoamaka draws attention to the gender bias and segregation embedded in the school system, especially for women of her class background. For women of lower classes, the influence of teachers and school managers was crucial in making career decisions. Since they usually have no one at home to give them advice on career choices, women like Uzoamaka often turn to the school staff. Uzoamaka regarded her teachers, especially, as counselors who would be able to help her make the right career decisions. But these teachers did not operate in a vacuum. The advice they handed out to Uzoamaka and other schoolgirls was a reflection of the social values attached to Igbo and Nigerian women's education. The teachers and school authorities Uzoamaka encountered probably operated on the basis of the gendered expectations of schooling already set in place in the larger society. That the teachers did not seem overly concerned about students' subject combinations suggests that, if anything, they did not question the prevailing social expectations about women's place in modern society. Uzoamaka and her schoolmates were to be equipped with the kind of training that would complement their primary role as homemakers and also provide some economic security in marriage. Therefore any assortment of subjects, however random, would have fetched them a degree in teaching, a profession they could conveniently combine with future domestic responsibilities. In fact, if they "married well" they could leave their careers behind and immerse themselves in marital bliss! In contrast, their male counterparts were being groomed for their role as the future breadwinners of elite households.

It is also evident that these women's families reinforced in many ways the social expectations that dictated how their daughters and sons should be treated. Even at present, most Nigerian parents have had little or no formal education. Fathers, on average, are more likely to have received more schooling than mothers.[11] A father's traditional prerogative, in addition, places him in the best position to make decisions about the children's schooling. It is therefore not surprising that all the four profiles portray a strong paternal presence in the decisions made about education and career. Uzoamaka, for instance, was basically pushed into a teaching career, while her brother was encouraged to pursue a medical career. To her father, it made perfect sense for Uzoamaka to study education, and her brother medicine. Chika was groomed along similar lines, albeit in more subtle form. With both female and, especially, male siblings following closely behind, she had no recourse but to accept, just like Uzoamaka, whatever was available. On the whole, Chika and Uzoamaka, despite their own personal ambitions, had a good idea of what careers were socially acceptable for them. Uzoamaka, in particular, appeared to accept the fact that male and female siblings were in noncompeting groups. The rationale for their training was not the same. The fact that her brother was encouraged to pursue a career in one of the male preserves while she was expected to move into a pink-collar occupation, despite her discomfort with the choice, was not lost on her. Indeed, Uzoamaka's parents could easily have shown a similar discomfort had their son opted for a pink-collar occupation. For her father, it was simply a question of placing his male and female children on the right path to adulthood in contemporary elite circles.

Both Uzoamaka and Chika set out with their own personal ambitions, which over time were molded by social expectations and boundaries, with their attached constraints of time and resources. Chika quickly came to terms with the economic constraints facing Igbo women of their social background. She could not afford to repeat a university class or pursue another degree at her family's expense. Chika also knew that despite her personal reservations about marriage, she had to consider the implications of postponing what seemed to be inevitable, not only to them but also to their immediate and extended families. Uzoamaka contested the inevitable for a while, and predictably the pressure only increased with the passage of time. Interestingly, she did assume the often calculated pose of her female counterparts—weighing academic and career options against marriage prospects before taking any step. Society employed the usual weapons and badgered her about marriage. But she did not exactly give in to social pressure. She weighed her options and stretched her resolve until she found the right suitor. Even her recourse to the Sandwich, and subsequently the business program, could be considered prudent decisions for an Igbo girl in her position. Unlike the regular full-time programs, these part-time programs afforded her the opportunity to stay close to home and keep her job. She earned a higher degree without pricing herself out of the marriage market by appearing independent and overeducated to potential suitors. But now that she is engaged to be married, she is, in principle, free to pursue her studies under a man's roof even though, as in the case of Alice and Chika, it may be a long wait before this dream is achieved. For now, Uzoamaka must place her career plans on the back burner while she establishes a strong presence in her home. She will have to seek out ingenious ways to keep this dream alive as she juggles career ambitions with the demands of marriage. How soon these ambitions will be realized, of course, depends largely on how soon her body responds to predetermined procreative requirements.

Of the four women, Uchenna is perhaps the one whose life and career paths have taken the most radical of turns. She deeply laments her father's absence and the support he could have given. In her view, this paternal influence would not only have sustained her ambitions but also enabled her to achieve them much earlier. But the fact that she did not have to battle against this strong male presence may have worked to Uchenna's advantage. Although, like Chika and Uzoamaka, Uchenna was never interested in any of the pink-collar occupations, she was the only one who sustained this initial ambition. Currently, she is not only better placed economically but is also competing with many of her male peers at work. The strong disapproval expressed by her female peers at the onset of her professional training clearly reveals the intensity of the pressures that counteract Igbo women's efforts to move up the ladder. As the details of her profile convey, Uchenna demonstrated exceptional strength of character and determination in a social setting where she was not expected to be a high achiever. Obviously, she was mindful of her place in the natal family as a woman, knowing that her brothers' progress was crucial to establishing her father's lineage within the extended family. But even as she toiled to uplift their status, she managed to keep her own dreams alive.

Uchenna may have achieved beyond her female peers, but this enviable status appears to have been achieved at great personal cost. She is competing with male peers but not on an equal footing. Unlike the young bachelors she rubs shoulders with every day at work, she worries about finding the right man to begin the procreative journey as soon as possible. Unlike the male colleagues with whom she is running the rat race, she cannot afford to go too fast and must stop at intervals to assess her options.

Obviously, Uchenna wants to get married and is taking great pains to present a low career profile to potential suitors. She could further her career by moving to Lagos, but that would seriously endanger her chances. Given her religious background and social class, polygamy, in whatever form, is out of the question. Moving to Lagos means moving further away from the pool where most eligible young Igbo men concentrate on finding a bride. Although many of these men do move to big cities to seek their fortunes, they would likely come home to find the proper bride. Uchenna's effort to maintain the demeanor of a "well brought up girl" may be costing her some steps up the career ladder, but this potential loss cannot be compared with the need to find the right partner in time. Uchenna knows that with her age, socioeconomic status, and life experience, which includes having lived abroad, she is already pushing her luck. Without the "shelter" a husband provides, her present status is already casting doubt over her moral reputation.

These profiles clearly assert a growing reality. Contemporary elite Igbo women are not satisfied with assuming their primary role, as constructed in different historical periods. Despite the constraints they confront, they manage to find cracks in existing social structures and trends in order to advance their status. Despite the rigidities created by the coexistence of old and new social institutions and the continuities and contradictions introduced by social transformation over time, these women continue to question their subordinate position. In some cases they manage to use the very boundaries erected against them to reshape and usurp the opportunities often reserved for men. While this struggle invites significant concessions in various forms, it also demands their resilience in contesting contemporary visions of womanhood inimical to their progress.

Chapter 6

Making It in Paid Employment

Formal and Informal Barriers, New Economic Realities, and Coping Strategies

That bit of economic independence a working woman has helps
. . . to an extent.

—Nnenna

The man may provide all your needs now, [but] what about to-
morrow? What if he dies? . . . Who will I fall back on?

—Uchenna

I know we're comfortable, but I can't abandon my career. . . .
You have to think of the future; something to work towards beyond a husband and kids.

—Chinelo

Men no longer want liabilities [in marriage]. They want
women who can help out financially.

—Chika

In this chapter Igbo career women share their experiences of working
outside the home. They begin with the reasons they work at all and
their rationale for pursuing a career. Both the single and married
women go on to discuss at length the challenges they face at work as
well as the strategies they employ to maintain their economic and
professional niches. Their experiences portray both the overt and subtle biases that characterize the relations of gender and class in paid
employment.

Nnenna, the thirty-four-year-old legal manager in a commercial
bank, reiterates the importance of paid work as a source of income
that is not directly tied to her relationship with the male authorities in
her life. She is married to a university professor, and they have two
young daughters. By society's standards, her husband is doing well

and is certainly in a position to take care of his family. But as Nnenna explains, wives who are totally dependent on their husbands enjoy financial security at the expense of their personal freedom. As she points out, the basic assumption in Igboland is that a wife belongs to her husband, along with whatever she owns. She insists, "That bit of economic independence a working woman has helps . . . to an extent." Paid employment provides, at least in principle, direct income that goes straight into a woman's purse—"her" money. Ifeyinwa, thirty-eight and a civil servant with five children, agrees with Nnenna. She is married to a well-to-do businessman but does not hide her cynicism for the bliss of full-time domesticity elite Igbo women presumably enjoy. According to Ifeyinwa, most elite couples neither manage financial resources jointly nor have equal access to the family income. The unemployed wife is therefore at the mercy of her working husband. "It is not that I earn much, but . . . you can't depend 100 percent on a man. If you need one naira [Nigerian currency] for toilet paper, you go to him. If you need five naira to buy a lipstick, you go to him."

Women like Ifeyinwa obviously attract the envy of the female majority outside the elite circles—not so much for their professional standing but for the commonly held belief that their husbands can provide them with many comforts. But much as female salaried workers like Ifeyinwa appreciate the economic security of being married to an able breadwinner, they are well aware that there are no guarantees for the future. Uchenna is thirty-four, single, and a professional banker. When her father died prematurely, her mother was unprepared to take on the family burden:

> There is no question about a woman not working in this country. The man may provide all your needs now, [but] what about tomorrow? What if he dies? . . . Who will I fall back on? . . . Even if he left something behind most men don't often discuss their investments with their wives. In many cases, the wife will not know the extent of his business dealings. . . . Even if a man left his estate to the wife . . . the [in-laws could] easily wrest control from her and make her beg for whatever she needs. . . . I know that there are women who are living in luxury on account of their husbands' wealth . . . , but let's face it, such women are few. . . . I don't feel comfortable with not having my own money.

Apart from conferring economic autonomy, paid work, for a good number of these women, also satisfies their desire to pursue a career.

These women are not mere wage earners. A good number of them are well established in their careers. Even some of the younger single women are far up on the ladder in their professions. Their married counterparts are not doing badly. Chinelo, for instance, is an accountant in a commercial bank and the mother of two young children. She intends to keep her job even though her husband, a wealthy businessman, would prefer she stay home with the children. She feels "it is quite boring just staying at home, taking care of kids. . . . Of course, he doesn't see what I'm making out of my job. I know we're comfortable, but I can't abandon my career. I love banking and would like to make something of it. You have to think of the future, something to work towards beyond a husband and kids."

Indeed, the fact that these professional women are pursuing careers for personal fulfillment, among other reasons, challenges the established structure of gender roles and may very well threaten the status quo. A closer look at their individual experiences, however, also reveals the care with which they approach paid work and especially the professional quest. Chinelo, for instance, has so far managed to maintain both her professional ambitions and her domestic obligations. Her husband, of course, has no cause for worry. He still remains the boss at home and his wife knows her place both at home and in the company of her husband's family and friends.

The present economic situation underscores the need for elite women's economic contributions to the household. Igbo women's economic importance may have declined during periods of economic boom, but their income remains a crucial part of the family budget. Few have husbands like Chinelo's. In any case, few elite women, regardless of their husband's economic status, are comfortable with going to their husband for every financial need. That element of culture that prescribes separate financial structures (chapter 8) for spouses continues to resonate in elite Igbo households. The current economic climate only lowers the barrier that kept apart the management of each spouse's financial resources. According to Chika, the schoolteacher with three children who is married to an architect, the harsh economic realities are also hitting men. In the current economic decline, she explains, "Men no longer want liabilities [in marriage]. They want women who can help out financially. In fact, these days, it is the woman's salary that is used to meet most of the immediate domestic needs like food, medical bills, school fees, and clothes, while the man keeps his own money for major projects like building a house." Uju points out, in addition, that a wife's economic status improves her bargaining position at home and determines the extent to which she can protect her most important investment in the union—children. She is a thirty-eight-year-old schoolteacher married to a senior civil servant and they have five young children. Regardless of the limited financial independence afforded by paid work, Uju explains, many working mothers are primarily concerned about their children's welfare: "Although I'm also concerned about my husband's welfare, I try extra hard because of my children . . . , to give them whatever they need as long as I can afford it. . . . I don't earn much, but I struggle to keep them healthy and to see to it that they get a good education."

Except for Onyeka, who was expecting her second baby, each of the married women in the study has at least two children. As couples, these women and their spouses may share household responsibilities but do not necessarily pool their incomes. With the worsening economic situation, there is increased pressure from the extended families, especially their husbands' relatives. Dealing with extended family demands has always meant a constant reworking of divided loyalties.

The Challenges of Holding a Career

According to these Igbo career women, the already deeply ingrained gender segregation in paid employment is increasingly reinforced by discrimination and corrupt practices. From their own experiences and personal observations, they cite many examples of segregation in paid work, especially in the middle and higher ranks.

Uchenna, the thirty-four-year-old accountant, points to cases of discrimination in her bank, especially in the foreign exchange department, where she works. According to her, the bank tends to transfer the female officers in this section to other departments once they become eligible for the "sensitive" positions:

> As for the men . . . they think that there are jobs made for them and jobs made for us. It's okay if we are clerks, messengers, and secretaries and at best supervisors. Once you get into the officer cadre, it is no longer a woman's job, especially in foreign exchange. It is tolerable for women to be administrative and personnel officers . . . but foreign exchange? The men think that you'd block their plans of striking highly lucrative business deals with businessmen. They could also insinuate that your relationship with these customers isn't strictly official.[1]

As a number of social critics noted in chapter 3, the roots of bribery and corruption within and outside paid employment are deeply ingrained in Nigerian society. But Uchenna's experience reflects society's discomfort with contemporary transgressions of gendered spaces that previously situated men and women differently and specified criteria for their interaction. Evidently, corruptive practices in formal employment feed on already established gender inequalities. Although the boundaries of gender segregation may seem unclear in some cases, they still limit, to some extent, the prospects of ambitious women. Even with credentials and expertise similar to men's, female applicants might prefer to compete on their own turf, deliberately opting for pink-collar positions. Indeed, the stiffer competition for available jobs in the present economic climate makes the situation worse for women, especially in the private sector. Nnenna, the thirty-four-year-old legal manager, draws from her own personal experience in a private bank. She explains that men would prefer to run an all-male club: "The men prefer to work with their fellow men at any time if they can get away with that. . . . the men in . . . [our bank] dread working in departments where there are many women."

It is not surprising that men would not want to work with women in a private firm, such as a commercial bank. Igbo men do not see career women like Nnenna as colleagues but primarily as women who should either be working with other women or running their households. It may be difficult for male colleagues to treat their female counterparts as fellow workers and competitors in the professional ranks. Obviously the rigid definitions of gender roles in elite circles, which initially placed women in the domestic sphere as homemakers and men in the public sphere as breadwinners and decision makers, continue to cast a shadow on the relations of gender in paid work.

It seems that in many cases, beyond the basic qualifications for entry, other attributes define the nature of the job requirements within. In Uchenna's bank, for example, both the foreign exchange staff and bank customers, who are mostly men, maintain an informal but mutually beneficial relationship. The relations that further the economic interests of male bankers and businessmen are quite understandable if not well accepted. In contrast, the female staff's misgivings about such relations reveal their awareness of boundaries beyond which their professional integrity, unlike men's, could be questioned socially. Both the male and female staff are well aware of the different and unequal moral scales of evaluation. While the men worry about female intruders who are not prepared to do business with customers, the women worry about their professional integrity in terms of the business ethics that govern these staff-customer relations.

All the women unanimously cite the local, state, and federal cabinets that house the office of the chief administrator at each level as sites of gender segregation. They admit, of course, that, as in other parts of the formal employment sector, there are certain positions in these cabinet offices that may not be suitable for women, especially working mothers. But as Onyeka points out, it is difficult to make such distinctions in situations where the working environment builds in a redefinition of roles to men's advantage. Onyeka, a thirty-one-year-old civil servant married to a protocol officer, speaks from personal observations. According to her, the cabinet offices have maintained a gross segregation of gender that remains unquestioned within the ranks. Protocol officers are responsible for the chief administrator's social profile. They manage his regular social schedule and in many cases answer directly to him. For instance, Onyeka notes, protocol positions are largely reserved for men based on a widely held assumption that their female counterparts cannot deal with some of the requirements, such as extended working hours and regular travel, that come with such jobs. Such requirements could eliminate married women from the pool of prospective applicants. Onyeka admits that "married women may not be able to handle all that [the job calls for]." She insists, however, that "some . . . single women want just that. [But] even if they can do the job, they are not likely to be hired. The men at the top will not be convinced of their competence. They'd still prefer to hire their fellow men." Obviously, as long as the cabinet offices maintain a hostile posture toward female "intruders" they will remain a preserve of the "boys." Obviously, the cabinet offices have no problem with female secretaries and receptionists. At these much lower ranks, female staff cannot threaten the camaraderie shared by men. As Nnenna equally notes in the case of private banks, men do not have a problem with female subordinates. Women pose a problem only when they invade men's working space as competitors or higher-ups to whom the men must defer.

Single female applicants find that the social expectations built around women's primary role significantly affect their prospects even before they enter the labor market. Mma's experience provides a very good example. Forty and divorced, with no biological children of her own, her marital status was a critical factor in deciding her fate as the legal adviser in a commercial bank. She relates her experience with the all-male panel that interviewed her for her first position at the bank:

> They asked about my husband and I told them that we were separated. Then they asked, "Is there any chance of your getting back together?" I said no. You can see how selfish men can be. They said, "What about children?" and I said, "I have none." Then they asked me, "Suppose you decide to start having children?" I told them that I came from a strict Christian family; that such a situation would not arise. . . . Eventually, I got the job and was later handed the minutes of the meetings where they discussed my appointment. There it was clearly written that "even though I am a woman, they could not pass up my excellent credentials, but that happily enough I didn't have any encumbrances." . . . But they all have wives and children at home, and because they are men, those are not encumbrances on their part. . . . So, I wouldn't have been given the job if I had still been married or had children at the time.

It is not surprising that many employers, especially those in the private sector, are not prepared to take chances with women, especially working mothers. The panel in question was obviously concerned about the quality of service Mma could render. The members were well aware that the current structure and organization of formal employment in Nigeria have made only very limited allowances for women's domestic "encumbrances." Working wives and mothers entering Mma's position would have to make substantial private arrangements to stay on the job. In other words, the discrimination Mma refers to is more far reaching than simply a private firm's gender preference. For instance, Christie, a forty-nine-year-old assistant director in a government department, observes that many senior male civil servants do not want to work with female assistants. These men go to great lengths to avoid working with women, especially married women, whose domestic responsibilities, they feel, would spill over into their job. Christie has seen many internal memos in which men specify their preference. Where many women continually strive to maintain that precarious balance between their responsibilities at home and at work, gender discrimination and segregation are likely to operate in both subtle and overt terms. Employers pounce on this "problem" as one good reason to simply avoid hiring women or placing them in the higher ranks. Indeed, the fact that most of these women, especially those who work in the private sector, are holding on to their jobs and progressing through the ranks, however slow the climb, is mainly due to their own personal resilience.

Establishing and Guarding Your Niche:
IM and Bottom Power

The crisis in the labor market only strengthens the corruptive networks endemic to the rank and file of formal employment. The allotment of employment quotas along ethnic and religious lines further complicates the gender politics of paid work in Nigeria. But besides the quotas, the politics of IM—whom you know—also appears to be flourishing within the ranks of paid employment. Uju, a thirty-eight-year-old French teacher and mother of five, stresses the importance of this practice in today's Nigeria, where too many people are competing for too few jobs: "IM is very important because too many people are qualified. If you have a godfather, an uncle, brother, or guardian who is highly placed, or if you know any such person . . . that may help push your case." Ijeoma, a thirty-year-old single bank accountant, concedes that the influence of her father, who was the chief executive officer of a commercial bank, helped a great deal in securing her present job. Although Ngozi's father died a number of years ago, his name still commands some influence among his colleagues in the banking industry. When she was interviewed for her present job, Ngozi was well aware that she had an edge over the other candidates. Access to such a lucrative position, Ngozi admits, often requires influence at the top. Nnenna, the legal manager in a commercial bank, agrees with Ngozi: "Since the employment embargo of the mid-1980s, most of those who got employed had relations or godfathers here. Officially, they will advertise the positions, but it is those who know people that will be considered. The result is that merit rarely comes in. You find that a lot of [the staff] are mediocre. . . . Of course, there are basic qualifications, but beyond that IM takes over."

The larger hiring quotas, less rigid employment requirements, and loose hiring procedures in public service provide a fertile ground for IM to flourish unquestioned. Rose, an assistant director in a civil service department, refers to a recruitment exercise for teachers carried out in 1988: "We had vacancies in specific disciplines like Igbo and Yoruba languages, maths, and physics. There was a long list from 'above' . . . and the vacancies were filled based on this directive. . . . The members of the [education] commission were mad, but what can they do? The list came from the powers that be. They dared not question the decision."

Chika, thirty-eight and mother of three children, who transferred from the teaching field to the school board, shares her experience as an insider in a process that unfolds regularly in her present place of work: "Somebody just shows up with a letter from the government house with the instruction, 'Recruit this person.' The person is automatically hired. Getting into teaching now depends on . . . who you know. They give you a piece of paper and you start work, while those who graduated years before are still hanging around. In fact, the letter may even stipulate that the new teacher be posted to a school of his or her choice."

For those who have no godfathers bribery is an equally viable option. As chemistry teacher Erimma remarks, "You know Nigeria. No vacancy, [they say]. But vacancy may exist if you grease a few palms." The culture of corruption in high places, which nurtures its own relations of power within the state machinery and across the rank and file of paid work, is hardly a new phenomenon in Nigeria. While the same can be said of much of Africa, Nigeria seems to rank at the top, and the current economic crisis only exacerbates the situation. The experiences of these Igbo career women put a face on the problem, exposing the ramifications of these corrupt practices, which subvert social progress. Christie, forty-nine, an assistant director with the education board, unveils some of the negotiations that occur in the corridors of power: "[IM] comes in at some point. . . . If we're hiring and our director is interested, there is no way we can stop him from sending his candidate. . . . Of course they [directors] do sponsor candidates. Some may even write to the chairman of the panel or give the candidate a note the day before the interview saying, 'I'm interested in this candidate.' . . . That's where the lowering of standards comes in. You have to oblige the director."

In the private sector, employers obviously look for much more impressive credentials. Compared to the public sector there are much fewer positions available and the need to assert one's influence at the top is much greater. Mma, the legal adviser and company secretary of her bank, provides an inside view of an accepted process. Hiring in most banks often relies on oral and written tests for candidates. A short list is drawn from top performers on the written test. The short-listed candidates are then invited for the oral interview. According to Mma, "Members of the board or the management sometimes indicate their interest in certain candidates. Such candidates will definitely be considered if they sailed through the written tests. The oral interview is where the bigwigs have the chance to use their position."

The mass promotion of teachers and civil servants limits the need for a godfather to intervene in the normal channels of advancement. Public-sector workers expect to be promoted at periodic intervals, except in situations where gross dereliction of duty is reported. In that case, highly placed advocates may be called on to help reverse the official verdict. But godfathers could play a crucial role in the recruitment, transfer, and appointment of workers to special positions in public service. For instance, some form of influence may be needed to avoid being placed in or transferred to "unpleasant environments," particularly the rural areas. However, with the schools becoming a distinct ghetto for those without better options, even the conditions of service in the public sector increasingly divide teachers and "civil servants." Igbo career women in this book lament, for instance, the fact that, unlike the case with other civil servants, the government no longer endorses the promotion of teachers every three years.[2]

A godfather looks after a candidate's or an employee's interests. He usually has significant clout by virtue of his position in either the establishment or the larger society. He bestows favors to nurture longstanding and mutually beneficial relationships he has with individuals or groups of people (e.g., family, community, and in-laws). Although godfathers are not usually family members, parents, older relatives, and siblings in such positions can play a similar role, especially by providing the right contacts for their wards. In the more competitive private sector, with its more rigorous assessment process, Chinelo, the bank accountant with two children, believes that IM helps a lot. As she puts it, "You can't rule out the Nigerian factor. If you have a godfather—brother, uncle, father, or friend—he will give you special attention, ensure you get the breaks and help push you up the ladder. . . . It happens everywhere. Our bank is no exception."

What happens to those who have neither godfathers nor the financial means to grease the palms of the powers that be? That is where, these Igbo career women explain, the "politics" of gender come in. According to the participants, some women may be compelled to give sexual favors in return for a job or promotion. As Ngozi, the accountant, points out, "Things are no doubt rough for men who have no [godfather], but when it comes to overall representation, they are at an advantage. Who are the military officers, directors, commissioners, and managers? Men, of course. . . . [Bottom power—sexual attraction] evens things out to some extent." Men and women tend to accept these sexual relations as part of the dynamics of gender relations in the workplace, and as one of the options women may exploit to find a niche in paid work. Nnenna, who like other professionals puts in extra hours, remarks, "We have had incidents when you go to the office in the evenings only to find the boss with a girl sitting on his lap. It happens. If he can't attend to you then you come back later." Speaking from her experience of what happens in the education board where she now works, Ifeyinwa knows that "by getting 'acquainted' with the boss, the girl will now get to know somebody and he will in turn influence things in her favor. She will now be coming in through somebody. But she will be dreaming if she relies on just the interview, hoping that someone will pick out her name."

It is possible, the women agree, that in these hard economic times the politics of gender may come in handy for some female applicants and employees. Uju, the vice principal, agrees that "things are very hard in Nigeria today . . . and most [university graduates] want a job at all cost." Both IM and bottom power, these career women argue, reinforce sexual harassment in formal work settings. Female employees often find their own strategies to avoid being made a target. In the case of civil servants, Onyeka remarks, the competition for available positions may force women who do not make the short list to use bottom power.

The general assumption is that unattached women are more likely to exploit bottom power than are working wives. Married women face a much higher risk, given the potential penalties such a step could bring. But married women are certainly not excluded from the game. Citing several instances from her workplace, Nnenna exclaims, "Eh, some married women do this too, not just the single ones. . . . they do it because they need the job or they want a promotion."

Drawing from her experience as a seasoned administrator in the public service, Christie believes that the organizational lapses within a much less monitored public sector help to encourage bottom power. This peddling of influence, she claims,

> breeds indiscipline in the [civil] service because the person that came into the ministry through the director may flout rules as long as that man is still at the helm of affairs. You know that bureaucracy is based on rules and regulations, but [workers who have godfathers] may not for instance come to work early most of the time. There are people here who are regarded as sacred cows. These people have either godfathers or some big shots behind them. When they flout rules nothing

happens, but when you do the same, you're in trouble. These days many young girls are getting away with such behavior.

Although these Igbo career women describe various instances of bottom power in the workplace, they insist that the practice is highly overrated. In their view, it is an option only a few women succumb to. Women who resort to bottom power, they remark, are often looked down upon by both male and female colleagues. This is especially true when the female employee who succumbs to bottom power is forced to repeat the favor for an indefinite period. Most female wage earners, they insist, struggle to be recognized and rewarded on the basis of their expertise. They would rather suffer dire consequences than resort to sexual attraction. Career women in this book also reiterate consistently that just because the conditions of paid work at present make room for this practice does not mean that merit has been completely annihilated. They all agree with Nnenna, who maintains that "most of the time the women involved are not serious about the job or are not even interested enough to try." Even though in some instances, "merit becomes underrated, to the detriment of the hardworking staff," Nnenna argues, the long-term consequences will still catch up with the mediocre female employee who thinks she can use bottom power to get ahead. Women who resort to bottom power, she warns, must be prepared to weather the storm. They must keep away from their critics and ignore the stream of gossip that easily invites complaints against them. Any woman who allows herself to be exploited knows that bottom power does not provide any guarantees. And in many cases, the affair does not stop with merely securing the job. As Uju, the vice principal, points out, "The girl can go to the boss's office. . . . They can just do it in there in the office and then the girl is hired. The problem is that if you subject yourself to that kind of treatment, he may continue to pester you for more sexual favors simply because he helped you to get the job."

It would therefore be misleading, these career women caution, to suggest that most women (and men) in desperate situations succumb to either bottom power or IM. These practices certainly present themselves as options in many instances, but they attract only those who are desperate enough to be morally swayed. While the women decry IM, they accept it as a ready option for those who are lucky to have the privilege. Nobody anywhere in the world, they argue, would hesitate to use IM to help him or herself where the system offered it as a viable option. Although most of the career women who share their views here argue in defense of women who opt for bottom power, none of them admits to ever falling victim to the practice. The resort to bottom power by a negligible female minority, these women argue, is only one response to existing barriers.

While none of the women defend either IM or bottom power, they seem to accept them as opportunist and desperate measures the structure and organization of formal employment in Nigeria encourage. What they strongly decry is the shadow of suspicion cast on innocent men and women. They resent, in particular, the impression bottom power has created—that women are less capable than men and cannot make it to the top on their own.

Juggling Family and Career

As these Igbo career women pointed out earlier, working mothers prefer to stay in the public sector simply because of the rather flexible schedule it affords them. A career in public service enables them to accommodate many conflicting but serious domestic concerns that private-sector employers would not consider. Of course, such privileges are not officially condoned, but working mothers often work out agreeable arrangements with their bosses. Uju, the schoolteacher with five children, has a good working arrangement with her (female) boss, the school's principal. According to Uju, the principal knows that in order to get the best from them she has to help married female employees like Uju maintain the "rear":

> Naturally, the married [women] often have to deal with emergencies like sick children or husbands having to leave in a hurry for unscheduled trips. You have to work closely with them [the working mothers] and earn their trust, otherwise they will just sneak out of school only to return later with a medical excuse issued by a doctor. Of course, you know that at the right price some Nigerian doctors would easily do such favors. However if these [women] know that informing you will not cost them their job or attract a rebuke, they will be frank with you. But some of them would prefer to deal with the domestic emergency first and later look for any excuse . . . they can get away with.

Working mothers like Uju must equally find ways to fit official work policies into rigid domestic demands. Given the gender division of labor at home, Uju comments, it's only "natural" that the working mother finds creative ways to manage her home at work. She accepts that it is usually her own schedule that must be stretched whenever necessary to accommodate the services she must render to her husband and children.

With the economic crunch, few Igbo career women can afford to quit their jobs or even take a leave of absence. Even the few with husbands who can financially support the family are well aware of the cost of losing their economic autonomy—for themselves and their children. Hence, many of these female wage earners have to rely on the cracks within the system. For instance, those in the civil service can stretch their lunch hour to do some food shopping. The indulgence of those in authority is also crucial in terms of how far individual women can push the boundaries. As long as they respect certain acceptable limits, most working mothers manage to find time for domestic business by exploiting the official cracks. Chidimma, thirty-one and a home economics teacher, is a good example. She had all five children without any breaks in her employment.

> They [school principals] know [a daily absence] is official when you get a letter from a doctor. However, . . . an unsympathetic principal would not condone long absences from school. In my former school, the principal could not tolerate that and she had me transferred to another school. You know how ladies treat one another. She said, "What kind of baby do you have in your stomach? Pregnancy is not an illness." She insisted that I report for work, but I was not fit enough. So she submitted my name for transfer. The principal in my present school is very understanding.

Chidimma is married to a medical doctor and, as she openly admits, their social status gives her some clout when it comes to dealing with those in authority at work. As most of the public servants openly admitted, their immediate bosses cannot go very far in the tedious bureaucratic process to effect a termination of their appointment. Most school principals, for instance, would simply ask for an uncooperative staff to be transferred. The teachers, in particular, insist that the government has no right to demand better service from them. As far as they are concerned, their performance is hardly rewarded. The motivation to work hard in the present state of affairs, they argue, is hardly material. Working mothers like Chidimma admit that tedious as the schedule might be, public-sector employment is perhaps the most convenient work for them, at least in their childbearing years:

"You have to have a properly organized schedule. A lot of the time I could not rest. For instance, I had to personally wash the children's sterilizing units in the morning and I had to be at school on time unless I was on maternity leave. Anyway, I was mostly on maternity leave in those days because, once I resumed duty after leave, I could leave the school after twelve noon until my baby was six months old. But by the end of the six months, I would be expecting another baby."

There are hardly any day care facilities for children under two years of age in Nigeria. Infants can be left with maids for intervals of only two or three hours between breast-feedings. In order to gain more time, therefore, expectant mothers aim at pushing the effective date of leave as close as possible to the delivery date. After delivery, most mothers in the public sector resume their duties but simply end their workdays at noon. Many have no personal means of transportation. Onyeka, the thirty-one-year-old public servant married to a protocol officer, admits that "although the policy says one hour for six months, some nursing mothers would not change their schedule after six months and most would leave the office at noon. It is just not convenient to work within such a tight schedule." The deterioration of general working conditions has stripped paid work of much of the economic security it previously provided. In fact, many female workers now combine their job with a "little business" on the side. Ngozi, the accountant, points out that women's part-time petty trading can really augment the family income: "The allowance from their husbands rarely goes halfway into the month. They use very ingenious ways to augment like selling jewelry, dresses, and wrappers in the office." The timing and extent of a husband's contribution to the family's upkeep are no longer constants, and wives must "come up with very ingenious ways" to steady the family monthly budget.

Often these businesses are advertised by word of mouth. The actual display of wares during office hours is usually frowned upon and may invite a serious reprimand, especially for workers in the private sector. Wares may be viewed on request, usually at home after working hours. Many female public-sector workers frustrated with the growing economic gap are turning these "sidekicks" into elaborate commercial ventures. According to Ifeyinwa, "Lagos is too near for the more daring women. I know a woman who works in a [public] research institute. Between July and now [December] she has traveled overseas twice to buy the things she sells in her shop. . . . Many women operate on a smaller scale, like retailing trinkets. Some men are in this too. It's not only women and school teachers that engage in these side ventures."

But part-time petty trading can hardly reverse the widening gap in remuneration packages between the public and the private sectors. In fact, this gap is already visible even between seasoned public servants (and those in academe) and university graduates who find jobs in the private sector. According to Rose, the fifty-seven-year-old assistant director in a government department, this gap is disturbing because it is gradually eroding established hierarchies. "It starts from the top. The university staff is poorly paid. But their students graduate and within a year of working in a bank become car owners while many of their professors can barely afford to pay for a taxi ride." Of course, the fortunate ones are the few with the right connections to fetch them lucrative positions in the new financial establishments. Most university graduates must bid for the much less desirable positions within a shrinking public service. The rest are left unemployed or underemployed, with only a few that can draw on familial economic support to establish viable private business ventures. These dismal economic prospects have great potential for leading highly educated men into uncharted and dangerous paths to wealth accumulation.[3]

For women, especially those with children, stiff competition for available positions means that they are likely to end up with unattractive options. Ifeyinwa, who left teaching for a desk job, comments, "The rate at which [Nigerian] women are rushing into teaching and government work [desk jobs] is alarming. At this rate, you will hardly find a single man in the civil service in the next ten years. You rarely find men these days in the federal teachers colleges. They are more interested in making quick money." Obviously, men who take this route have the opportunity to try for better opportunities elsewhere. Women stay behind not because they are not interested in more lucrative jobs but because their domestic responsibilities prevent them from competing with men for these opportunities. As Erimma, the thirty-four-year-old chemistry teacher, laments, "We are so many that even one naira for each teacher runs into thousands." According to her, teachers are engaged in a constant battle with the authorities for unpaid entitlements. Veronica, a fifty-five-year-old school principal, concurs. Although civil servants also suffer the same fate, teachers may go for indefinite periods with no salaries and benefits.

This list of grievances, in addition to constant harassment by school principals, students, and education authorities, is turning the teaching profession into a camp for disgruntled workers with no fringe benefits to cushion the effects of the economic crunch. Chika points out, for instance, that civil servants "in the poultry department of the Ministry of Agriculture are given some concessions like buying chicken or fertilizer at cheaper rates. Banks equally give loans to their workers at lower interest rates. You never get such benefits in teaching." The potential for such extras, the other career women agree with Chika, now distinguish the "masculine" from the "feminine" jobs in the public sector. As the masculine jobs in the public service increasingly disappear, the new lucrative enclaves in the private sector are quickly turned into male preserves. It seems that the gender divide is constantly redefined as the labor market shrinks, squeezing women into the least favored positions.

The short-term measures taken by working mothers cannot effectively address the economic gap between public- and private-sector employment. These coping strategies cannot alleviate their burden in the long run. These women are already saddled with more domestic chores than men, even with the assistance of domestic hands. Since employers often assume that these responsibilities are bound to encroach on the formal work settings, most female wage earners, especially women of childbearing age, are kept away from the lucrative preserves. Indeed, the coping strategies adopted by working mothers tend to reinforce, if not justify, the discriminatory treatment they receive in the labor market.

The women agree, however, that further training is the most viable strategy for escaping the public-service ghetto. However, women who consider major career moves as a potential career exit must carefully weigh their options. What may seem like a positive development has to be examined in the light of its prevailing labor market implications. Those who are presently pursuing this option are hoping that more education will get them into more lucrative and satisfying careers at a time when education has declined in value as a means of gaining access to highly paid positions in contemporary society. A university degree no longer translates into the economic status and social prestige it has in the past. Not only is more training hardly a guarantee for social mobility, but its potential value depends on the particular type of training pursued. For public-school employees who have no professional training, an education degree may be important for purposes of promotion or appointment into management positions. But these positions are few today compared to the number of qualified candidates. In the private sector, those who pursue professional degrees in business and law, at least, extend their options far into the male preserves. Evidently, educational qualifications now constitute only a basic prerequisite for entrance into formal employment. Beyond that basic requirement, a host of additional factors come into play.

Undoubtedly, higher education and formal employment will continue to provide the stepping-stone for elite Nigerian women's entrance into the elite circle. These assets provide them with some impetus to assert rights that are accorded to other women only in principle. The younger women in this study are confronting the conflicting expectations of a hybridized social order. But their experiences also point to the limits to which they can contest the boundaries of social opportunities available to them. These experiences call for a reexamination of the value of education and paid employment per se as assets for Nigerian women's social mobility. Economic decline means not only fewer opportunities than before, even for the highly educated, but also a diminished value attached to such training. It means that schooling for women, even as a prerequisite to social mobility, has to become more specific in terms of level and specialty. Beyond the aspiration of making it to the tertiary level, Nigerian women also have to diversify their educational options in preparation for the challenges of a changing labor market.

7

Balancing Act

Igbo Working Mothers and the Domestic Division of Labor

> Even as children, we know that girls have to help at home. As you grow up, society cushions the impact and nothing comes as a surprise.
>
> —*Nnenna*

> The fact that I'm a school principal has nothing to do with my responsibilities at home.
>
> —*Veronica*

> When I'm sick, I still manage to cook the soup. My husband is very particular about that.
>
> —*Onyeka*

> If you want your moi moi sand free, you have to do it yourself.
>
> —*Rose*

With the expansion of public schooling, the large pool of extended family relatives that elite Nigerian families drew from in the past had all but dried up. But the illusion of an abundant supply of cheap labor readily available for the use of elite households prevails. This assumption has rendered invisible the challenges that domestic work presents for working mothers in African cities. Igbo working mothers explain that they must find a balance between career ambitions and domestic obligations. All the women I interviewed cite domestic demands on their time as the major constraint to their professional advancement. Those in public service, in particular, cannot seek more lucrative and professionally challenging employment. And the three working mothers in private establishments have had to scale down their career ambitions because of domestic obligations. Alice, forty-eight and a lawyer and mother of five children, maintains a small practice but does not want to expand despite the more attractive prospects that have come her way. Similarly Nnenna, the thirty-four-year-old legal manager, married with two young children, settled for a managerial position in the legal department of a commercial bank instead of going after more lucrative options in either private practice or the merchant banks. Chinelo, the thirty-one-year-old accountant and mother of two young children, refused a more attractive offer as an auditor in another private company. She felt the job would be very demanding and accepted instead a low-key administrative position in a commercial bank. For these three women, even the advancement prospects of their current positions are significantly curtailed by the demands of their primary roles as mothers and wives. For example, they claim, many working mothers seldom attend seminars, workshops, or short-term training programs outside Enugu. They find it virtually impossible to make time for these professional requirements in their already chaotic work lives. Those who speak out here insist that their stories are not unusual. The implications of limited childcare services and a highly skewed gender division of domestic labor in men's favor weigh heavily on any working Nigerian mother's decisions about the nature and level of participation in paid work. Without any other viable options such as part-time or home-based employment, most Nigerian working mothers must accept the limitations of the formal employment opportunities available to them.[1]

The Sharing of Domestic Labor among Women: Relatives, House-Helps, and Maids

Given the various kinds of relationships among women that both the indigenous and colonial patterns of household arrangement have instituted in contemporary Africa, it would be a misnomer to generally label the pool of domestic laborers at the female wage earner's disposal simply as maids. Domestic workers are usually females (see chapter 2) and indeed, the mistress-and-maid model that has come to characterize the relationship also simplifies a complex set of relations based on the different statuses that a domestic laborer can assume within the elite household. Perhaps the term *house-help* provides a general label for this labor pool whose relationship with the elite household can produce different configurations. Only the highly placed, a very small minority in Nigerian society, can afford the conventional housemaids whose terms of employment include a package of official fringe benefits. With the employment of elite women becoming increasingly crucial to family subsistence, the challenge of managing the home with the added responsibilities of paid work has created further domestic laborers. But meeting this demand with available hands means that the content of domestic work and strategy for managing its various components has to be carefully worked out. Working women often try to find house-helps to suit their individual schedules, responsibilities, and budgets. The typical housemaid, who receives a regular salary, is affordable to only a few elite women.

The domestic labor pool, or house-helps, potentially available to Igbo female wage earners can be divided into three major groups. The first group comprises experienced workers, a diminishing pool, hired by the top echelons of elite society, and a fairly stable bank of semiqualified house-helps, the supply of which extends to neighboring countries such as Chad, Niger, and Cameroon. The second group consists mainly of the tiny pool of unpaid relatives who are in high demand, despite the conflict they can easily create. The third and increasingly prevalent source of domestic help consists of nonrelatives from rural areas closer to the city. This group provides services under specified conditions agreed on by their parents, the employers, and a broker who brings the elite and rural families together. As part of the contract for house-helps in this group, the middlemen often extract at least a firm guarantee from an employer that the house-help will attend school or receive private vocational training at some point during her service. House-helps in this group may receive regular financial stipends, especially in a situation where their full service is demanded without the option of attending some kind of formal training. The second and third groups often include girls as young as eight years old. Hence they are often unskilled in comparison to the average colonial maid or her counterparts in contemporary African settings. Their training often starts with initial steps to familiarize them with the elite household.

Since the large pool of extended family relatives that can offer a full day's service has been virtually depleted, the assistance of middlemen who procure the service of nonrelatives from the rural areas has become very important. Increasingly aware of the importance of literacy and economic opportunities for their children in the modern economy, parents in the rural areas now insist on some form of training. For those who can afford the cost of one or more full-time caregivers, nonrelatives who can offer full-time service for a stipend have become a better alternative. But the majority of elite couples now settle for house-helps, relatives or not, who provide limited service in exchange for some training. Unlike in advanced industrial countries, most of these house-helps are young, untrained, and expected to learn on the job. While some expertise may be expected from those hired on full-time stipends, the experiences of career Igbo women in this book clearly show that the existing ideologies of domestic work place some cultural limits on the range and quality of services house-helps should provide. Both the material conditions of domestic work and the ideological construction of certain tasks make it impossible for the working mother and wife to completely extricate herself from her domestic obligations regardless of how competent her house-helps might be.

Only three of the twelve married women who tell their stories here have house-helps who are related either to them or to their husbands, although most of the house-helps do not receive a regular salary. Instead, they are usually either enrolled in the public schools or train for vocations such as sewing and hairdressing in private institutions. Except for Chinelo, the accountant with two children, none of the women has a full-time house-help on salary. In general, classes in the schools or vocational centers run for six to eight hours every weekday. These institutions offer both morning and afternoon sessions, which provides some flexibility for elite households to organize their daily routine around two maids.[2]

The Organization of Domestic Labor: Does This Man Live Here?

The organization of domestic work in the elite Igbo household is unquestionably gendered and this broad gender division fundamentally shapes both the working mothers' participation in paid work as well as their relationship with house-helps. Their husband's share of domestic work is minimal and tends to be restricted to nonrepetitive tasks, especially minor household repairs and, in some cases, his own personal laundry. Men's assistance at home is negligible compared to the large burden that the working mother and her house-helps must carry. As in most of Africa, domestic work in elite Nigerian households often includes the care of relatives in addition to childcare and housework.

With very few labor-saving devices at home and the supply of electricity unsteady, domestic work in the elite household is more open ended than often assumed. Female professionals and their house-helps are immersed in this process from morning till night but may not characterize some of their activities as work. During my discussions with professional women in their homes, the process was hardly disrupted by my presence. Often there was a pot of rice cooking on the stove or the house-help interrupted with the shopping list for dinner before leaving for the nearby evening market. Of course the children were always around, and keeping an eye on them was not seen as work. Unlike their counterparts in villages, young urban children, including teenagers, do not seem to be appreciably involved in domestic work.[3]

The daily routine can be chaotic, especially for women who have both preschool and school-age children. Preschool children are usually left with the house-helps during working hours. The weeks immediately after the six-week maternity leave can be very challenging, for the nursing mother must find time to go home and feed her baby. Working mothers share much of the childcare at this time with domestic hands. The care of infants involves a lot of washing and cleaning.[4] Disposable diapers are relatively expensive and are therefore not widely used. House-helps normally do the washing of cloth diapers. Working mothers often concentrate on the more complex tasks, such as the washing and sterilization of infants' feeding units, and must therefore undertake or closely supervise the care of infants to ensure safety and good hygiene. Given their age and experience, most house-helps cannot handle such responsibilities on their own.

Working mothers without private transport have, in addition to their domestic responsibilities, to deal with inefficient commercial alternatives. It is not surprising that poorly paid civil servants incessantly complain about the lack of motivation to invest in their careers. Managing the household essentially involves the organization of specific tasks to do with cooking, shopping for food, cleaning, and planning for social activities. Juggling the obligations of domestic and paid work requires careful planning and scheduling. The endemic problem of unreliable power supply makes it difficult to plan ahead or keep most bulk supplies for more than a few days. Even basic labor-saving devices such as refrigerators, gas cookers, and blenders cannot be relied on. This means frequent cooking, regular trips to the market, and a standby alternative to the cooker: the kerosene or wood stove. Often, labor-intensive tasks such as pounding foufou, grinding red pepper for soup, and doing the laundry have to be done manually. Much of the food processing and preparation are still done manually at home since most people tend to have their meals at home, except for midday snacks at work. Moreover, cooking is more tedious in Nigeria than in the West because the basic ingredients for food preparation—such as vegetables, meat, and fish—are often not packaged for ready use.

The day begins at 5:30 A.M. for most of the career women and their house-helps and ends around 10 P.M. This daily schedule often extends to 11 P.M. on Friday, when the weekly bulk cooking begins, although the more flexible weekend schedule often means an additional hour of rest for career women. The working mothers usually undertake the preparation of the major meal components for the week, such as soup and stew. House-helps often prepare the ingredients beforehand or as the cooking progresses. Simpler cooking tasks such as boiling rice, making breakfast cereal, and warming prepared food can be delegated to house-helps, especially during the workweek. Bulk cooking starts on Friday evening and often extends to Sunday, with other activities spaced in between. Working mothers must also find time over the weekend to prepare the weekly schedule for bulk cooking and household cleaning. As most of the women point out, the weekend break enables them to tie up the loose ends accumulated over the workweek. It is also a time to give the family a treat to compensate for the divided attention the female wage earner gives to her husband and children on weekdays.

Working mothers have to do the bulk shopping over the weekend, with their house-helps on hand to carry the purchases. Husbands may purchase bulk supplies such as rice and beans during their visits to the village,[5] but the regular daily purchase of perishables presents quite a challenge to the female wage earner. Career Igbo women who shared their views and experiences point out, however, that the prevailing economic conditions have forced them to become involved in virtually every aspect of household spending for childcare and housework. In these harsh economic times, they admit, every woman strives to control the family budget. Those in the civil service can stretch their lunch hour to squeeze in a quick trip to the open market for perishables. As Onyeka, the civil servant with two young daughters, bluntly asserts, "The break period is about the only time I have to go to the market. Every female civil servant does it. Even our *ogas* [bosses] know about it, but they understand. In fact, some of them who are not living with their wives often send their typists to get them foodstuffs at the local market." Many working mothers in the private sector cannot afford such risks since their work schedules are often closely monitored. For most of them, this means a regular stop at the market on their way home after work.

House-helps are responsible for a substantial part of the household cleaning. General cleaning on Saturday mornings may start as early as 5:30. According to the women in the study, the family bedroom, living room, and delicate laundry are strictly the responsibility of the madam of the house.[6] Grown children clean their own rooms, and the house-help is largely responsible for cleaning the kitchen and bathroom and doing the rest of the laundry. The Saturday schedule usually ends in the afternoon in order to make way for social events. Apart from socializing with the family, working mothers often attend social events such as weddings, christenings, and funerals with their spouses. These events involve a good deal of planning and preparation. The help of female friends and relatives is often expected.

The efficiency of the workweek schedule depends very much on what the working mothers can achieve during the weekend. The house-helps act mainly as deputies on weekdays, acting on delegated authority. The basic morning schedule on weekdays revolves around preparing the children for the day (e.g., bathing, feeding, packing lunches). The house-helps assist with the specific tasks, but the working mother has to supervise the entire operation. On weekdays working mothers who have personal cars do the morning and afternoon school runs. Seven of the nine women with school-age children have their own cars. The husbands of the other two women do the school run. Mothers also attend to the children's social life, homework, school activities, and school requirements, such as fees, uniforms, and books.[7]

In addition to childcare and regular house chores, working mothers and their house-helps may have to cater to relatives either occasionally or on a regular basis. While extended family members may help out with domestic work and childcare, they may also exert both financial and emotional strain on the elite household. Onyeka, a young mother in her early thirties, had three of her husband's relatives staying in her home barely two years into her marriage: "As much as one upon getting married would expect to cater to a family that would enlarge over time, [this] 'sudden increase' without planning gets you destabilized, for some time. That's the part that worries me. Ideally, you need to plan for large families. It's one thing to plan for the children and the [house-help], it's another thing to plan for adults. Sometimes, you can't concentrate at work, thinking about the family, how to make ends meet."

The care of parents-in-law, especially mothers-in-law, is a top priority, according to the women. As noted in previous chapters, the dynamics of this relationship can produce various scenarios. Parents-in-law have considerable influence on the stability of the nuclear unit and a wife's status within her husband's extended family. Chika, for example, considers herself very fortunate. For one thing, her mother-in-law does not live with them in the city. For another, she and the older woman seem to get along quite well. Chika explains that there is nothing typical about the workday schedule when her mother-in-law is visiting:

> I go in to greet her first thing in the morning . . . and inform her that the [house-help] will attend to her whenever she is ready for food and a bath. When I come back from work, I have to make time to chat with her. . . . I might suggest a visit to some relatives and, if she desires, take her myself. It's also nice to buy, on your way home from work, fruits and other little things you know she likes. . . . And then you have to shop for the items she might like to go home with. . . . My husband comes [back from work] when the woman is already in bed. The only time he sees her will be when he's getting ready for work in the morning.

For businessmen and their counterparts employed by private firms, the workday can extend to eight or nine in the evening. It is not uncommon, this career woman notes, for the male elite to stop in a bar after work and hang out with their friends for an hour or more before heading home. For the elite wife who does not have a good relationship with her mother-in-law, this period after work can be very trying. But regardless of the quality of the relationship, all the women agree, it is the additional household responsibility they have to share with their house-helps that they dread. Iruka, thirty-two, a schoolteacher and mother of one little girl, describes her experience nursing a dying father-in-law in a two-bedroom apartment. The man "was very sick and bed-ridden. He took an entire room and we [husband, daughter, and house-help] had to squeeze into the other room. It wasn't easy. According to our culture, I shouldn't complain, but sometimes I did, venting my anger on my husband. I'm human! He did understand, though. He consoled me, reminding me that it would be for just a while." Interestingly, all the working mothers accept such responsibilities as theirs. In such situations, they agree, the father-in-law, especially, should come back to his son. None of the working mothers questioned the fact that their sisters-in-law, who should be closer to their own parents, seemed to wash their hands of such a burden.

Depending on the level of care demanded, the relationship between nuclear and extended families comes with its strains and stresses. As the working mothers explain, the potential for conflicts is higher on the side of in-laws because of their cultural status as wife to all the members of the husband's family. Members of a husband's family, especially the parents and siblings, may insist on relating to a son or brother's wife as a subordinate, who must place their needs above hers. While the Igbo wife and mother seeks various ways to nurture her relationship with the natal family, any assistance she renders is received with the understanding that her loyalty, at least overtly, lies primarily with her husband's people. Thus, these working mothers' experiences with in-laws capture, to some extent, the ideological construction of wifehood in elite Igbo circles.

Apparently, the division of household tasks significantly shifts the physical labor and tedium to the house-helps. But despite the volume of domestic work that house-helps can be held accountable for, the working mother must carry a considerable portion of domestic obligations alongside her job. Even with the house-helps' assistance, a good portion of domestic work, particularly childcare, cannot easily be accommodated by the working mother's rigid schedule. For instance, it is the working mother who stays at home when a child is ill and needs the attention of a parent. Moreover, health care delivery is inadequate and inefficient, and the time spent taking children to the clinic or hospital can easily run into hours. The daily shopping for perishables and traffic holdups during school runs can easily cut into the daily work schedule.

The need for close supervision greatly reduces the extent to which working mothers can fully delegate domestic tasks to house-helps. For most elite households, who cannot afford trained full-time caregivers, house-helps can serve as a solution only to a point, even under normal conditions. By virtue of their backgrounds, most house-helps are not conversant with the quality of service demanded in elite homes. For instance, the standard of hygiene is higher in the cities than in the villages because water and electricity are readily available in the former. As Rose, fifty-seven and an assistant director in a government department, points out, "If you want your moi moi [bean cake] sand free, you have to do it yourself."

Older women are often reluctant to leave the peace and quiet of village life to become city nannies. Older girls are not preferred because they may prove to be more difficult to control and more expensive to maintain than younger girls.[8] House-helps who are family relatives may have a freer rein than nonrelatives. Family relatives must be handled with care in order to avoid any bad feelings among members of the extended family, especially where such ties are still relatively strong. In general, house-helps are not trusted with large sums of money, especially because of their age. In these harsh economic times family expenses must be closely monitored in order to meet the monthly budget. The women in the study also drew attention to the high turnover rate of house-helps, especially in families with very young children. These families often have a heavy domestic workload, which most house-helps often try to avoid.

Besides the quality of service provided, these career women also worry about the influence these house-helps can have on their children. For instance, many of the house-helps speak the more comfortable pidgin English at home,[9] especially when they are alone with the children. Like their counterparts in other African countries, these career women are not comfortable with the long periods of time their children spend with maids.[10] But the absence of a better alternative means that they have to settle for a patriarchal bargain that provides them with some degree of economic autonomy but leaves them holding the short end of the stick.

Working Mothers, House-Helps, and the Ideological Construction of Husband Care in the Elite Household

Of the various aspects of domestic responsibilities the Igbo working mother must carefully balance with paid work, the care they give their husbands vividly portrays the patriarchal contract she must adhere to in return for her participation in paid work. In our discussions, all the working mothers agree that there are certain tasks that must not be delegated to house-helps. Soup preparation is, perhaps, the most notable among these tasks. According to them, this is one of those tasks a woman must perform as a wife to the head of the household. As Christie, the forty-nine-year-old assistant director in a government department and mother of two, explains, "Of course, that is the period in your life that it is absolutely necessary you be the one to do it. Most men won't eat soup prepared by the house-help." Onyeka, the civil servant with two young daughters, confirms this view: "When I'm sick, I still manage to cook the soup. My husband is very particular about that. As far as he is concerned, I have to be the one to prepare

the soup. I can't remember ever falling so sick as not to cook the soup."
And Veronica, fifty-five, points out, "If he [my husband] is around, I
wouldn't stay here and let the girl [house-help] cook. If both of us are
watching TV and the girl is cooking, he wouldn't like that. He would
rather I finish with the cooking first before coming to relax in the living room. They [husbands] also want to be served by the wife. If I'm
tired, I could let her boil the rice or yam, but never the soup. . . . He
would still like to see that I care about what he eats. The fact that I'm
a school principal has nothing to do with my responsibilities at home."

These experiences significantly depart from the picture painted in
earlier literature on colonial housewives-at-leisure. Social transformation and the more recent economic decline have thrown many elite
women into the paid labor market. The special attention they must
give to their husbands and children means that female wage earners
must combine a substantial part of their domestic obligations with
paid work. Most of the women believe that the unequal gender division of labor in the household, if unnatural, cannot be easily changed.
Although many voice their discontent with the situation, they made it
clear they are not in a position to question men's noninvolvement.
Nnenna, the legal manager, certainly agrees: "[Women] are made to
withstand more stress [than men]. Even as children, we know that
girls have to help at home. As you grow up, society cushions the impact and nothing comes as a surprise. Here in Nigeria everyone accepts the fact that men must be men."

Christie, the forty-nine-year-old director, is not happy with the
situation but admits, "We are raised in this country and we are raised
to accept these hardships. The Nigerian man does not do anything at
home. . . . Once again, we see tradition coming into the equation. It's
the woman's place to take care of the home. Of course, when you push
too far they say you're a feminist, that you want to convert the man
into a maid. But I can tell you that women are not happy about it.
They are complaining, but we haven't been able to take any action. We
don't want to be branded feminists."

Christie fears being branded the man in the family. She is more
highly placed in the civil service than her husband. It is therefore important to her that she projects a subordinate stance in the domestic
setting. She says she needs to sustain the impression that her qualifications and position at work have not gone to her head. As she hu-
morously points out, "Yes, I may be his boss in the office, but in this
house he will remind me he is the master." These working mothers
must face the fact that society views the domestic domain as their re-

sponsibility. The married woman's economic importance is recognized only to the extent that it does not threaten the gender equation at home. Chika, the schoolteacher with three young daughters, feels,

> In this environment, the man is not interested in how you cope or what you must go through to get the home running smoothly. All he cares is that he gets his meals on time. He is not interested in the fact that you have to wake up at 2 a.m. in order to do this. . . . The typical Igbo man does not bother with such [domestic concerns]. He sees them as the woman's responsibility and if he has to help out on occasions, you have to really talk to him and explain why you cannot do it yourself. That way, he is sure you know it is your responsibility. So he does it for that day and shifts it back to you.

Nnenna, the legal manager, equally voices her disapproval of the situation, but sadly accepts the reality of her domestic status. Regardless of a woman's professional status, the double standard, according to her, is hardly questioned and many elite men would not accommodate any readjustments that might upset the daily routine.

Nnenna, for instance, says that her husband, a professor of microbiology, expects her to defer to his own professional expectations. His feelings about her career emphasize that employers know where the working mother's loyalty lies (see chapter 6). He apparently expects such an understanding in his wife's case: "He [my husband] objects when [my career] gets in the way. There was this day I came home late and he asked me to go and tell my employers that I'm a married woman and that I have a family to look after. . . . Of course, I felt very bad. I said to him, 'When you go to work or on one of your research trips, I'm often very supportive and concerned about how they turn out, but when it comes to me, it's another story.'"

Uju, the schoolteacher with five children, argues, in the same vein, that many Igbo female wage earners often end up taking jobs they do not like because they are more compatible with their domestic duties: "It's a fact that's affecting a lot of women. . . . They're influenced by their husbands. As for what they actually want to do, these women will do something different, left on their own."

Bringing Up the Rear:
Ideological Realities of the Juggling Act

The subordinate status women occupy not only rigidifies the gender division of labor but also does little to open up cracks for resistance in the younger generation. Most of the women have younger children who apparently are waited on by house-helps. The few households with grown-up children have already made the gender divide, in which much of the domestic work, especially cooking, has been shifted to the daughters as future homemakers—in contrast to their brothers, who are being raised as future breadwinners.

The gender division of labor in elite households points to the conditions under which women are allowed to gain status in the mainstream social order. These women do not take on the burden of domestic work simply because they are economically dependent on their husbands. Four of the women are in senior positions, earning substantially higher incomes than many of their male peers. Indeed, each of the twelve women devotes a significant portion of her income to family upkeep. Hence, the analysis of the gender division of domestic labor in these households has to be placed within the larger structure of social relations. Regardless of their economic status, these women have a list of requirements to meet as subordinates in the marital union. Domestic labor is merely one aspect of these requirements. But unlike the need for a male heir, for instance, it is an ongoing requirement. The division of domestic work is bound up with the responsibilities a wife has to her husband, her husband's people, even her natal family (who has to ensure they bring up a marriageable daughter), all of which reinforce her subordinate status in the larger society. John Caldwell points out,

> A significant redefinition of conjugal roles with increased sharing of domestic duties may require, as a precondition, the development of stronger nuclear families with closer emotional ties between spouses. . . . The Nigerian extended family deliberately depreciated emotional relationships between spouses because it was important for family solidarity that the husband gives primary consideration to the wishes of his kin rather than of his spouse. If a husband attempted to assist his spouse with "female" domestic tasks, his mother or kin would intervene and would warn him of the unnatural influence of his spouse.[11]

Moreover, the underlying power relationship between the elite wife and her husband cannot be overlooked. The responses of women in the study clearly suggest that there is a connection between the services they provide at home and their marital security. Preparing soup, for instance, is not just one of the chores necessary in order to make it through the workweek. Admittedly, it is in part an expression of affection for a spouse. However, this food-love connection is constructed in a manner that reinforces a wife's subordinate position.

The social construction of domestic work as women's domain shields and legitimizes the exemption of men from participation. It tends to create a facade that trivializes the skills, volume, and sheer tedium of the work involved given the limited range of labor-saving devices available. This facade hides the continuum of inherently oppressive relations that the working mother must maintain with her house-helps in order to hold on to the economic autonomy that schooling and paid work offer. The relegation of domestic work to women and their house-helps gives it a trivial status. This trivial status devalues the house-help more than her madam, nullifying her crucial role in maintaining the unequal bargain a working mother strikes with both her husband at home and her employer at work. In fact, the women's description of husband care almost idealizes what the working mothers do, projecting their services as a labor of love[12] without accounting for the tedious aspects of this burden carried by house-helps.

This feminization of domestic labor and the class inequalities it generates among women in elite Igbo circles points to the patriarchal continuities and contradictions of postcolonial social arrangements that African women must contend with in their struggle to carve out a niche for themselves. These patriarchal continuities and contradictions must now be understood in the light of broader relations of power that mediate the lives of different groups of women. House-helps are exploited not merely as a cheap pool of female labor for elite women, but also as a group who have no better options. Their social background, age, and lack of skills reinforce this exploitation. To most of these house-helps, living in an elite household is a step closer to a better life. The arrangement creates a firm female hierarchy, the dissolution of which would necessitate a fundamental restructuring of the elite social order. With the present organization of paid work, especially professional employment, house-helps remain the only option for women who work outside the home. It seems that as the traditional support system for domestic work crumbles, Igbo women, like those in the West, tend to resort to alternatives that will not upset the patriarchal structure of the family. Igbo working mothers inevitably exploit a vulnerable pool of young girls in return for formal training that may improve their lives, but is not likely to catapult them into elite society. Their Western counterparts shift some of the burden to a feminized and underpaid domestic work force. None of these alternatives results in any appreciable restructuring of the domestic relations of gender.

Many female wage earners may fit the loose description of female elite but shoulder a substantial part of the domestic burden despite the assistance of house-helps. Most Igbo working mothers would keep one or more house-helps at home since the extent to which they can embrace formal employment depends on their capacity to drag the "domestic rear" along.[13] The demands of their primary role are bound up in a subordinate status, which is both materially and ideologically constructed. Domestic labor is only one expression of that subordinate status but it is a very important one. For the Igbo working mother, the use of house-helps as a stopgap does not significantly upset the nature of husband care, even with her increasing contribution to the family income. It could therefore be inferred that Igbo men's acceptance of their wives' career pursuits may have more to do with the need for a second income to meet the family budget than with an appreciation of women's extradomestic ambitions.

Much as this domestic arrangement enables female wage earners to participate in formal employment and improve their economic status, it reinforces the patriarchal continuities and contradictions that define women's membership in elite society. More important, the availability of house-helps does not in any way change the gender division of domestic work. The gender division of labor in the elite household places an extra burden on female wage earners, and the cheap labor provided by house-helps adds a twist to the dynamics of gender relations at home. It not only weakens the female wage earner's bargaining status at home but also provides a solid anchor for class divisions among women as long as it remains crucial to maintaining that balance between home and paid work for the female wage earner. As in advanced industrial societies, this arrangement creates a sharp gender divide that reinforces the existing domestic labor ideology. But, in contrast, working mothers in most advanced industrial societies have at their disposal a range of labor-saving devices that considerably ease the double burden. They can also rely on day care centers for children and other family members rather than on live-in caregivers during working hours. In their case, class relations with caregivers outside the domestic sphere are muted and the rigid gender division of labor at home has weakened comparably. In the African context, the range of labor-saving devices is greatly limited and the domestic sphere is largely contained within the household where the female wage earner, her husband, and the house-help closely interact. This interaction brings into closer view the oppressive sets of relations in which domestic work is embedded.

The organization of domestic work in the present elite household suggests that Igbo women's progress in both the school system and formal employment has not remarkably altered the relations of gender at home and in society. As the experiences of the working mothers in this study show, the asymmetry between home and paid work still presents a difficult challenge for Igbo women who plan to pursue a career in addition to fulfilling their primary role. Meeting the requirements of this crucial responsibility—getting married, bearing a male heir, having an acceptable number of children—easily compromises the woman's career goals. Those employed in the public sector are in a much better position to weather the balancing act. It is therefore not surprising that most working mothers end up in the public sector.

The dilemma faced by these working mothers, however, does not justify the class divisions among women created by the organization of domestic work in elite households. These class divisions cannot be overlooked simply because they allow some women to establish and nurture an economic niche. Such class divisions allow women to hang on to privileges offered by the elite society rather than claiming their right as full-fledged citizens. Hanging on to these privileges means that elite women must defer to the dictates of elite men. This is a difficult position for a female minority, who are in the best position to question the gender inequities that constrain women's lives in contemporary society.

8

Ours Is Ours but My Own Is My Own

Nuclear Households, Separate Purses, and Shared Responsibilities

The Nigerian man has not reached the point where he can sit down together with his wife and jointly make financial decisions.

—*Rose*

I never believed in joint accounts . . . and I'm not the busybody type . . . what he does with the rest of his income is his business.

—*Christie*

For most Nigerian men, an educated wife . . . a [university] graduate, is a threat. They will not openly admit this but it often comes out in their behavior.

—*Nnenna*

You want to help your relatives without giving your husband the impression that every kobo you earn goes to your family.

—*Chika*

The principle of separate resource structures (SRS) has considerable impact on conjugal relations within the Igbo nuclear household.[1] SRS gives Igbo women a customary right to manage their own finances, but the nature of their family responsibilities largely determines how much autonomy that control affords them. The case of married female wage earners only introduces a new twist to these dynamics.

Separate Resource Structures: Patriarchal Continuities and Contradictions

Whatever form SRS take, the practice appears to be perpetuated by the conflicting loyalties embedded in the structure of elite marriages. Depending on their individual circumstances these conflicts often create mixed feelings between elite husbands and wives about SRS.

For elite husbands, SRS may prove beneficial in a number of ways. First, the practice shields them from having to make joint decisions with their spouses on financial matters. Igbo men often face the conflict of providing financially for the nuclear and extended families. In Igboland children are encouraged very early in life to accept responsibility for the well-being of family members, particularly one's parents. In a cultural sense, children never really leave home and parents are expected, if need be, to sacrifice their own lives for their children's future. Without a formalized social net, children remain the most important source of investment for old age. Since Igbo culture is largely patrilineal, the incessant requests for financial assistance from one's relatives often weigh heavily on elite men, who must balance these external pressures with the needs of the nuclear household. As Chika, in her late thirties, a civil servant and mother of three little girls, points out, "men would rather not have you nose into their business. My husband tries not to involve me in discussions about giving [financial] assistance to his family. He feels that if I get to know what he gives them, I might start complaining that all the money is being forwarded to his people. That might not be the case, but oftentimes that's where the trouble starts."

Most of the working mothers reported that their husbands send a monthly allowance to one or two parents, but only one woman knew the specific amount. The average elite husband earns more than his wife and may not feel comfortable giving up his dominant position in family decision making in return for a partnership of some sort. Moreover, conjugal decisions over finances may expose the elite husband's personal interests, especially those that seriously conflict with the couple's commitments to the nuclear family.

According to the women, extramarital relations also represent another conflicting aspect of an elite Igbo man's life he would prefer to keep to himself. The women admit that a good number of elite husbands do not pursue such interests. But they also point out that extramarital liaisons are not unusual among elite Igbo men, who normally try to keep their tracks covered. Some men in monogamous marriages may also keep "outside wives" in residence away from the nuclear household. Such relationships may result in the birth of children, who traditionally belong to the man. Even if such unions are not formalized in the strict sense of the word, men are usually expected to provide some financial support for their "outside family."[2] Such appendages, the working mothers in this study insist, are a man's exclusive business and must not compete with the nuclear family's interests.

Despite the freedom SRS allow elite men, they can also present some challenges for them. Given the cultural demands on their financial resources, most elite men could certainly do with some financial help in the present economic climate and must accept some kind of partnership with working wives. According to the working mothers, a wife in a high-paying job is certainly a good economic asset to her husband, particularly one with many dependents. But as Nnenna, the thirty-four-year-old bank manager with two young children, points out, such a wife also poses a serious threat to the elite man's unquestioned dominance in the household: "For most Nigerian men, an educated wife . . . a [university] graduate, is a threat. They will not openly admit this but it often comes out in their behavior . . . They will say things like, 'Why are you so proud? Are you the only lawyer around here?' Yes, I'm a threat to him [my husband], even to his relatives [elder siblings]. . . . Often he will try to impress this upon me by putting his foot down during arguments, no matter how unreasonable his stand."

The growing number of highly educated Nigerian female wage earners reflects elite women's progress in contemporary society. But this progress is undermined by the increasing financial burden they bear in the family. While women's rising socioeconomic status and contribution to family may strengthen their bargaining power, they do not appear to threaten men's dominance in the elite household. Rose, fifty-seven and the mother of three grown children, reflects on her experience with SRS over the decades. She is at present an assistant director in a public department and one of the few Igbo female university graduates of the early 1960s. She joined the civil service in 1962 with a degree in history and subsequently got married. Her early marital experience is very revealing:

> The Nigerian man still feels that he owns the woman. . . . He is not ready to accept you [his wife] as a partner. . . . Many of us resisted pressures to surrender our paychecks. Do you know that there are still some Nigerian women who are forced to do that? . . . My husband tried . . . but I was adamant. In fact, I saw this as an achievement because in those days, the moment you [got married] . . . you'd be asked to regularly explain what you did with your salary. I made it clear to my husband then that he should forget the marriage if he was interested in my money. I was allowed to spend my own money the way I chose. . . . The Nigerian man has not reached the point where he can sit down together with his wife and jointly make financial decisions.

Since elite men are expected to provide financially for their nuclear and extended families, many of them might take for granted a wife's primary commitment to the immediate household. But a potential conflict exists in terms of how working mothers choose to distribute their earnings between household and nonhousehold demands. With no direct access to his wife's income, the elite husband must give way to some form of negotiation, which might also mean some degree of joint financial management. Such a cooperative stance on his part does not necessarily translate into equal partnership in making financial decisions for the household and the extended families.

For female wage earners, SRS may prove advantageous in a number of ways. Foremost, the elite woman's economic status can strengthen her bargaining position in her marital home. The participants in this study unanimously stressed the need for women to maintain some degree of personal financial independence. Nnenna, the bank manager, echoes the feelings of the younger female wage earners: "It's a basic attitude of Nigerian men. Everything that belongs to a wife is theirs. As long as you're their wife you should be dependent on them. That bit of economic independence a working woman has helps."

An Igbo woman's control of her earned income is crucial to the protection of the most important investment in her marriage: children. While men, by custom, "own" the children, the primary responsibility for their welfare usually falls on women. Even the highly paid woman does not lose sight of the fact that her children remain the strongest allies in both the nuclear and extended families. Women's ties to their natal families also strengthen their support bases and bargaining power in marriage, and the highly educated female wage earner is in a very good position to foster those ties with the financial resources at her disposal. Maintaining those ties often involves the exchange of gifts and money. Depending on her financial capacity, the female wage earner may take on major financial responsibilities in her father's compound. But the elite woman must be careful about how she relates with her natal family since, by custom, her loyalty lies first with the family she married into. Chika, the civil servant and mother of three, puts it this way:

> Being a woman, you want to help your relatives without giving your husband the impression that every kobo[3] you earn goes to your family. For instance, you don't tell your husband that you purchased George [an expensive cloth wrapper] for your mother. He might not be happy

to hear that. If you begin to inform him whenever you give some assistance to your family, you might be asking for trouble. In fact, he might even begin to think that you're spending the family's allowance on them. . . . To make sure that you don't get into all that, you do your own thing secretly. If he decides at any time to help your family, just thank him.

Despite the advantages SRS provide for women, the Igbo female wage earner may not totally embrace the practice for a number of reasons. For instance, some female wage earners would want to pool resources with their spouses in order to foster a closer emotional bond. Those who earn very little income compared to their husbands may go for a common purse in order to safeguard their children's economic welfare. Close nuclear ties are also invaluable to the woman who would like to assist her poor natal family without causing any trouble in her own home.

The conflicts SRS present to elite couples appear to have given way to a redefinition of the practice as a compromise of sorts. Usually couples share the responsibilities within the nuclear household but maintain a respectable distance from their spouse's extranuclear interests. However, this financial arrangement has its own caveats. For women especially, managing their own finances does not necessarily imply spending their incomes any way they choose. It is important to remember that husbands can overrule their wives' decisions, especially when their points of view differ.

The differing responses to SRS by the working mothers in this study reflect their individual bargaining stances. Those with the highest-paying jobs, such as Christie, insist on separate purses and are not bothered about their husbands' financial dealings as long as the husbands meet their own household responsibilities. Christie is forty-nine and a mother of two young children. She is an assistant director in a government department and, like her husband, has substantial financial responsibilities in her extended family. In her own case, she states, "I never believed in joint accounts . . . and I'm not the busybody type. Once he gives me his part of the family allowances we agreed on, what he does with the rest of his income is his business." As Christie notes, this arrangement may actually prove much more beneficial for the highly paid woman in an inequitable marital arrangement, where there is great potential for controversy over conflicting loyalties and degrees of financial autonomy. Unlike the four highly paid married participants in the study, the other eight, who earn more moderate salaries, appear to have closer financial dealings with their husbands. Their responses reflect both their financial status and economic importance in the family. For example, Iruka and her husband have agreed on meeting certain financial obligations in their respective extended families. The total burden, however, is much heavier on her husband's side. The couple must, therefore, work out the monthly budget well ahead of time in order to ensure they cover the regular financial demands from his younger siblings. As she admits, "Of course you don't feel good when they keep making demands. You sit down to draw up a budget for the month with your husband and he begins to list the [financial] demands from his brothers. . . . You feel cheated, like you're slaving away for some other persons besides your husband and children. The money is not even enough for us!" Often family members congregate around relatives who are in a position to help out. The burden can be quite daunting if only one or two members are well placed to respond. As the Igbo adage says, "The fortunate sibling should sponsor a father's burial; the first son didn't kill him." In other words, those who are able should help, since fate does not necessarily distribute wealth according to age and position in the family.

In contrast to Iruka, Chidimma is married to a wealthy medical doctor and enjoys a much higher standard of living than her income provides. According to her, she has opted for a more subordinate stance than many of her contemporaries. She is thirty-one, a schoolteacher, and mother of five children. Her husband is the second son in his family and is partly responsible for the education of six younger siblings. Chidimma admits that she is not in a position to question how her husband handles his finances:

> [My husband and his siblings] normally keep me out of such discussions. When his brothers visit, they hold private discussions with him. I know that he has given them some money, but not the exact amount or what it's for. He would not, for instance, tell me that he has given them school fees or pocket money. Occasionally, I do come across their letters to my husband. Then, I have an idea of what is going on. Normally, I don't make any noise about it. Once you start complaining he becomes more secretive about his financial dealings with other people and begins to confide even less in you.

Chidimma does not want to jeopardize the trust her husband places in her and the emotional bond that has created. After all, she reasons, it is his money and he can spend it any way he wants. Such a stance clearly portrays a cultural facet of the marital contract in elite marriages. The monogamous nuclear household is still strongly embedded in a sociocultural milieu with many indigenous features that reinforce men's dominant status. These indigenous features also find a strong support base in the rigidities of an arrangement, which have proved unresponsive to its Western transformations over time.

SRS certainly present their own challenges, but elite Igbo women also seek out their own strategies to advance their financial autonomy. It is important to note that despite the responsibilities that come with extended family relationships, elite men also have a considerable stake in protecting the nuclear union. Elite couples share some concern for each other's welfare and, regardless of the competing claims being made on their resources, their children's well-being is the top priority. Moreover, elite men like Iruka's husband need their wives' earnings to make ends meet. They may therefore be more cooperative than their better-placed colleagues.

The Division of Financial Responsibilities in the Elite Household

In the elite household men are expected to take care of major expenses for school fees, rent or maintenance of the family home, utilities, hospital bills, food, and car repairs. Ideally, women's income is not to be used for any of the expenses mentioned. The participants in this study unanimously agreed that men should bear most of the household responsibilities, advancing various reasons for this view. Chika, thirty-eight, a schoolteacher with three children, is married to an architect. She argues that husbands should remain the primary breadwinners: "It is his responsibility in the first place to cater to his family. If I was not working, he would still have to find a way to fulfill this responsibility. ... But since I work, well ... he would expect me to pitch in something. That seems reasonable enough." Ifeyinwa, thirty-eight, a civil servant and mother of five young children, agrees with Chika: "It is the man's responsibility to pay his children's school fees. After all, the children don't bear the woman's maiden name. They belong to the man."

Of course these women are only restating the patrilineal underpinnings of Igbo culture in a contemporary context. The children belong to their father, along with the responsibility for their well-being. The elite marital arrangement has restructured a mother's direct responsibility for her children, making any possible contribution on her part only a supplement. Based on the same argument, a husband is also primarily responsible for rent, hospital bills, utilities, and repairs around the home. In addition, he is expected to give his wife a monthly allowance for the family's upkeep, which the female wage earner can augment with her own salary. According to the women, a good portion of the entire allowance goes toward the food budget.

Although the welfare of women and children in elite homes was never guaranteed, legally or otherwise, the colonial legacy of dependent full-time housewives is indelibly etched in the social image of contemporary elite families. But the views and experiences of these career women show that this social image is only a myth that does not reflect present-day realities. In any case, the housewife model is largely Western and has never accommodated the peculiarities of Nigerian cultures. In fact, the financial responsibilities Igbo women in paid work carry barely raise an eyebrow because they complement rather than contravene traditional expectations of women's contribution to family subsistence. Traditionally, Igbo women's access to economic ventures was tied to their responsibility for children and depended on their relationship with men, usually husbands, who provided the means of production. In other words, husbands delegated responsibility for their children to their wives, along with access to productive resources. Within this context, the differential allocation of rewards and entitlements in men's favor seems justifiable.

The shift in the traditional arrangement posed very little conflict in the early stages of colonization, when women had little or no access to paid work. The conflict arises in the present context because paid labor affords female wage earners an independent economic base without a commensurate status in making household financial decisions. Indeed, the gender division still allocates more rewards and entitlements to elite men. Given their economic base, working women's contribution to family subsistence cannot therefore be translated into a response to delegated authority. The women in this study recognize the patriarchal contradiction as a basis for men's larger share of the financial burden.

However, the actions of these women suggest that this basic stance has weakened in present times. Nigeria's economic decline, it appears, has significantly reshaped the practice of SRS in the nuclear household. In principle, the women stand by their arguments for allocating the major responsibility for the family's well-being to men. However, when it comes to the details of monthly household expenses, it becomes clear that the actual distribution of gender responsibilities differs remarkably from their initial stance.

Usually the total household income is spread over the family's upkeep, individual allowances of spouses, major projects, assistance to relatives, and personal investments of each spouse.[4] The proportion of each woman's monthly income that goes into the family's upkeep depends on both the total family income and her income relative to her husband's (table 8.1). The twelve married women are placed in three categories based on their average monthly income.

The women in group 1 have high-paying jobs in either the civil or the corporate sector. Two of them, Christie and Nnenna, actually earn monthly incomes comparable to or higher than those of their husbands. The four women in this group contribute more financial resources toward the family's upkeep than their spouses do. The six women in group 2 are mainly schoolteachers and middle-level civil servants. They earn a little more than half of their husbands' income but contribute about half of the entire family expenses. The two women in group 3—Chinelo, thirty, an accountant, and Chidimma, thirty-one, a schoolteacher—are married to a wealthy businessman and a medical doctor, respectively. Both women spend more than half their income on the family's upkeep. Unlike the women in the first two groups, however, their contributions hardly match those of their spouses.

The data in table 8.1 deviates remarkably from the women's stance on the spousal division of family financial responsibilities but reflects the married working mother's vested interests, particularly in these harsh economic times. Despite their feelings about the unequal division of rewards, these women take direct responsibility for their children's welfare. Along with the rigid schedule of paid work, working mothers are responsible for the day-to-day running of the home with

Table 8.1. Women's Monthly Income and Proportional Financial Burden (%)

Economic ranking of married female wage earners	Group 1	Group 2	Group 3
Wife's income as percentage of spouse's income	80	57	15
Percentage of wife's income allocated to family expenses	55	80	60
Wife's contribution as percentage of total family expenses	55	45	20

Source: Compiled from data on income and family expenditure provided by the twelve married women in the sample.

its never-ending stream of unbudgeted expenses. In the Nigerian context, that responsibility presents some peculiar challenges. First, it is difficult to budget for the family's upkeep with the usual "disruptions" from extranuclear family attachments. Most of the women were quite amused when they were asked how they handle such uncertainties. Chika (group 2), the schoolteacher with three children who is married to an architect, responded with a shrug, "There isn't much to decide on because, often, they don't inform you that they are coming. You either meet them at your doorstep or they are already in the house when you arrive from work."

Dealing with relatives is an accepted reality of life in urban Nigeria, and elite Igbo households are not immune from the attendant pressures. However, as two of the women indicated, drawing from their own personal experiences, not all families have an open-door policy. Many elite families no longer have strong ties to the extended family and the elite wife certainly has a good idea how far she is expected to go in meeting such obligations. In addition to irregular expenses, the working mother also has to deal with the skyrocketing inflation since the onset of the SAPs in the 1980s. The women point out that, in many households, a wife's earnings are increasingly needed to meet what have become regular shortfalls in what her spouse provides. It has become increasingly difficult to keep track of the unstable market prices, which rise almost daily. The situation creates further problems since the elite wife cannot even count on a regular allowance from her husband. For instance, Chika's husband, a self-employed architect, can no longer guarantee his full monthly contribution. Private business ventures have become highly unstable with the economic downturn. The situation is different for Iruka, Onyeka, and Uju (group 2), whose husbands are civil servants with perhaps smaller, but regular, contributions the family can budget around.

These women are well aware that their husbands cannot shoulder the financial burden alone and increasingly find themselves trying to balance conflicting demands. In fact, most of the women in groups 1 and 2 must now accept at different times some responsibility for major household expenses such as rent, the children's school fees, and hospital bills. A few of the women now shoulder some of these financial responsibilities on a regular basis. In spite of their beliefs about the gender division of financial responsibilities within the family, they appear quite willing to make more sacrifices than before. Uju, thirty-eight, a school vice-principal and mother of five, aptly explains,

"Although I'm also concerned about my husband's welfare, I try extra hard [to provide for] . . . my children. . . . I don't earn much, but I struggle to keep them healthy and ensure they get a good education."

Christie (group 1) is equally concerned about her children's well-being. She married at thirty-four and has risen to a higher rank at work than her husband. She has two children, a daughter and a son, but her husband has other children from a previous marriage. Her marriage, she remarks, has been a constant struggle to assert herself, and her economic status has provided a strong support base. She has resolved that her daughter and female relatives in her care learn from her experience so that they may have the same leverage that she now has in her marriage: "I'm very particular about the girls' education. . . . They must be able to fend for themselves. . . . These days, no man is prepared to marry a woman who is idle. I keep telling my daughter, 'Just go on and read. Don't look back. Keep going. This is your only route to independence.'"

A good education, most of the women emphasize, provides children, especially girls, with a more secure future than they otherwise might have. Young women cannot easily embrace the risks attached to the economic opportunities their male counterparts now pursue instead of formal schooling. Thus, the uneducated woman remains severely disadvantaged compared to her peers who have acquired some formal training.

Besides the added financial responsibilities that came with SAP, many working mothers must also make the necessary allowance to accommodate their house-helps, financially and otherwise. Although most of the house-helps are not employed on salary, the family budget must make room for their basic needs such as food, clothing, and toiletries. Husbands may help out with the fees for their formal training either in the public schools or in nonaccredited vocational centers. Only three of the women received such assistance in full. In any case, a good number of them had mixed feelings over their husband's intervention. A female wage earner's capacity to assume this financial responsibility, they point out, not only enables her to decide the type and number of house-helps to bring in but also gives her the power to exert full rein over them. For instance, Onyeka, thirty-two and a civil servant, had one house-help before the birth of her year-old daughter. With another baby arriving, she needed her husband's financial support for an extra house-help. He refused, insisting that one live-in house-help was enough. It took the intervention of her mother-in-law to change his mind. The situation is different for the women in group 1, who assert that the number of house-helps they choose to keep is their own business since they, not their husbands, will foot the bill. Regardless of who pays the bill, working mothers strive to maintain close supervision and control over their house-helps. Many are especially wary of the likelihood of extramarital liaisons in the elite circle. According to Nnenna (group 1), the bank manager, "Some women are unfortunate. Their husbands sleep with the [house-helps].[5] That creates problems, especially if she gets pregnant. In that case, you have to deal with your husband, the maid, and her people. . . . My husband leaves everything concerning the [house-helps'] welfare in my hands. I buy their clothes, I pay their fees, and I discipline them if they misbehave."

Like Nnenna, women in monogamous unions have to watch out for any threats to their marriage in a society where men's extramarital liaisons are not strongly frowned upon. It is important for the elite Igbo woman to guard against setting the seduction scene herself, given that many less privileged women would not hesitate to step into her shoes or even accept a less formal arrangement with her husband. The female wage earner's financial responsibility for a house-help indicates to the latter that her employer can make or break her should she take a wrong step.

In terms of major financial outlays the working mothers assist their husbands in major family projects such as building a new house, renovating or furnishing the family residence, fixing the car, or starting a business. Ten out of the twelve married women have been involved in a number of such projects. Those in group 1 have made direct cash contributions to major projects. In fact, of the four women, three provided the furnishings (chairs, curtains, rugs) for the family's residence. The fourth woman, Rose, a fifty-seven-year-old assistant director in a government department, bought the land for the family's residence at Enugu. The rest of the women spend most of their income on regular family expenses, especially those in group 2, who must deal with the shortfalls arising from their husbands' irregular contributions.

As all the working mothers admit, their husbands' customary claim to the family property does place them in a vulnerable situation when it comes to long-term investments. However, they appear to accept the risk involved, as reflected in the financial support they are willing to provide. In fact, three of the women in group 1 actually initiated the idea for a family-owned residence and pressured their husbands into taking the first steps. These women's support for such projects clearly demonstrates their faith in the stability of their marriage. Evidently the women and their children also benefit from such projects. As part of the man's nuclear household, each woman enjoys the comfort and social prestige attached to the family home(s) and car(s). The village residence in particular is often located in the husband's village and remains unquestionably his property. But that enclosure, however modest, is for the visiting elite wife from the city—a safe haven that shields her from the prying eyes of less privileged relatives.

In terms of a budget for personal needs, most of the women spend only modest amounts on luxuries such as cosmetics, clothing, and jewelry. Again, women with higher incomes or wealthy husbands (or both) tend to spend more money on these items than those on tighter budgets. Women in group 3 have very little income compared to their husbands, who in many cases foot the bill for luxuries.

Despite their financial commitments to family projects, these working mothers also find various means to strengthen their individual economic status, especially in the long run. Those with fewer resources tend to invest mainly in their children. For instance, women in groups 2 and 3 often have little left for personal savings by the time the financial responsibilities of the nuclear and natal families are met. But those with higher incomes may in addition undertake capital investments. For instance, Rose (group 1), who owned the land on which the family residence was built, recently purchased another piece of land, for what she considers very good reasons: "The CIO [certificate of occupancy] is in my name so that if anything happens, I can sell it or build a house on it. . . . You have to make plans . . . acquire properties or shares in your own name. . . . Such precautions save you from going under if anything happens. If you're lucky, it [divorce or separation] may not come at all. Knowing that it could happen and society will not see anything wrong with [your being disinherited] you'd better prepare yourself from the word go by putting certain measures in place."

According to the working mothers, the married woman is expected to seek her husband's consent for major expenditures. But, as Rose explains, ventures like hers might meet with stiff opposition. She has therefore decided to go on with her plans and find a way to sell the idea to her husband later. Similarly, Nnenna, the bank manager, is currently "working on" her husband to get his permission to make major repairs on her car. She has secured a loan from her bank for the expenses, but her husband insists that she spend the money otherwise: "He asked me to purchase tires with all the money instead. Of course I don't want to do that. Now he's threatening that I must not go ahead. So I have to gradually steer him around to see things my way without causing trouble. Yesterday I bought all the things needed for the job. I haven't told him yet."

To gradually win her husband over, Nnenna has adopted a nonconfrontational strategy. She has to tread carefully because she earns as much as he does, if not more. As she points out, this is not simply a question of car repairs versus buying tires. It is not only her husband's feelings that must be considered but also those of his immediate relatives and friends. It is not fashionable, she points out, for a wife to flaunt her economic independence in a society where a man should be calling the shots in his own home.

In balancing the conflicting interests of the nuclear and natal families, the proportion of her income the female wage earner spends on her natal family is largely influenced by her economic status relative to other members. For instance, women such as Chidimma who have financially comfortable parents and siblings escape any direct obligations to family and kin. Having elite parents also weakens considerably any existing ties to the larger extended family. In contrast, Chika has an aged mother and a younger brother in school to provide for. In addition to a younger sister who lives with her, Uju is also supporting a number of older relatives. Christie has already seen two distant relatives through secondary school. She has two children of her own but has also taken under her care a niece and a nephew. In addition, she extends financial assistance to some aged relatives, though not regularly.

Nuclear Units, Separate Incomes: Women's Bargaining Power and Economic Security

The gender division of responsibilities and entitlements clearly portrays the dual status of partner and subordinate assumed by the married female wage earner in Igboland. As partners, women are inclined to invest in the nuclear unit, assume considerable responsibility for the children's welfare, and "jointly" accumulate capital with their spouses. As subordinates, it is important that they secure their own future through their children and, possibly, personal capital investments. But the struggle to strengthen their bargaining power and

personal autonomy is strongly undermined by the actual gender distribution of financial responsibilities. This arrangement seriously
erodes their attempts to maintain a balance between providing for the
household and for their own personal economic security in a union
whose long-term stability is anything but certain. The majority of the
working mothers are saddled with a myriad of seemingly trivial
household expenditures that easily drain their monthly incomes. In
the uncertain economic climate they live in, it is difficult to keep track
of and plan for these expenses ahead of time. Even the highly paid
woman must maintain this balance between familial and personal economic needs in order to save for the future. Going by their actual contributions relative to their incomes, most of the women are certainly
more than mere financial helpmates to their husbands. But the bulk of
these contributions remain in a sense invisible. The invisibility of
their economic importance in the family conveniently reinforces men's
dominant status at home and the special privileges that go with it.

In contrast, elite men's financial responsibilities in the household
tend to be limited to major or predictable items such as fixed monthly
allowance, school fees, building or renovating a home, and car purchases. These expenditures are quite visible; women's contributions
pale in comparison. Even when women shoulder some of men's responsibilities, it is perceived as merely lending a hand to the main
breadwinner.

In effect, men can easily pass on some of their own responsibilities
to their wives without endangering their dominant position in the
family. In fact, men do not necessarily have to account for or seek their
wives' approval for other expenses outside the family. This may not be
the case for all couples, but, in general, men nevertheless have the prerogative to keep their financial dealings personal. These women's involvement in family projects would be justified even more if their
rights with regard to the property would be adequately protected.
But, as subordinates, these working mothers realize that their contribution to the family's well-being and future social status might, at
least, safeguard their children's future and perhaps strengthen their
bargaining power in the household. Even for the highly paid women
in group 1, the surplus after their contributions to the family is not
entirely under their control. Their economic status notwithstanding,
these women value their marriage security for very good reasons.
Paid labor merely improves, to some extent, their subordinate position in marriage. Their financial burdens may be increasing with the

economic situation, but not necessarily their bargaining power. Rose, the assistant director, sums it all up: "They [husbands] will make you spend every kobo of that money on the family. You will be the one to spend your money all right, but you will be forced to use it to maintain the home. You may even end up with nothing to give your parents. However, I would still prefer to be the one giving out the money."

The invisibility of these women's economic importance in the family conveniently keeps in place the various facets of an oppressive structure of gender relations. Obviously, it is those fundamental assumptions of society that stipulate a subordinate status for Igbo women that prescribe accordingly the attendant roles and obligations. The contemporary elite Igbo family now struggles with the continuities and contradictions of social transformation, and women appear to bear the brunt of these developments. The present social arrangement in many ways supports the oppressive structure of gender relations, justifying the accommodations women make in order to secure a niche in the elite circle.

But, as the experiences of women analyzed here portray, Igbo female wage earners are carving out their agency and seeking out viable strategies to establish a strong economic base and future. Despite the rigidities of the structure they find themselves in, these women display remarkable resourcefulness. They appear to be exploiting every crack in the system to safeguard their interests and those of their children. These working women clearly recognize that their overall wellbeing in society is inextricably linked with their position at home and at work. Hence they exploit any available opportunities in both settings to improve their situation. These women recognize the contradictions embedded in the marital contract, and those well positioned can expand their economic autonomy outside the strictures of elite marriage.

9

Looking to the Future

Nigeria's Educated Women as Nation Builders

The experiences of Igbo career women strongly affirm the enormous impact of patriarchal continuities and contradictions from colonial to contemporary Igboland. Patriarchal continuities are evident in the school system, the family, and the labor market. But patriarchal contradictions also mediate the definitions of gender roles, the specific requirements attached to them, and the rewards accruing from individual efforts. In fact, the complex interaction of continuities and contradictions are vividly revealed in conflicting social expectations—widening career options with rigid domestic roles; malestream work structures and work practices with policies unresponsive to domestic demands; and an autonomous source of income undermined by the gender division of financial responsibilities and rewards. Since the hybridized social order reinforces a double standard that favors elite men, these women are forced to wrestle with a persistent ideology underlying female education in Nigeria: women should benefit from formal education only as subordinates to men.

The experiences of Igbo career women in this book provide crucial insights about gender relations in Africa—not in terms of the taken-for-granted burden of indigenous and foreign discrimination they carry but rather in their understanding and rejection of spaces and positions in which society places them. It is obvious that despite the varied extents to which women within this group applied wit and resilience, there were critical redefinitions of the status quo in each case.

Each of the career Igbo women in this book articulated experiences and a worldview that were mediated by gender, age, and class, among other factors. The choices they made indicated some degree of resistance, however mute, to layers of ideologies they were not prepared to wholly accept.

In general, the lives of these university-educated career women reflect some of the major impacts of colonization and capitalist expansion on elite women across Africa, which include subordinate status in elite circles, poor school enrollment, gendered segregation in higher education and formal employment, tensions in managing inflexible responsibilities in domestic and public spheres, and the inherent challenges of riding the economic, political, and social trends of the past two decades.[1] Capitalist expansion has opened up new opportunities and invariably created what may be seen as cultural boundaries. Women's access to these opportunities entails the complex negotiation of power and privilege.[2] The range of views and experiences captured in previous chapters does not permit any general conclusions. It is important to recognize, however, that the significance of the analysis here lies more in the authenticity of these women's voices and the originality of the knowledge base from which they articulate their worldviews. While one cannot make generalizations based exclusively on research that explores the lives of a small group of Nigerian women, it is safe to claim that their stories provide insights that could contribute to a better understanding of broader patterns across the continent.

The voices of Igbo women in this book speak to the gross marginalization of African women in tertiary education, which social researchers, development organizations, and African governments continually lament.[3] Despite the significant strides African women have made in higher education in the past three decades, they have yet to even approach parity with men.[4] Igbo career women in this book give a face to issues and problems that statistics cannot reveal. They give us a picture of what it takes for the female minority to achieve success. As these women persistently declare, formal training, especially at the tertiary level, still remains the most viable path to social mobility in Africa. African women with tertiary educational credentials constitute a privileged minority. Such women are, in a sense, survivors, given the range of social weapons that keep young girls from aspiring to or staying in school beyond the primary and secondary levels.

For each Igbo career woman in this book, the journey to higher education highlights one crucial issue—African women's participation in higher education is not simply a matter of expanding structures and facilities to accommodate the numbers. Of course, public subsidies are crucial to boosting women's enrollment. Without the necessary infrastructural and financial support, the school system would have to deal with a much higher female dropout rate. But, as Eva Rathgeber logically extrapolates, "If fewer women complete primary and secondary schooling . . . fewer will be found at the tertiary level. If girls are encouraged to marry early, to be burdened with household responsibilities and defer their own educational aspirations in favor of their brothers' [and husbands'], then again, it is clear that they will be under-represented at the tertiary level."[5] It is important to recognize that the mere expansion of access to schooling for women cannot in itself improve their representation. Any efforts aimed at increasing African women's numbers in higher educational institutions must begin with breaking the barriers that limit their progress.[6]

The profiles of Igbo career women in this book also highlight the importance of women's distribution across the disciplines. If women are to participate fully and effectively in tertiary education, adequate provision has to be made for both access and distribution in various fields. Most African women who pursue higher education must accept the fact that, compared to their male counterparts, any kind of training at this level, in material and social terms, would fetch them much lower returns. African women's access to paid work, for instance, mirrors not only their low profile in school systems across the continent but also the social expectations regarding the utility of their training. Certainly, women have made considerable progress in paid work in other African countries such as Botswana and Mauritius, where they constitute 38 percent and 37 percent of the workforce, respectively. But again, the average female participation in paid work in Africa remains a mere 22 percent, with women in countries such as Chad and Niger constituting only 5 and 9 percent of the workforce, respectively. On average, African women's representation in formal employment reflects a dismal share compared to the situation in other developing regions of the world, such as Latin America, with an average of 40 percent.[7] Any significant improvements in African women's participation in formal employment must include some radical efforts at opening up male preserves in academia and professional careers. Policies for women's education have to go beyond providing more places for women. Both the level and the kind of training have to be considered if women are to be properly equipped with the skills necessary for a changing labor market.[8]

The Igbo career women who share their life experiences here also expose the overt and covert biases that not only reinforce gender segregation but make formal employment an endeavor many women pursue with substantial reservations. The very structure of jobs, the organization of work, and working conditions are still in many respects tailored to male workers. As all the women admit, paid work still remains a malestream environment that merely accommodates women. Unfortunately, one cannot expect any remarkable improvement if the relations of gender in the family remain unchanged. The situation Igbo working mothers find themselves in is in part a reflection of the rigid and unequal division of domestic responsibilities women deal with across the continent.[9]

African women's participation in higher education should also do more than provide economic autonomy. Training at this level should also prepare them to take their place alongside men in nation building. The career profiles of Igbo women in this book clearly show that gender segregation across the disciplines is an integral part of socialization even before boys and girls enter the school system. In many ways, the school system is nurturing the seeds already sown by society, co-opting teachers, at times, into the process. The equitable distribution of African women across the disciplines would facilitate their participation in nation building not only in terms of social mobility but also as a prerequisite for generating a much-needed database. Their participation in higher education, especially their representation in the male preserves, entails the breakdown, however gradual, of a global stereotype. Women across the world, but more so in developing countries, are stereotyped as followers. Men are seen as natural leaders, and therefore the responsibility of managing the social order and charting future paths for change rest on their shoulders. Charlotte Bunch, a renowned international social activist, asserts:

> Women are not expected to take control, and in consequence, are not encouraged to think analytically. In fact, critical thinking is the antithesis of women's traditional role. Women are supposed to worry about mundane survival problems. . . . We are not meant to think analytically about society, to question the way things are, or to consider

how things could be different. Such thinking involves an active, not passive, relationship with the world. It requires confidence that your thoughts are worth pursuing and that you can make a difference.[10]

If African leaders are serious about improving African women's participation in higher education, they must begin to cast this half of the population in a new light. Higher education should empower African women to be equal citizens with men rather than an essentially subordinate group that enjoys paternal privilege under well-specified conditions. Tertiary training should equip women with access to and control of productive resources to enable them to take their place with men, not as their aids and consorts but as equal partners in the nation-building process. Research on the global feminization of poverty, for instance, clearly indicates that women's material lack is traceable to an "insufficient access to resources, a lack of political rights and social options, and greater vulnerability to risks and crises."[11] At the very core of African women's struggle for social emancipation is their denigration, apparent and subtle, in a contemporary society where women's potential as productive citizens is exploited rather than nurtured for social progress.

Women's representation in the professions, therefore, cannot be separated from their place in academia as teachers, researchers, and administrators. The African university is still characterized by a heavy, if not foreboding, cloud of patriarchal authority that continues to mediate the experience and prospect of higher education for both female students and faculty. If higher education must do something for African women, it should provide at least the scholarly forums where they can interrogate their social status and demand answers from society.[12] As Nigerian scholar and social activist Ayesha Imam asserts, the task, for those who challenge the gender biases and other social inequalities inherent in contemporary African societies, is not simply to develop knowledge, "but is also necessarily and simultaneously profoundly a political struggle over power and resources."[13] In generating knowledge about gender and social organization, the African university cannot settle for mere descriptions of African women's lives with the usual call for aid attached. Scholarship on African women must ask questions that may not sit well with certain power groups and establishments—questions that may even confront the interests of some groups of women. As active participants in higher education, women should be at the forefront, developing knowledge that the struggle for social emancipation must necessarily feed on.

African women's full participation in higher education also demands a rethinking of what the curriculum is meant to achieve. The very content of women's education, from the primary level, must be questioned. Liobi Moshi argues, "There is an assumption that formal education is the ultimate liberator of women in Africa. However, we need to bear in mind that much of what is taught in formal education is like a double-edged sword—for the most part it is foreign and has affected societal values for the worse. Although formal education can be used to raise women from the shackles of poverty and inequality, it can also make the same women victims of continuous criticism for abandoning cultural and traditional values."[14]

African women's education is often presented as a monolithic product. Public debate revolves around their access to this seemingly monolithic asset and their progression through its ranks. Nobody questions the gender biases, foreign or indigenous, that come with the package. The curriculum is expected to provide both the basic training that enables individuals to function as adults and the critical thinking skills that force them, as they progress through the system, to question various facets of social relations. The curriculum should not merely present African cultures and customs to both male and female children as the social dictates of the time but should also encourage them to ask some pertinent questions: Is culture perpetually stagnant? Must things remain the way they are for no clear reasons? Should tradition serve us or must we serve tradition? Must we bow to tradition regardless of the burden it places on the shoulders of certain groups? Might tradition be invoked in some instances as a platform on which we can stand to fight our causes?

Critical reconfigurations of the content of higher education should not simply integrate women's struggles into the system, but should also draw from their knowledge bases, which remain undervalued. Despite the time-tested skills they have acquired, African women are rarely consulted for their input on policies about food production, natural resource management, and medical science. At present, the social and economic demarcations between elite and nonelite circles, formal and informal sectors, haves and have-nots, mean that these knowledge bases essentially reside in women who are even further marginalized in today's society. These knowledge bases will remain untapped if the younger generation of women is not trained to extract this invaluable information.

None of the Igbo career women in this book seemed to harbor any political ambitions. Not even the older women, who have long established their careers, expressed any desire to enter formal politics. The brief review of the general pattern across the continent (chapter 1) reflects this apathy. Obviously, African women's minimal political representation is not necessarily due to the lack of higher education credentials. Whether reinforced by tradition or the legacy of colonial sexism, women's political representation in Africa reflects the narrow niche carved out for them in a contemporary society where they are expected to harness their efforts toward family subsistence and register their presence in the public sphere only to the extent that it does not challenge their subordinate status beside men as brothers, fathers, husbands, and leaders who hold the fort and chart the path. Evidently the paternal culture of formal politics in Africa, which cultivates various forms of corrupt practices, creates barriers that female groups and individuals cannot easily break through. But the very structure of gender relations within and outside the home already make formal politics a boys' club with ladies in waiting. In order to make any dents in the current state of affairs, higher education must begin with transforming itself from a bastion of male authority to a true ivory tower where the search for knowledge has no boundaries.

The challenges African women face in accessing higher education and utilizing its credentials also need to be reassessed in global terms. In an increasingly globalizing world, Africa's problems cannot be understood only in terms of what is happening in the continent. Although the full ramifications of their impact have yet to be ascertained, a number of trends are already shaping the future of higher education in Africa. The optimistic vision of education, for instance, as an engine of modernization and economic growth, has all but virtually disappeared in much of sub-Saharan Africa. The worsening economic situation has radically reduced state funding and its capacity to absorb school graduates in search of formal employment. But with educational training still representing the major prospect for the good life, an overwhelming demand for places in higher education continues to grow, undiminished by shrinking public subsidies. The recent mushrooming of private higher education institutions, many with questionable standards, is therefore not surprising.[15] This expansion, experts observe, is further linked not only to the demand for quality that financially strapped public institutions can no longer maintain but also to the need to diversify options for a young generation competing in a changing labor market.[16] However, the blunt economic rationales by international financial institutions have also introduced new directions in higher education policies across the developing world, including Africa. What was conventionally perceived as a public good—crucial to the development of human capital and technical capacity for national development—is now increasingly being heralded as an equally private one which bestows considerable prospects that recipients cannot receive at society's entire expense.[17]

What is slowly emerging is a continuum of higher education options from cost-sharing public schools to for-profit tertiary institutions. Current debates on the future of higher education in Africa have yet to unravel the ramifications of this development with respect to the concerns of social equity and national planning. In the meantime, the fates of over 50 percent of Africa's school-age population, whose life chances depend on public intervention, hang in the balance. How well the new private institutions are doing is an important factor, which is already generating its own controversies. Experts in the field agree, however, that the privatization of higher education in Africa only complicates existing questions surrounding access, funding, autonomy, accountability, and quality—especially with the rising internationalization driven by information technology.[18] Despite some notable peculiarities found in specific countries, Africa's economic decline has placed a huge financial burden on both higher institutions and their students in meeting the challenges of increased demand for training. Indeed, access to tertiary education, particularly entrance into specific fields of specialization, could become increasingly marked by gender in addition to an already existing urban-rural divide. The privatization and diversification of higher education programs in many parts of the continent certainly represents a turning point for African women in their struggle to improve their mobility and be recognized as partners with men in nation building. With market forces making inroads into Africa's higher education, the pressure for improvements in women's representation, which was formerly directed at the state, must now extend to private territories. How legitimate the argument for gender equity in these private institutions can be made is another matter.

Other global trends, such as the evolution of information and communication technology, are gradually separating Africa from the rest of the international community, and their implications for higher education in Africa are slowly emerging.[19] It is safe to argue, however, that the impact of these trends on African men and women will still be shaped by the dynamics of social relations. Higher education cannot be removed from life in other social spaces including the home, formal work settings, and political forums. The highly educated Igbo women who share their stories in this book vividly portray the varied forms and settings of social relations in which their lives are immersed. Their overall well-being entails, at least, the negotiation of power and privilege across various social groups. Their status as career women in elite circles derives meaning from the content and nuances of these social relations.

But any attempts by women to transform the dynamics of social relations for the better must involve women's mobilization as collectives that can speak with a common voice. Individual women can employ resilience in their own personal struggles. They can stretch themselves with every resolve to slip through the cracks even as they welcome the little miracles that fate brings their way. They can celebrate their victories and pat themselves on the back for battles won, even while accepting many of the boundaries society has drawn. But any fundamental improvements in the quality of their lives as daughters, wives, mothers, career women, and partners with men in nation building can be achieved only through a fervent commitment. The experiences of Igbo career women in this book vividly portray the distance between a privileged minority in elite circles and their unfortunate sisters in the informal economy. These women's credentials and professional status, as useful assets in the struggle for social emancipation, have clearly distanced them from most of their less educated or illiterate counterparts. In order to make a difference in the struggle to improve women's social status, especially the living conditions of the larger female population, elite Igbo women must renegotiate their relations with the male ruling class. In order to position themselves as leaders in the struggle for female emancipation within in the larger female collective, they have to form partnerships in which women outside their privileged circles are represented as equal stakeholders and not as beggars. Elite women should be at the forefront of this struggle. They are the group best equipped to champion women's struggle for their rights and privileges within and outside marriage. They are the group best positioned to push for an expansion of women's access to social opportunities and status, not only in education and formal employment. The struggle for social change cannot achieve immediate results. However, highly educated women in elite circles are much better placed to negotiate with the bastions of male privilege and power in society for a fairer deal in future generations.

Without a change in the priorities of the male collage of African governments and policymakers, however, women's efforts at mobilization can go only so far. As the experiences of various groups of women across the continent bear out, African leaders and governments cannot accomplish much without a strong resolve to confront the intricate social structures that maintain the status quo. Such an intervention should go beyond expanding African women's participation in schooling and paid work. It has to muster the political resolve to integrate them into the process of nation building—as equal partners with men. African governments cannot claim to stand behind women in their struggle even as they ignore, and in many instances reinforce, the structures that keep them down. As the experiences of Igbo career women in this book convey, the boundaries created by the rigid structures of social relations have tended to constrain African women's capacity for resistance in overt terms. It is therefore not surprising that African women's response is, for the most part, reflected in their resilience, endurance, and varying degrees of collaboration with social norms and expectations.

In the Nigerian case, political leaders and policymakers are only gradually waking up to the small but rapidly growing literature on gender relations. They have yet to recognize the need for studies of this nature and the importance of harvesting insights from women's voices—beyond statistical figures, surveys, and forecasts. In tandem with their counterparts across the continent, major decision makers are quick to assert their commitment to uplifting women's status but are not yet prepared to translate these assertions into concrete action. The emphasis on women's primary roles and rhetorical acknowledgements of the heavy burden of family subsistence they bear continues to undermine any political will that will enable women to register their contributions beyond the domestic sphere.

If African governments and policymakers are serious about improving the conditions of women's lives across the continent, they should give an ear, at least, to the voices that dare to speak out. Obviously, more in-depth investigations about women, which project women's viewpoints and experiences, are needed in order to the build a database that will inform social policy. The sheer thinness of such a database at present renders the conclusions of existing research findings tentative at best. The experiences of working Igbo women here clearly show that we must go beyond material analyses of where women are and what they are doing in order to understand the full impact of formal education and paid employment on their lives. Evidently, culture and social ideologies shape the material relations of gender within and outside the family. For reasons stated earlier, the analysis here is limited to university-educated women. It is my hope that future investigations in the field should also include the experiences of men and women across classes, ethnic groups, religious origin, and other mediating factors. Obviously, the analysis here focused mainly on gender relations within a privileged group. A comparison of Igbo career women and men in the lower classes, for instance, would certainly reveal another layer of social relations. Not withstanding the importance of giving voice to women's experiences, it is also important to reflect men's perspective. This volume is only one contribution to the development of an impressive database that all scholars of Africa, as well as her sons and daughters who have joined in the search for a renaissance, can be proud of.

Appendix

Interview Format

As noted in chapter 1, my interview format was semi-informal. I prepared my questions in advance and, with the use of prompts, explored the issues under study in great detail. Although I met these career women in person either at their workplace or at a friend's house, most of them preferred to be interviewed at home. I introduced myself and my research to each woman at our first meeting and sought her formal consent before making arrangements to come to her home for the interviews. I went to each woman's home with my tape recorder and interview format for interview sessions that lasted between three and four hours. I deliberately avoided mealtimes, when other adult family members, especially the husbands of married subjects, were likely to be around. A typical Igbo man would not hang around his wife and her female acquaintances at other times unless invited.

Our discussions were conducted in a mixture of standard English, Igbo, and pidgin English. My familiarity with this amalgam of languages made the interviews much easier. The single women lived in either rented apartments or a rooms in their parents' residences. Hence my interviews with them took place with little or no interruption. Interviewing married women who had young children, however, meant having these children as an "active" audience. I had to continually wrestle my tape recorder from the tiny hands of little ones who found my small radio a very fascinating toy. Many of them insisted I record their own speeches so they could hear the playback before I left the house. Many times during my interviews with the young mothers, they stopped midsentence to take care of family domestic matters— call the children to order, comfort a crying child, or shout instructions to their house-helps in the kitchen. Knowing the culture as I do, such interruptions seemed quite normal.

The interviews were quite interesting, although the preparations for each session presented many challenges. The venue, time interval, and audience were largely outside my control. With many unpredictable factors, such as duty calls and family emergencies, on the part of the women, inefficient local transportation, and rain, I had to reschedule appointments on many occasions. Despite the difficulties presented, I accepted their choices of where to be interviewed, knowing that these women were also trying to make the necessary adjustments in their daily schedule in order to give me an audience.

The following format consists of questions and prompts for my interview sessions with Igbo career women. Specific prompts appear in brackets; directions to myself appear in italics. I prepared the format in advance in order to maintain the proper focus as well as ensure that all issues would be covered with each respondent. Since specific topics were often addressed as they arose during the interviews, the sequence of questions was not followed rigidly.

First Interview:
Education and Initial Labor Market Experience

My interest here is in examining the range of things that happen to you at home and in your job as they affect your work life. I will be asking you questions that may entail your taking time to elaborate. Please ask for further explanation if you do not understand my question.

A. Demographic Details

(Show index card with a range of options.)
1. Name, age, religion, and marital status of respondent.
2. Members of the household, relationship, sex and age distribution.
3. Educational background and employment record.
4. Salary range of respondent and spouse (if any).

B. Current Job Situation *(general information)*

1. Tell me what you did today: how you prepared for work, what you did at work, and what happened after work. [specific tasks done, with whom, departures from daily routine, e.g., illness]
2. If I were in your office today, what would I have seen you doing with your colleagues? [general impressions of colleagues, organizational structure at work, division of tasks among workers, departures from daily routine]

3. How do you find your job generally? [hectic, fun, boring, interesting?]

C. *Work History*

(Use chart to pin down basic information.)

Now, I want us to go through your work history, from your first job to where you are presently.

1. For each job, where appropriate: [source of information about job, procedure for getting employed, conditions of service, job description]

2. What made you take the job? [positive or negative influences of people, parents, siblings, husband, teachers; gender, marital status; typical features of job—e.g., teaching young people, lucrative; economic constraints—e.g., need to cater to self and dependents; personal aspirations; reasons for quitting]

D. *Educational Experience*

1. We will return to your job later. For now we will review in more detail your educational background in relation to where you are now. Tell me about your primary and secondary education until you got to the university. [which school did you attend? public/private/religious organization in charge; where? urban/rural/north/south; duration; qualifications]

2. You said you attended [tertiary institutions]? What made you opt for [specific subjects or area of specialization]? [influence of people—parents, siblings, husband, peers—economic factors, features of the course, etc.]

3. Looking back at your thoughts and goals while at school, how have your dreams worked out?

4. What would you say are the educational factors that brought you to your present position in your job? Tell me first about the factors that gave you strength. (They may be bad experiences, like someone's death, or people doing things that encouraged you, or opportunities presented by events like the oil boom or free-education policy.) What were the things that discouraged you?

5. If you were to do it all over again, how would you have handled university? [marriage and career decisions]

Second Interview: Current Labor Market Experience

(Give transcript or summary of first interview to respondent to confirm, correct, or add new material.)

Today we will be discussing in detail various issues concerning your present job. I will be asking you questions about hiring, leave, transfer, training, and so on. You may not know much about some of the underlying management policies. I just want us to discuss the factors that affected you and why.

A. Interaction in the Workplace

Before we get into specific issues concerning your job, I want us to talk a little bit more about people you work with. [respondent's relationship with workmates, junior/senior colleagues, boss]

B. Hiring

1. Now, tell me what you know about hiring in your job. [specific individuals involved (men/women), official and perceived unofficial criteria, workers in other categories, perceptions of current practice]
2. Looking at what happens in [place of work], do you see that as the general pattern of hiring in other places?

C. Financial Entitlements

I want you to tell me a little bit about the various entitlements in your job, such as salary and fringe benefits. *(show chart from salary scale document to indicate range of salary, housing and leave allowances, car loan, etc.)* [differences due to gender, marital status; workers in other categories, respondent's perception of policy]

D. Tax

What range does your monthly tax fall into? What deductions are you entitled to? *(show index card with a range of options)* [Probes: differences due to gender, marital status; workers in other categories, respondent's perceptions of official tax policy]

E. Leave

Let's take a few moments to discuss the various kinds of leave available to workers at your level. [for each level: details of procedure, official and perceived unofficial criteria for eligibility, influence of gender, marital status, respondent's experience, case of colleagues/workers in other categories, personal perceptions of current practice]

F. Maternity Leave

Let's now talk about maternity leave. I realize that policies differ in various jobs and they can make it easier (or more difficult) for women to obtain maternity leave. It is also possible that there may be a difference between the official policy and what actually happens in the workplace. [influence of marital status, personal experience, case of other colleagues' perceptions of current practice]

G. Training

What do you know about training in your job? [organization, eligibility, influence of gender, marital status, personal experience, case of other colleagues, other kinds of training, perceptions of current practice]

H. Promotion

Tell me what you know about the promotion policies for workers with your qualifications. [Probes: eligibility, official and perceived unofficial criteria, influence of gender, marital status, personal experience, case of colleagues, perceptions of current practice]

I. Transfer

Thinking about your work life in general, I want you to tell me what your experience has been with transfers. [number of and reasons for transfers, effect on job—e.g., opportunities for training, promotion]

J. Professional Associations

Do you belong to any professional associations? [for each: organization, gender and marital status distribution, respondent's degree of involvement, perceived impact of association on respondent's career, case of male and female members]

K. Summing Up

1. I asked you this question before, but now we have discussed what happens to your job in more detail. Thinking about your own experience now, what would you say are the things you did that put you where you are today? [productivity- and nonproductivity-related factors, comparison with colleagues]

2. How would you do things if you were to start over now?

3. What are your plans about work in the next five years? [specific goals, possible constraints, strategies for tackling them]

Third Interview: Job and Family Life

(Present transcript or summary of second interview for comments.)

A. *Current Situation*

1. General information [current residence, rented or owned, distance from workplace]

2. Describe for me a typical working day in your family life. [division of tasks among respondent, spouse, children, housemaid, other household members; routine on nonwork days]

B. *Childcare*

We are now going to talk about the way caring for your children has affected your working life both in the past and presently.

1. How do you organize the care of your children during the week (or during working hours, if different)? [i.e., care of babies and preschool children and/or care of school-age children (getting ready for school, making lunches, PTA meetings, conferences, homework, care for a sick child, school holidays)]

2. What arrangements have you had in the past?

3. What was/is the effect on your work life? [strategies at home/work for coping]

C. *Care of Relatives*

1. I want us to discuss your own experience of caring for others in the household besides your children. [where appropriate: parents, parents-in-law, siblings, extended family, unexpected situations]

2. What arrangements have you had in the past?

3. What was/is the effect on your work life? [strategies for coping]

D. *Housework*

COOKING

1. I want you to focus on how you would normally plan a typical week, balancing home and work commitments. Now describe for me a typical one-week cooking schedule. [division of tasks among respondent, spouse, children, maid, and other family members; disruptions from normal routine]

2. What was the case in the past?

3. What was/is the effect on your work life? [strategies at home/work for coping—e.g., lunch break shopping]

HOUSECLEANING

1. I want you to think about a typical week in your life as a working woman. Then, describe for me the typical things that are done

within the course of one week, the division of tasks among family members, describing them as they fit into your work life.
2. What was the case in the past?
3. What was/is the effect on your work life? [strategies at home/ work for coping]

LEISURE
1. We have been talking about the myriad things you have to do at home and at work. I am left wondering about time for relaxation. What do you do for leisure? [activities engaged in: job/nonjob related, how organized, other participants—husband, children, colleagues]
2. What was the case in the past?

E. Decision Making
In this last section, I want to discuss how decisions are made in your household. The important thing here is how decision making in your household has affected your work life.

MONTHLY BUDGET
I would like to start with how you spend your monthly income. Can you tell me how this is usually broken down? *(show chart of possible expenses to get discussion going)*

MAJOR FINANCIAL DECISIONS
How was the decision arrived at? How was it financed? Any connection (negative or positive) with your work life? [major purchases—cars, house repairs, household appliances; investments; inheritance; etc.]

JOB-RELATED DECISIONS
Earlier on we talked about the times when you had to embrace or forego certain opportunities at work [e.g., training, conferences, appointments, a transfer]. For each opportunity: How did you arrive at this decision? How do you think it affected your career?

OTHER DECISIONS
[Where appropriate, children's schooling—e.g., choice of school; hiring and firing of house-helps; prompt for relevant issues not thought of.]

Final Summary: Prompts, Clarifications, and Recollections

Notes

Preface

1. Organization of African Unity (OAU), *New Partnership for Africa's Development* (NEPAD) (Abuja, Nigeria: OAU, 2001); Gwendolyn Mikell, ed., *African Feminism: The Politics of Survival in Sub-Saharan Africa* (Philadelphia: University of Pennsylvania Press, 1997); Michael Kevane, *Women and Develoment in Africa: How Gender Works* (London, Boulder: Lynne Rienner, 2004).

2. Ifi Amadiume, *Male Daughters and Female Husbands: Gender and Class in an African Society* (London: Zed Books, 1987); Oyèrónké Oyewùmí, *The Invention of Women: Making an African Sense of Western Gender Discourses* (Minneapolis: University of Minnesota Press, 1997).

Chapter 1

1. The analysis here cites references to intellectual discourses and development policies of the past three decades. The UN-sponsored meetings that now assess global efforts at five-year intervals have also helped to sustain that momentum.

2. See Organization of African Unity, *New Partnership*, especially references to women's education.

3. C. E. Smock, *Women's Education in Developing Countries: Opportunities and Outcomes* (New York: Praeger, 1981); Grace P. Kelly, ed., *International Handbook of Women's Education* (New York: Greenwood Press, 1989); Valentine M. Moghadam, "Development and Women's Emancipation: Is There a Connection?" *Development and Change* 23, no. 3 (1992): 215–55.

4. Roberts Fatton, "Gender, Class and the State in Africa," in *Women and the State in Africa*, ed. Jane L. Parpart and Kathleen A. Staudt (London: Lynne Rienner, 1989), 47–66; Claire Robertson, "Women's Education and Class Formation in Africa, 1950–1980," in *Women and Class in*

Africa, ed. Claire Robertson and Iris Berger (London: Africana, 1996), 92–113; Marianne Bloch, Josephine A. Beoku-Betts, and B. Robert Tabachnick, eds., *Women and Education in Sub-Saharan Africa: Power, Opportunities, and Constraints* (Boulder: Lynne Rienner, 1998).

5. Marnia Lazreg, *The Eloquence of Silence: Algerian Women in Question* (New York: Routledge, 1994); Oyewùmí, *The Invention of Women;* Obioma Nnaemeka, ed., *Sisterhood, Feminisms, and Power: From Africa to the Diaspora* (Trenton: Africa World Press, 1998).

6. Tiyambe Zeleza, "Gendering African History" (book review), *African Development* 18, no. 1 (1993): 99–117.

7. Barbara Rogers, *The Domestication of Women: Discrimination in Developing Societies* (London: Tavistock, 1980); April Gordon, *Transforming Capitalism and Patriarchy: Gender and Development in Africa* (Boulder: Lynne Rienner, 1996); Margaret Snyder and Mary Tadesse, "The African Context: Women in the Political Economy," in *The Women, Gender, and Development Reader,* ed. Nalini Visvanathan, Lynn Duggan, Laurie Nisonoff, and Nan Wiegersma (London: Zed Books, 1997), 75–79.

8. I use the word *seemingly* because I am mindful of the fact that some of these biases have been tainted so much by social transformation that it is really difficult to ascertain how much of their content can be solidly defined as indigenous.

9. Janet M. Bujra, "'Urging Women to Redouble Their Efforts . . .': Class, Gender and Capitalist Transformation in Africa," in *Women and Class in Africa*, ed. Claire Robertson and Iris Berger (London: Africana, 1986), 117–40; Simi Afonja, "Changing Modes of Production and the Sexual Division of Labor among the Yoruba," in *Women's Work: Development and the Division of Labor by Gender,* ed. Eleanor Leacock and Helen Safa (South Hadley, MA: Bergin and Garvey, 1986), 122–35; Maria Nzomo, "Beyond Structural Adjustment Programs: Democracy, Gender Equity, and Development in Africa, with Special Reference to Kenya," in *Beyond Structural Adjustment in Africa: The Political Economy of Sustainable and Democratic Development,* ed. Julius Nyang'oro and Timothy Shaw (New York: Praeger, 1992), 99–117.

10. Bade Onimode, *Imperialism and Underdevelopment in Nigeria: The Dialectics of Mass Poverty* (London: Zed Books, 1982); Georges Nzongola-Ntalaja, *Nation-Building and State-Building in Africa,* occasional paper no. 3 (Harare: SAPES Books, 1993), 17.

11. Critics of Western feminist literature have done a great job of exposing the biased interpretations of African cultures as well as the elements of Western culture that reinforce African women's oppression.

Very few scholars (e.g., Simi Afonja) have attempted to put the African side under similar scrutiny. The contradictions, in particular, have not been adequately addressed as an integral part of a postcolonial social order.

12. Mahmood Mamdani, *Citizen and Subject: Contemporary Africa and the Legacy of Late Colonialism* (Kampala: Fountain Publishers, 1996); Margaret Jean Hay and Marcia Wright, eds., *African Women and the Law: Historical Perspectives*, Boston University Papers on Africa, no. 7 (Boston: Boston University, African Studies Center, 1982).

13. Afonja, "Changing Modes," 122, 134.

14. Women had access to farmlands but only through men who (as fathers, husbands, brothers, etc.) had direct control over ancestral land. Obviously, this custom curtailed the boundaries of women's economic autonomy as food farmers and traders. It needs to be noted, however, that men's control of land was communal. Unlike women, who were expected to marry and join another lineage, men stayed within their lineages and therefore were better placed to protect this communal asset.

15. Dorothy Hodgson and Sheryl McCurdy, eds., *"Wicked" Women and the Reconfiguration of Gender in Africa* (Oxford: James Currey, 2001).

16. Amadiume, *Male Daughters*, 4.

17. See Nicole Willey, "Ibuza vs. Lagos: The Feminist and Traditional Buchi Emecheta," *Journal of the Association for Research on Mothering* 2, no. 2 (Fall/ Winter, 2000): 155–66. Willey points out that African women's progress in the struggle for social emancipation depends greatly on their capacity to adapt to and negotiate the patriarchal continuities and contradictions of the hybridized social order.

18. Morley Gunderson and Craig Riddell, *Labor Market Economics: Theory, Evidence and Policy in Canada*, 2d ed. (Toronto: McGraw-Hill Ryerson, 1988), 364–89.

19. Ibid., 234–36.

20. Walt Rostow, *The Stages of Growth: A Non-Communist Manifesto* (Cambridge: Cambridge University Press, 1960); Theodore Schultz, *Transforming Traditional Agriculture* (New Haven: Yale University Press, 1964).

21. Smock, *Women's Education*, presents a broader analysis of women's experiences in the developing world.

22. Philomina Okeke, "Postmodern Feminism and Knowledge Production: The African Context," *Africa Today* 43, no. 3 (July–September, 1996): 223–33.

23. Bujra, "'Urging Women'"; Fatton, "Gender, Class."

24. Anthonia Kalu, "Women and the Social Construction of Gender in African Development," *Africa Today* 43, no. 3 (July–September, 1996): 269–88; Amadiume, *Male Daughters.*

25. Chandra T. Mohanty, introduction ("Cartographies of Struggle: Third World Women and the Politics of Feminism") to *Third World Women and the Politics of Feminism*, ed. Chandra T. Mohanty, Ann Russo, and Lourdes Torres (Bloomington: Indiana University Press, 1991), 1–47; Vidyamali Samarasinghe, "The Place of the WID Discourse in Global Analysis: The Potential for a 'Reverse Flow,'" in *Color, Class and Country: Experiences of Gender*, ed. Gay Young and Bette Dickerson (London: Zed Books, 1994), 218–31; Lazreg, *Eloquence of Silence.*

26. P. Okeke, "Postmodern Feminism," 225.

27. Onimode, *Imperialism and Underdevelopment;* Okwudiba Nnoli, *Ethnicity and Development in Nigeria* (Brookfield, VT: Ashgate Publishing, 1995).

28. Lamont D. King, "State and Ethnicity in Pre-colonial Northern Nigeria," *Journal of Asian and African Studies* 36, no. 4 (2001): 339–60.

29. This does not suggest a common agreement among Igbos. In fact, some parts of Igboland claim a "foreign" origin and may consider others inferior to or different from the rest. The Onitshas and some Igbo groups living around the Niger River are good examples.

30. Marcellina U. Okehie-Offoha, "The Igbo," in *Ethnic and Cultural Diversity in Nigeria*, ed. Marcellina U. Okehie-Offoha and Matthew N. Sadiku (Trenton: Africa World Press, 1996), 66.

31. Individuals and groups were ostracized, among other reasons, for having a hand in the murder of a relative, disobeying clan agreements, and committing incest.

32. Sebastian M. Obi, *How to Solve the Osu Problem* (Owerri: Agape Education Resources, 1994); Victor Dike, *The Osu Caste System in Igboland: A Challenge for Nigerian Democracy* (Sacramento: Morris Publishing, 2002).

33. Flora Kaplan, ed. *Queens, Queen Mothers, Priestesses, and Power: Case Studies in African Gender* (New York: New York Academy of Sciences, 1997).

34. Amadiume, *Male Daughters.*

35. Molara Ogundipe-Leslie, "Women in Nigeria," in *Women in Nigeria Today*, ed. Women in Nigeria editorial committee (London: Zed Books, 1985), 124.

36. Nzongola-Ntalaja, *Nation-Building*, 17.

37. Okechukwu Ikejiani, "Education for Efficiency," in *Nigerian Education*, ed. Okechukwu Ikejiani (Lagos: Longmans of Nigeria, 1964), 83–92.

38. Hugh H. Smythe and Mabel M. Smythe, *The New Nigerian Elite* (Stanford: Stanford University Press, 1960), 93.

39. Such camaraderie in Igbo elite circles is captured in Ikejiani, *Nigerian Education.*

40. Ibid., 93.

41. Bujra, "'Urging Women.'"

42. Jane Guyer, *Family and Farm in Southern Cameroon*, African Research Studies, no. 15 (Boston: Boston University, African Studies Center, 1984); Jane Guyer, ed., *Feeding African Cities: Studies in Regional Social History* (Bloomington: Indiana University Press, in association with International African Institute, 1987); Christina Gladwin, ed., *Structural Adjustment and African Women Farmers* (Gainesville: University Press of Florida, 1991).

43. Sylvia Leith-Ross, *African Women: A Study of the Ibo of Nigeria* (London: Routledge and Kegan Paul, 1939); Bolanle Awe, "The Iyalode in the Traditional Political System," in *Sexual Stratification: A Cross-Cultural View*, ed. A. Schlegel (New York: Columbia University Press, 1977); Judith Van Allen, "'Aba Riots' or Igbo 'Women's War'? Ideology, Stratification, and the Invisibility of Women," in *Gender in Cross-Cultural Perspective*, ed. Caroline Brettell and Carolyn Sargent (Upper Saddle River, NJ: Prentice Hall, 1997), 513–28.

44. LaRay Denzer, "Female Employment in the Government Service of Nigeria, 1885–1945," in *Symposium on Women's Studies in Nigeria: The State of the Art Now* (Ibadan: University of Ibadan, Women's Research and Documentation Centre, 1987); Cheryl Johnson-Odim and Nina Mba, *For Women and the Nation: Funmilayo Ransome Kuti of Nigeria* (Chicago: University of Illinois Press, 1997); Fatton, "Gender, Class."

45. Bloch, Beoku-Betts, and Tabachnick, *Women and Education*.

46. Guyer, *Feeding African Cities*.

47. Amina Mama, "Feminism or Femocracy? State Feminism and Democratisation in Nigeria," *African Development* 20, no. 1 (1995): 40.

48. UNECA, *African Charter for Popular Participation in Development* [Arusha Declaration] (Addis Ababa: UNECA, 1990), 19–20.

49. UNECA, *African Platform for Action: African Common Position for the Advancement of Women, Adopted at the Fifth African Regional Conference on Women, Dakar, Senegal, 16–23 November 1994* ([Addis Ababa?]: UNECA, 1995); Organization of African Unity, *New Partnership*.

50. Aili Tripp, "Women's Movements and Challenges to Neopatrimonial Rule," *Development and Change* 32 (2001): 33–54.

51. Julius Ihonvbere, "From Movement to Government: The Movement for Multi-Party Democracy and the Crisis of Democratic Consolidation in Zambia," *Canadian Journal of African Studies* 29, no. 1 (1995): 2.

52. Amrita Basu, ed., *The Challenge of Local Feminisms: Women's Movements in Global Perspective* (Boulder: Westview Press, 1995); Philomina Okeke, "The First Lady Syndrome: The (En)Gendering of Bureaucratic Corruption in Nigeria," *Council for the Development of Social Science Research*

in Africa Bulletin 3, no. 4 (1998): 16–19; Kathleen Staudt, "Gender Politics in Bureaucracy: Theoretical Issues in Comparative Perspective," in *Women, International Development, and Politics: The Bureaucratic Mire*, ed. K. Staudt, (Philadelphia: Temple University Press, 1997).

53. Mama, "Feminism or Femocracy?" 38.

54. Philomina Okeke and Susan Franceschet, "Democratisation and 'State Feminism': A Comparison of Gender Politics in Africa and Latin America," *Development and Change* 33, no. 3 (2002): 439–66; Kole Shettima, "Engendering Nigeria's Third Republic," *African Studies Review* 38, no. 3 (December 1995): 61–99.

55. Lisa Aubrey, "Gender, Development, and Democratization in Africa," *Journal of Asian and African Studies* 36, no. 1 (2001): 104.

56. P. Okeke, "First Lady Syndrome."

57. Maryam Babangida, *The Home Front: Nigerian Army Officers and Their Wives* (Ibadan: Fountain Publications, 1988).

58. Bolanle Awe, *Nigerian Women in Historical Perspective* (Ibadan: Sankore/Bookcraft, 1992); Shettima, "Third Republic"; Mama, "Feminism or Femocracy?"; Amina Mama, "Khaki in the Family: Gender Discourse and Militarism in Nigeria," *African Studies Review* 41, no. 2 (1998): 1–18; Philomina Okeke, "Interrogating Tradition on African Women's Status: Beyond the Critique of Western Feminism," *Black Studies Journal* 2 (1999): 65–76.

59. Shettima, "Third Republic"; Mama, "Feminism or Femocracy?"

60. Kema Chikwe, *Women of My Era* (Owerri, Nigeria: Prime Time, 2003).

61. Hussaina Abdullah, "'Transition Politics' and the Challenge of Gender in Nigeria," *Review of African Political Economy* 56 (1993): 27–41; Hussaina Abdullah, "Wifeism and Activism: The Nigerian Women's Movement," in *The Challenge of Local Feminisms: Women's Movements in Global Perspective*, ed. Amrita Basu (Boulder: Westview, 1995), 209–25.

62. Staudt, "Gender Politics."

63. Tripp, "Women's Movements."

64. Aubrey, "Gender Development, and Democratization," 90–91.

65. Robertson, "Women's Education."

66. Claire Robertson, "Developing Economic Awareness: Changing Perspectives in Studies of African Women, 1976–1986," *Feminist Studies* 13, no. 1 (1987): 127.

67. Oyèrónké Oyewùmí, ed., *Reflecting on the Politics of Sisterhood* (Trenton: Africa World Press, 2003).

68. The oil boom in Nigeria occurred between 1973 and 1979, when the high price of crude petroleum in the world market yielded an unprecedented amount of foreign exchange to the country. This period was also

characterized by increased public funding of education, which boosted school enrollment. Those with credentials in higher education were rewarded with lucrative opportunities as the relatively small formal employment sector opened up to both indigenous and foreign private enterprise. But the oil glut at the close of the decade brought declining revenues that led to huge reductions in public funding for social services, including education.

Chapter 2

1. Jane L. Parpart, "Wage Earning Women and the Double Day: The Nigerian Case," in *Women, Employment and the Family in the International Division of Labour*, ed. Sharon Stichter and Jane L. Parpart (London: Macmillan, 1990), 163–64.

2. Peter Lloyd, *Power and Independence: Urban Africans' Perception of Social Inequality* (London: Routledge and Kegan Paul, 1974); Claire Robertson, *Sharing the Same Bowl: A Socioeconomic History of Women and Class in Accra, Ghana* (Bloomington: Indiana University Press, 1984).

3. Janet M. Bujra, "Class, Gender and Capitalist Transformation in Africa," *African Development* 8 (July 1983): 35.

4. Parpart, "Wage Earning Women," 162.

5. Christie C. Achebe, "Continuities, Changes and Challenges: Women's Role in Nigerian Society," *Présence africaine: Cultural Review of the Negro World* 120 (1981): 7; Parpart, "Wage Earning Women"; Philomina Okeke, *Is Development a Good Thing? Women and Wage Labour in a Developing Economy*, Pearson Public Interest Series (Halifax: Pearson International Institute for Development, Dalhousie University, 1993).

6. Okehie-Offoha, "Igbo," 75.

7. Kristin Mann, *Marrying Well: Marriage and Social Change among the Educated Elite in Colonial Lagos* (Cambridge: Cambridge University Press, 1985), 78.

8. Yam is a status-enhancing crop, a mark of prosperity, and a major item presented at traditional ceremonies, such as the conferment of titles on socially acclaimed men and women.

9. Ifeyinwa Iweriabor, "Women in the Family, Labour and Management: What Can Be Done?" in *Women and the Family in Nigeria*, ed. Ayesha Imam, Renée Pittin, and H. Omole (Dakar: CODESRIA, 1985), 146.

10. Mann, *Marrying Well*; Nina E. Mba, *Nigerian Women Mobilized: Women's Political Activities in Southern Nigeria, 1900–1965* (Berkeley: University of California, Institute of International Studies, 1982).

11. Genesis 2:24 (New International Version).

12. Ester Boserup, "The Economics of Polygamy," in *Perspectives on*

Africa: A Reader in Culture, History and Representations, ed. Roy R. Grinker and Christopher B. Steine (Cambridge, MA: Blackwell, 1997), 506–77; Sheila Clarke Ekong, "Continuity and Change in Nigerian Family Patterns," in *Social Change in Nigeria,* ed. Simi Afonja and Tola Pearce, (Essex: Longman, 1986); Mann, *Marrying Well.*

13. Political memorandum, 1913–18, cited in Alfred Kasunmu and Jeswald Salacuse, *Nigerian Family Law* (London: Butterworths, 1960), 17.

14. Although the practice of child marriage was more common in the Muslim north, the age of marriage for girls across the ethnic groups was significantly lower than the British norm. Even the subsequent amendments of the legal minimum did not impose any firm prescriptions. For instance, the 1947 legal review left the age of lawful carnal knowledge for girls at thirteen, far below the prescribed age of marriage, eighteen. Nigeria, *The Laws of Nigeria,* rev. ed. vol. 2, cap. 42, nos. 214–25 (January 1948), 99–103.

15. Kasunmu and Salacuse, *Nigerian Family Law.*

16. D. S. Obikeze, "Son Preference among Nigerian Mothers: Its Demographic and Psychological Implications," *International Journal of Contemporary Sociology* 25, no. 12 (January–April 1988): 55–63.

17. See Nigeria, *Law Reports: A Selection of the Cases Decided in the Full Courts of the Gold Coast Colony, of the Colony of Lagos and of the Colony of Southern Nigeria* (Lagos: Government Printer), vol. 1 (1915), 15–23; vol. 2 (1915), 41–45; vol. 3 (1937), 89–93; vol. 5 (1938), 50–55.

18. Ester Boserup, "The Economics of Polygamy," in *Perspectives on Africa: A Reader in Culture, History, and Representation,* ed. Roy R. Grinker and Christopher B. Steiner, 506–17 (Cambridge, MA: Blackwell, 1997); Thérèse Lauras-Lecoh, "Family Trends and Demographic Transition in Africa," *International Social Science Journal* 42, no. 4 (1990): 475–92; Sangeetha Madhavan, "Best of Friends and Worst of Enemies: Competition and Collaboration in Polygyny," *Ethnology* 41, no. 1 (2002): 69–84; Luigi M. Solivetti, "Family, Marriage, and Divorce in a Hausa Community: A Sociological Model" *Africa* 64, no. 2 (1994): 252–71.

19. Iweriabor, "Women in the Family"; Ogundipe-Leslie, "Women in Nigeria." For instance, Igbo women, married or not, are bestowed with the status of umuada (daughters of the extended natal family; chapter 1). This larger female circle of relatives within a lineage does have certain privileges and responsibilities, upheld by their male counterparts, but often the people they wield power against are the wives of the lineage, especially the younger ones.

20. Kasunmu and Salacuse, *Nigerian Family Law,* 290. See also Ekong, "Continuity and Change," 55.

21. Mann, *Marrying Well,* 83–84; Zahra Nwabara, "Women in Nigeria: The Way I See It," in *Women and the Family in Nigeria,* ed. Ayesha Imam, Renée Pittin, and H. Omole (Dakar: CODESRIA, 1985), 12–13; Jadesola

Akande, "Concepts of Women Development in Africa," *Nigerian Tribune* (Ibadan), April 8 (p. 4) and 10 (p. 13), 1991.

22. T. O. Elias, *The Impact of English Law on Nigerian Customary Law,* Lugard Lectures (Lagos: Ministry of Information, 1958).

23. Parpart, "Wage Earning Women."

24. See women's columns of newspapers in West African colonies, especially in Lagos. For instance, Kofo Moore's commentaries on the conditions of women's education in Nigeria were carried in the *West African Pilot* from November 29 to December 1, 1937; Stella Thomas and R. B. Marke, interviews by editor, *West African Pilot,* April 22, 1939, 4; August 21, 1942, 1.

25. Nigeria, Education Department, *Memorandum on Educational Policy in Nigeria* (Lagos: Government Printer, 1947), 92.

26. Nigeria, *Annual Report of the Federal Ministry of Labour, 1959–1960* (Lagos: Nigerian National Press, 1960), 20.

27. This social climate strengthened the negative attitude of Nigerian society toward women's education, especially in the north. A young Muslim girl of ten or eleven may be married off to an older affluent man and kept in seclusion, away from the moral dangers of the world outside her husband's compound. See Kasunmu and Salacuse, *Nigerian Family Law,* esp. chapters 2 and 3.

28. Ikejiani, "Education for Efficiency," 88–89.

29. For instance, see Parpart, "Wage Earning Women," 163–64.

30. Stella Thomas, interview by editor, *West African Pilot,* September 25, 1943, 4.

31. Achebe, "Continuities, Changes and Challenges," 7.

32. Safiya Muhammed, "Women, the Family and the Wider Society, " in *Women and the Family in Nigeria,* ed. Ayesha Imam, Renée Pittin, and H. Omole (Dakar: CODESRIA, 1985), 30.

33. Any girl can be called daughter (*ada*), but the first girl in the family is referred to as *the* ada. The importance of procreation, and thus the sensitivity of the society to women's age at marriage, often compel the ada to marry first. Many parents would prefer that their female children marry in age succession so as to avoid "putting the elder daughter on the shelf."

34. Obi, *Osu Problem.*

35. M. O. Ekiyor, "Formal Colonial Education: An Assessment of Its Impact on the Marriageability of 'Acada' Women in Southern Nigeria," in *Symposium on the Impact of Colonialism on Nigerian Women* (Ibadan: Institute of African Studies, University of Ibadan, 1989).

36. The term *son preference* is borrowed from Obikeze, "Son Preference."

37. Lena Ampadu, "Motherhood—A Joy? The Status of Mothers of African Descent in the Literature and Lore of Africa and the African Diaspora," *Journal of the Association for Research on Mothering* 2, no. 2 (Fall/Winter, 2000): 2.

38. John S. Mbiti, *African Religions and Philosophy* (Garden City, NY: Anchor Books, 1970).

39. Renée Pittin, "The Control of Reproduction: Principle and Practice in Nigeria," *Review of African Political Economy* 35 (1986): 40–53.

40. Wambui Wa Karanja, "Conjugal Decision-Making: Some Data from Lagos," in *Male and Female in West Africa*, ed. Christine Oppong (London: Allen and Unwin, 1983), 236–41.

41. Obikeze, "Son Preference." For names, see 60–61.

42. Marcellina U. Okehie-Offoha and Matthew Sadiku, eds., *Ethnic and Cultural Diversity in Nigeria* (Trenton: Africa World Press, 1996).

43. In some parts of Igboland, women had the weight of tradition behind them as female husbands to further their marital lineages. But the strong cultural tenets that reinforced this practice in the past have little import in contemporary elite circles. Amadiume, for instance, presents ethnography of an Igbo society in this regard. However, such practices, regardless of the power they afford individual women to assert themselves and hold on to their status in society, support the perpetration of the Igbo patriarchal lineage structure. Amadiume, *Male Daughters*.

44. Cited in Boserup, "Economics of Polygamy," 506; "Women in Traditional African Societies," *Report of the Workshop on Urban Problems* (New York: United Nations Economic and Social Council, 1963).

45. Boserup, "Economics of Polygamy."

46. Buchi Emecheta, *The Joys of Motherhood* (Ibadan: Heinemann, 1979), 123–24.

47. Willey, "Ibuza vs. Lagos," 156.

48. Wambui Wa Karanja, "Conjugal Decision-Making"; Wambui Wa Karanja, "'Outside Wives' and 'Inside Wives' in Nigeria: A Study of Changing Perceptions in Marriage," in *Transformations of African Marriage*, ed. David Parkin and David Nyamwaya (Manchester: Manchester University Press, 1987), 247–61.

49. Ekong, "Continuity and Change," 54.

50. Ogundipe-Leslie, "Women in Nigeria," 124.

51. Ekong, "Continuity and Change," 50–70.

52. Agnes Calliste, "Canada's Immigration Policy and Domestics from the Caribbean: The Second Domestic Scheme," in *Race, Class, Gender: Bonds and Barriers*, ed. Jesse Vorst et al., rev. ed. (Toronto: Garamond Press, 1991): 136–68; Tanya Schecter, *Race, Class, Women and the State: The Case of Domestic Labour* (Montreal: Black Rose Books, 1998); Bridget Anderson, *Doing the Dirty Work? The Global Politics of Domestic Labour* (London: Zed Books, 2000).

53. Esther Goody, "Some Theoretical and Empirical Aspects of Parenthood in West Africa," in *Seminar of the International Sociological Association Committee on Family Research* (Lome, Togo: 1976); Eleanor R.

Fapohunda, "The Childcare Dilemma of Working Mothers in African Cities: The Case of Lagos, Nigeria," in *Women and Work in Africa*, ed. Edna Bay (Boulder: Westview, 1982), 277–88; Mona Etienne, "The Case of Social Maternity: Adoption of Children by Urban Baule Women," in *Gender in Cross-Cultural Perspective*, ed. Caroline B. Brettell and Carolyn F. Sargent (Upper Saddle River, NJ: Prentice-Hall, 2001).

54. Nigeria, *Educational Policy*, 30.

55. Fapohunda, "Childcare Dilemma"; Bujra, "Class, Gender"; Parpart, "Wage Earning Women."

56. Fapohunda, "Childcare Dilemma"; Bujra, "'Urging Women.'"

57. Anderson, *Dirty Work*, 5.

Chapter 3

1. For a detailed chronology of Nigerian education see A. Babs Fafunwa, *History of Education in Nigeria* (London: Allen and Unwin, 1974) and C. O. Taiwo, *The Nigerian Education System: Past, Present, and Future* (Ibadan: Nelson, 1980).

2. Mann, *Marrying Well*, 91.

3. Mba, *Nigerian Women Mobilized*.

4. Phelps-Stokes Commission, *Education in Africa: A Study of West, South and Equatorial Africa by the first African Education Commission under the Auspices of the Phelps-Stokes Fund in Cooperation with the International Education Board, 1920–1921* (New York: Phelps-Stokes Fund, 1921), 160.

5. Nigeria, *Annual Digest of Educational Statistics* 2, no. 1 (1962): 17. Total enrollment excludes non-Nigerians.

6. Ibid., 15. Non-Nigerians excluded.

7. *Nigerian Blue Book*, W2–W3, 1938; W2–W5, 1931, cited in Denzer, "Female Employment," 40.

8. Especially in firms that produce cigarettes, other tobacco products, and cosmetics. See Nigeria, *Annual Report of the Federal Ministry of Labour, 1954–1955* (Lagos: Nigerian National Press, 1955), 24.

9. Ibid.

10. Nigeria, *Annual Report of the Federal Ministry of Labour, 1952–1953* (Lagos: Nigerian National Press, 1953), 35.

11. Ikejiani, *Nigerian Education*.

12. Nigeria, Commission on Post-School Certificate and Higher Education, *Investment in Education: Report* (Lagos: Federal Ministry of Education, 1960), 99.

13. Merchant banks came into prominence in the 1980s as the Nigerian currency, naira, suffered gross devaluation due to the introduction of SAPs. Unlike the usual commercial banks, which were open to the general public, the merchant banks focused more on special services such as

foreign exchange transactions and mortgages. See Robertson, "Women's Education"; UNECA, *Economic Report on Africa* (Addis Ababa, E/ECA/CM.16/3, 1990), 21–22.

14. ILO, *World Labour Report* (Geneva: ILO, 1989), 33–36.

15. UNECA, *Economic Report*, 21.

16. News report, *West Africa* 20–26 (April 1992), 683.

17. For a breakdown see Nigeria, *Annual Abstract of Statistics* (Abuja: Federal Office of Statistics, 1998), 250.

18. S. O. Dada, "Human Resources Training and Development: An Empirical Study of Its Problems and Gains in the Nigerian Banking Industry," *Nigerian Banker: Journal of the Institute of Bankers of Nigeria*, 1991, 6.

19. For instance, analyses of school enrollment trends in Igboland highlight the significant increase in the number of young men that shun higher education in favor of apprentice training for business opportunities—as a quicker route to economic prosperity. In fact, by the end of the 1980s the southeastern states recorded higher female enrollment at the secondary level—as indicated in Anambra State, *School Statistics* (Enugu: Statistics Division, State Education Commission, 1989), 22. This trend, however, is hardly representative of the national picture. Nigerian women's access to higher education and their distribution across the disciplines have not responded to any such new trends.

20. Mba, *Nigerian Women Mobilized*, 1982.

21. For instance, the British pattern mirrors the development of Canada's educational system. See Frank J. Mifflen and Sydney C. Mifflen, *The Sociology of Education: Canada and Beyond* (Calgary: Detselig, 1982), ch. 1; Cecilia Reynolds, "The Educational System," in *Feminist Issues: Race, Class, and Sexuality*, ed. Nancy Mandell (Scarborough, Ont.: Prentice Hall Allyn and Bacon, 1998), 233–48.

22. Women did not enter British universities until the late 1800s. Reynolds comments on a similar legacy of exclusion and separation for Canadian women. Reynolds, "Educational System."

23. Uduaroh Okeke, "Background to the Problems of Nigerian Education," in Ikejiani, *Nigerian Education*, 8.

24. Okechukwu Ikejiani and J. O. Anowi, "Nigerian Universities," in Ikejiani, *Nigerian Education*, 128.

25. Ibid., 130.

26. Iweriabor, "Women in the Family," 150.

27. Nigerian Archives, Ibadan, CS026/2/11833, vol. 2, Confidential GDSS, draft, 31.10.50, cited in Denzer, "Female Employment," 16.

28. Denzer, "Female Employment," 8.

29. Bujra, "Class, Gender," 33.

30. Canadian women suffered a similar fate. Reynolds, "Educational System," 235–36. For examples of the Nigerian experience, see Denzer, "Female Employment."

31. Robertson, "Economic Awareness," 102–3.

32. M. Awe, "Women, Science and Technology in the Colonial Era," in *Symposium on the Impact of Colonialism on Nigerian Women*, 1989.

33. Katherine Mamuddu, "Gender Perspectives in the Transformation of Africa: Challenges to the African University as a Model to Society," *Conference of Association of African Universities* (Legon: University of Ghana, 1992).

34. Eunice C. A. Okeke, "Nigeria," country profile in *International Handbook of Women's Education*, ed. Grace P. Kelly (New York: Greenwood Press, 1989), 43–64.

35. Kasunmu and Salacuse, *Nigerian Family Law*, 78.

36. Nigeria, *Educational Policy*.

37. M. Awe, "Women, Science," 1989.

38. Ekiyor, "Colonial Education."

39. Karen L. Biraimah, "Class, Gender, and Life Chances: A Nigerian University Case Study," *Comparative Education Review* 31, no. 4 (1987): 576; Rachel Uwa Agneyisi, "The Labour Market Implications of the Access of Women to Higher Education in Nigeria," in *Women in Nigeria Today*, ed. Women in Nigeria, 143–56 (London: Zed Books, 1985).

40. See Anambra State, *Civil Service Handbook* (Enugu: Civil Service, 1989) and Institute of Bankers, *The Collective Agreement between Nigerian Employers Association of Banks, Insurance and Allied Institutions and the Association of Senior Staff of Banks, Insurance and Financial Institutions* (Lagos: Headquarters, 1990).

41. Bujra, "Class, Gender," 33.

42. See Denzer, "Female Employment"; Patrick Uchendu, *Education and the Changing Economic Role of Nigerian Women* (Enugu: Fourth Dimension Publishers, 1995).

43. As recorded in Anambra State, *Civil Service Handbook*.

44. Announced during the president's 1992 budget statement.

45. Fapohunda, "Childcare Dilemma," 277–88; Eleanor R. Fapohunda, "Urban Women's Roles and Nigerian Government Development Strategies," in *Sex Roles, Population, and Development in West Africa*, ed. Christine Oppong (London: James Currey, 1988), 203–12; Parpart, "Wage Earning Women."

46. Aderanti Adepoju and Christine Oppong, eds., *Gender, Work, and Population in Sub-Saharan Africa* (London: James Currey, 1994); Bessie

House-Midamba and Felix K. Ekechi, eds., *African Market Women and Economic Power* (Westport, CT: Greenwood Press); Aili Tripp, *Changing the Rules: The Politics of Liberalization and the Urban Informal Economy in Tanzania* (Berkeley: University of California Press, 1997).

47. C. Gladwin, *Structural Adjustment;* Philomina Okeke, "Women's Movements," in *Encyclopedia of Twentieth Century African History,* ed. Paul Tiyambe Zeleza and Dickson Eyoh (London: Routledge, 2002).

48. E. Okeke, "Nigeria," 56.

49. Dan Agbese, "Corruption: The Palm Oil That Stains the Palm of the Giver and Receiver," *Newswatch* (Lagos), 1992, 14.

50. Zahra Nwabara, "Women in Nigeria," 11-12.

51. J. W. Hanson, "Developing a Federal Plan for Education," in Ikejiani, *Nigerian Education,* 25.

Chapter 4

1. Customarily, married women in Igboland and many parts of eastern Nigeria tie two wrappers (a cloth worn around the body) over a blouse. Single women are identified with one wrapper. Although such customs are no longer strictly adhered to, especially among elites, two wrappers still signify marital status, and older single women may tie them to command respect.

2. Achebe, "Continuities, Changes," 5.

3. Pittin, "Control of Reproduction," 49–50.

4. *Acada* is a corruption of the English word *academic.* Generally, it refers to one who is very studious or has high educational ambitions. It is also used derogatorily to describe highly ambitious women, especially career women who are single.

5. As noted earlier, an Igbo wife customarily "belongs" to all the members of her husband's extended family.

6. Robertson, "Women's Education."

Chapter 5

1. Achebe, "Continuities, Changes"; Muhammed, "Women, Family," 29–36.

2. Oluwatoyin Doherty, "Women in the Legal Profession in Nigeria," background data (Lagos: Nigerian Law School, 1990).

3. Due to the shortage of teaching staff some secondary school graduates were placed in secondary or primary schools, often on temporary appointment. The expansion of teacher training institutions in the 1970s and 1980s drastically reduced, if not eliminated, that shortage.

4. See Ikejiani and Anowi, "Nigerian Universities." Nigeria's political independence in 1960 precipitated a massive expansion of higher education after a long period of colonial suppression. As I pointed out in chapter 1, admission was open to women only in principle. However, the location of Nigeria's premier university in Ibadan proved a crucial advantage to Yoruba women. In Okoye's time, Ibadan offered short-term diploma courses that served as a stepping-stone for less qualified teachers.

5. In Nigerian elite circles today, teaching at the primary and secondary school levels is considered a profession for poor achievers, but one suitable for women.

6. Even with the economic decline, the banking sector, especially the merchant banks, has experienced unprecedented growth since the 1980s. Uchenna belongs to the new crop of professional women who are making inroads into this sector. The newer banks offer very attractive employment packages, but most are located in Lagos. See Dada, "Human Resources."

7. Uchendu, *Education.*

8. Mann, *Marrying Well.*

9. Mba, *Nigerian Women Mobilized.*

10. E. Okeke, "Nigeria"; Ekiyor, "Colonial Education," 9–17.

11. Oladimejo Alo and Selina Adjebeng-Asem refer to a 1977 report that puts female adult literacy at 6 percent and male at 25 percent. Alo and Adjebeng-Asem, "Women and National Development: A Socio-Cultural Analysis of the Nigerian Experience," in *Women, Development, and Change: The Third World Experience,* ed. Francis M. Abraham and Subhadra P. Abraham (Bristol: Wyndham Hall Press, 1988), 218. More recent studies clearly indicate that even with the considerable progress in women's education and public schooling in general, neither the gender imbalance nor adult literacy has shown much improvement. See also Deborah Oluwumi Otu, "Nigerian Women and Education: Issues, Concerns and Prospects for National Development," in *Conference on the Impact of Colonialism on Nigerian Women* (Ibadan: Institute of African Studies, University of Ibadan, 1989) and Nigeria, *Abstract of Statistics,* 183–244.

Chapter 6

1. See Katherine Mosley, "'Seizing the Change': Economic Crisis and Industrial Restructuring in Nigeria," in *Beyond Structural Adjustment in Africa,* ed. Julius Nyang'oro and Timothy Shaw (New York: Praeger, 1992); Olukoshi Adebayo, *The Politics of Structural Adjustment in Nigeria* (London: James Currey, 1993).

2. Official sources claim that between 1980 and 1992 the education authorities conducted two major mass promotion exercises for teachers in an attempt to catch up with their counterparts in the civil services, who have gone a notch or more higher.

3. I refer primarily to 419, a persistent international bank fraud named after the federal decree issued to arrest it, in which a scam artist poses as a wealthy businessman who needs to transfer large sums of money to a victim's account for a fee and for which Nigeria has been widely chastised since the early 1980s. It is still perceived as a risky but attractive option for many young men in a generation no longer impressed with the prospects of schooling and paid work. This lucrative scam dampens the measures presently taken to reverse the low male enrollment reported at the secondary school level in many parts of Igboland.

Chapter 7

1. Fapohunda, "Childcare Dilemma"; Parpart, "Wage Earning Women."

2. According to the respondents, there are actually nearby towns noted for supplying house-helps on contract. Often the elite household goes through an agent who establishes contacts with these families in the rural areas. The offer of some form of formal training is becoming a basic criterion for acquiring house-helps. While it is still possible to hire house-helps and pay them monthly or biweekly, most elite families cannot afford the cost, especially with the decline in real income.

3. Sharon B. Stichter, "The Middle Class in Kenya: Changes in Gender Relations," in *Patriarchy and Class: African Women in the Home and the Workforce*, ed. Sharon B. Stichter and Jane L. Parpart (Boulder: Westview, 1988), 177–204. In her study of similar households in Kenya, Stichter suggests that "the low level of child participation is mainly attributable to the competing demands of schooling, but may also be related to the increasing complexity of household tasks" (199).

4. *Omugwo* refers to the special care given to a woman who has recently given birth, especially by her mother. Like those in other Nigerian ethnic groups, an Igbo mother is expected to visit her daughter who has just delivered a new baby. During this visit, which can range from several days to a number of weeks, the (grand)mother helps out with housework and childcare, allowing the young mother enough time to recover and resume the management of her household. Being invited for the omugwo is an honor for a (grand)mother. Unfortunately, this cultural practice may die with younger generations as more women enter the labor force. For instance, two of the working mothers in the study have mothers who are

formally employed. They have to settle for part-time assistance from them or their mothers-in-law during their own omugwos.

5. The nature of the items to be purchased dictates the shopping schedule. For instance, items such as rice and beans are usually bought annually or biannually. Other items, such as meat and onions, may be purchased monthly in bulk and shared with other women. In fact, many of the working mothers belong to an office co-op for such bulk purchases.

6. Often, the maids are not conversant with the washing instructions for delicate fabrics. Moreover, some of them are quite young and may not be able to do heavy laundry or clean the house to these working women's satisfaction. The working mothers also handle the washing of underwear because they know that their husbands would frown on passing this responsibility to the house-helps.

7. A husband may actually provide the fees and the money for purchasing these items.

8. Fapohunda, "Childcare Dilemma," 279.

9. This corrupt form is often spoken by the less educated and is commonly used in public places such as open-air markets, parking lots, and bus stops.

10. Stichter, "Middle Class," 196–200.

11. John C. Caldwell, *The Socio-Economic Explanation of High Fertility* (Canberra: Australian National University, 1976), 107.

12. Meg Luxton, *More than a Labour of Love: Three Generations of Women's Work in the Home* (Toronto: Women's Press, 1980).

13. Stichter, "Middle Class"; Sharon Stichter, "Women, Employment and the Family: Current Debates," in *Women, Employment and the Family in the International Division of Labour,* ed. Sharon Stichter and Jane L. Parpart (London: Macmillan, 1990), 11–71; E. Okeke, "Nigeria."

Chapter 8

1. Although the patterns differ, this practice is not peculiar to Igboland. See Katherine Abu, "The Separateness of Spouses: Conjugal Resources in an Ashanti Town," in *Female and Male in West Africa,* ed. Christine Oppong (London: Allen and Unwin, 1983), 156–68; Fapohunda, "Urban Women's Roles"; David Iyam, "'Full Men' and 'Powerful Women': The Reconstruction of Gender Status among the Biase of South Eastern Nigeria," *Canadian Journal of African Studies* 30, no. 3 (1996): 387–409; Soniia David, "You Became One in Marriage: Domestic Budgeting among the Kpelle of Liberia," *Canadian Journal of African Studies* 30, no. 2 (1996): 157–83.

2. Fapohunda, "Childcare Dilemma," 1982.

3. One hundredth of a naira.

4. The respondents do not normally keep detailed records of their expenses. The information provided is based on estimates of family expenses during the fieldwork. This was fairly easy because the women kept the monthly contributions from both spouses and also monitored the family budget.

5. As noted in chapter 5, *house-help* is a general label for domestic hands, but in many cases elite women also use the older and far more restrictive term *maid*, especially for nonrelatives.

Chapter 9

1. Bloch, Beoku-Betts, and Tabachnick, *Women and Education;* Mairead Dunne and Yusuf Sayed, "Transformation and Equity: Women and Higher Education in Sub-Saharan Africa," *ISEA* 30, no. 1 (2002): 50–65; Eva Rathgeber, "Women's Participation in Science and Technology," in *Women in the Third World: An Encyclopedia of Contemporary Issues,* ed. Nelly Stromquist (London: Garland Publishing, 1998), 427–35.

2. Liobi Moshi, foreword to Bloch, Beoku-Betts, and Tabachnick, *Women and Education,* xi.

3. Philomina Okeke, "The Content and Research Base for Women's Education in Africa: Postcolonial Realities and Outcomes." *Journal of Postcolonial Education* 2, no. 1 (2003): 7–22; Organization of African Unity, *New Partnership;* UNIFEM, *Executive Summary,* www.undp.org/unifem/progressww/index.html (2002); World Bank, *Higher Education in Developing Countries* (Washington, DC: World Bank, 2000).

4. Dunne and Sayed, "Transformation and Equity."

5. Eva Rathgeber, "Women and Higher Education in Africa: Access and Choices," in *Women's Higher Education in Comparative Perspective,* ed. Gail Kelly and Sheila Slaughter (Dordrecht: Kluwer Academic Publishers, 1991), 57.

6. F. M. Hayward, "Higher Education in Africa: Crisis and Transformation," in *Transforming Higher Education: Views from Leaders around the World,* ed. M. F. Green (Phoenix: Oryx Press, 1997), 87–113; Bloch, Beoku-Betts, and Tabachnick, *Women and Education;* Philomina Okeke, "Negotiating Social Independence: The Challenge of Career Pursuits for Igbo Women in Postcolonial Nigeria," in *"Wicked" Women and the Reconfiguration of Gender in Africa,* ed. Dorothy Hodgson and Sheryl McCurdy (Oxford: James Currey, 2001), 234–51.

7. Collated from UNIFEM, *Progress of the World's Women 2000* at www.unifem.org/index.php?f_page_pid=123, chapter 3.

8. P. Katjavivi, "Empowering African Women through Higher Education," in *Women, Power and the Academy: From Rhetoric to Reality*, ed. Mary-Louise Kearney (New York: UNESCO/Berghahn Books, 2000), 59–70.

9. Ibid.

10. Quoted in bell hooks, *Feminist Theory: From Margin to Center* (Boston: South End Press, 1984), 114.

11. Birte Rodenberg, *Integrating Gender into Poverty Reduction Strategies: From the Declaration of Intent to Development Policy in Practice*, German Development Institute Briefing Paper no. 2, 2002, 1.

12. Ebrima Sall, ed., *Women in Academia: Gender and Academic Freedom in Africa* (Dakar: CODESRIA, 2000).

13. Ayesha Imam, introduction to *Engendering African Social Sciences*, ed. Ayesha Imam, Amina Mama, and Fatou Sow (Dakar: CODESRIA, 1997), 2.

14. Moshi, foreword to Bloch, Beoku-Betts, and Tabachnick, *Women and Education*, xi.

15. B. Thaver, "Private Higher Education in Africa: Six Country Case Studies," paper presented at African Universities in the Twenty-First Century: International Symposium, CODESRIA/University of Illinois, Urbana-Champaign, 2002; Q. Oula, "The Academic's Dilemma: Coping with the Neo-Liberal Reforms and the Intrusion of Money at Makerere University, Uganda," paper presented at African Universities symposium.

16. Thaver, "Private Higher Education"; Oula, "Academic's Dilemma."

17. World Bank, *Higher Education: The Lessons of Experience*, Development in Practice (Washington, DC: World Bank, 1994); World Bank, *Education in Sub-Saharan Africa: Policies for Adjustment, Revitalization and Expansion* (Washington, DC: World Bank, 1988).

18. Hayward, "Higher Education."

19. Dunne and Sayed, "Transformation and Equity."

Bibliography

Abdullah, Hussaina. "'Transition Politics' and the Challenge of Gender in Nigeria." *Review of African Political Economy* 56 (1993): 27–41.

———. "Wifeism and Activism: The Nigerian Women's Movement." In *The Challenge of Local Feminisms: Women's Movements in Global Perspective*, ed. Amrita Basu, 209–25. Boulder: Westview, 1995.

Abu, Katherine. "The Separateness of Spouses: Conjugal Resources in an Ashanti Town." In *Female and Male in West Africa*, ed. Christine Oppong, 156–68. London: Allen and Unwin, 1983.

Achebe, Christie C. "Continuities, Changes and Challenges: Women's Role in Nigerian Society." *Présence africaine: Cultural Review of the Negro World* 120 (1981): 3–16.

Adebayo, Olukoshi. *The Politics of Structural Adjustment in Nigeria*. London: James Currey, 1993.

Adepoju, Aderanti, and Christine Oppong, eds. *Gender, Work and Population in Sub-Saharan Africa*. London: James Currey, 1994.

Afonja, Simi. "Changing Modes of Production and the Sexual Division of Labor among the Yoruba." In *Women's Work: Development and the Division of Labor by Gender*, ed. Eleanor Leacock and Helen Safa, 122–35. South Hadley, MA: Bergin and Garvey, 1986.

———. "Changing Patterns of Gender Stratification in West Africa." In *Persistent Inequalities: Women and World Development*, ed. Irene Tinker, 198–209. Oxford: Oxford University Press, 1990.

Alo, Oladimejo, and Selina Adjebeng-Asem. "Women and National Development: A Socio-Cultural Analysis of the Nigerian Experience." In *Women, Development, and Change: The Third World Experience*, ed. Francis M. Abraham and Subhadra P. Abraham, 217–44. Bristol: Wyndham Hall Press, 1988.

Amadiume, Ifi. *Male Daughters and Female Husbands: Gender and Class in an African Society*. London: Zed Books, 1987.

Ampadu, Lena. "Motherhood—A Joy? The Status of Mothers of African Descent in the Literature and Lore of Africa and the African Diaspora." *Journal of the Association for Research on Mothering* 2, no. 2 (Fall/Winter, 2000): 166–75.

Anambra State [Nigeria]. *Civil Service Handbook.* Enugu: Civil Service, 1989.

———. *School Statistics.* Enugu: Statistics Division, State Education Commission, 1989.

Anambra State. Civil Service Commission. *Annual Report.* Enugu: Government Printers, 1989.

Anderson, Bridget. *Doing the Dirty Work? The Global Politics of Domestic Labour.* London: Zed Books, 2000.

Aubrey, Lisa. "Gender, Development, and Democratization in Africa." *Journal of Asian and African Studies* 36, no. 1 (2001): 87–111.

Awe, Bolanle. "The Iyalode in the Traditional Political System." In *Sexual Stratification: A Cross-Cultural View,* ed. A. Schlegel, 144–60. New York: Columbia University Press, 1977.

———. *Nigerian Women in Historical Perspective.* Ibadan: Sankore/Bookcraft, 1992.

Awe, M. "Women, Science and Technology in the Colonial Era." In *Symposium on the Impact of Colonialism on Nigerian Women.* Ibadan: University of Ibadan, Institute of African Studies, 1989.

Babangida, Maryam. *The Home Front: Nigerian Army Officers and Their Wives.* Ibadan: Fountain Publications, 1988.

Banderage, Asoka. "Women in Development: Liberalism, Marxism and Marxist Feminism." *Development and Change* 15 (1984): 495–515.

Basu, Amrita, ed. *The Challenge of Local Feminisms: Women's Movements in Global Perspective.* Boulder: Westview, 1995.

Bay, Edna, ed. *Women and Work in Africa.* Boulder: Westview, 1982.

Biraimah, Karen L. "Class, Gender, and Life Chances: A Nigerian University Case Study." *Comparative Education Review* 31, no. 4 (1987): 570–82.

Bloch, Marianne, Josephine A. Beoku-Betts, and B. Robert Tabachnick, eds. *Women and Education in Sub-Saharan Africa: Power, Opportunities, and Constraints.* Boulder: Lynne Rienner, 1998.

Boserup, Ester. "The Economics of Polygamy." In *Perspectives on Africa: A Reader in Culture, History and Representations,* ed. Roy R. Grinker and Christopher B. Steine, 506–17. Cambridge, MA: Blackwell, 1997.

———. *Woman's Role in Economic Development.* London: Allen and Unwin, 1970.

Bowman, M. J., and C. A. Anderson. "The Participation of Women in Education in the Third World." In *Women's Education in the Third World:*

Comparative Perspectives, ed. J. P. Kelly and C. M. Elliot, 11–39. Albany: SUNY Press, 1982.

Bujra, Janet M. "Class, Gender and Capitalist Transformation in Africa." *African Development* 8 (July 1983): 17–42.

———. "'Urging Women to Redouble Their Efforts . . .': Class, Gender, and Capitalist Transformation in Africa." In *Women and Class in Africa*, ed. Claire Robertson and Iris Berger, 117–40. London: Africana, 1986.

Caldwell, John C. *The Socio-Economic Explanation of High Fertility*. Canberra: Australian National University, 1976.

Calliste, Agnes. "Canada's Immigration Policy and Domestics from the Caribbean: The Second Domestic Scheme." In *Race, Class, Gender: Bonds and Barriers*, ed. Jesse Vorst et al., 136–68. Rev. ed. Toronto: Garamond Press, 1991.

Chikwe, Kema. *Women of My Era*. Owerri, Nigeria: Prime Time, 2003.

Cock, Jacklyn. *Maids and Madams: A Study in the Politics of Exploitation*. Johannesburg: Ravan Press, 1980.

———. "Trapped Workers: The Case of Domestic Servants in South Africa." In *Patriarchy and Class: African Women in the Home and the Workforce*, ed. Sharon B. Stichter and Jane L. Parpart, 205–19. Boulder: Westview.

Coles, Catherine, and Beverly Mack, eds. *Hausa Women in the Twentieth Century*. Madison: University of Wisconsin Press, 1991.

Dada, S. O. "Human Resources Training and Development: An Empirical Study of Its Problems and Gains in the Nigerian Banking Industry." *Nigerian Banker: Journal of the Institute of Bankers of Nigeria* (1991): 5–12.

David, Soniia. "You Became One in Marriage: Domestic Budgeting among the Kpelle of Liberia." *Canadian Journal of African Studies* 30, no. 2 (1996): 157–83.

Denzer, LaRay. "Female Employment in the Government Service of Nigeria, 1885–1945." In *Symposium on Women's Studies in Nigeria: The State of the Art Now*. Ibadan: University of Ibadan, Women's Research and Documentation Centre, Institute of African Studies, 1987.

Dike, Victor. *The Osu Caste System in Igboland: A Challenge for Nigerian Democracy*. Sacramento: Morris Publishing, 2002.

Doherty, Oluwatoyin. "Women in the Legal Profession in Nigeria." Lagos: Nigerian Law School, 1990.

D'Oyley, Vincent, Adrian Blunt, and Ray Barnhardt. *Education and Development: Lessons from the Third World*. Calgary: Detselig Enterprises, 1994.

Dunne, Mairead, and Yusuf Sayed. "Transformation and Equity: Women and Higher Education in Sub-Saharan Africa." *ISEA* 30, no. 1 (2002): 50–65.

Ekiyor, M. O. "Formal Colonial Education: An Assessment of Its Impact on the Marriageability of 'Acada' Women in Southern Nigeria." In *Symposium on the Impact of Colonialism on Nigerian Women.* Ibadan: Institute of African Studies, University of Ibadan, 1989.

Ekong, Sheila Clarke. "Continuity and Change in Nigerian Family Patterns." In *Social Change in Nigeria,* ed. S. Afonja and T. Pearce, 50–70. Essex: Longman, 1986.

Elias, T. O. *The Impact of English Law on Nigerian Customary Law.* Lugard Lectures. Lagos: Ministry of Information, 1958.

Emecheta, Buchi. *The Joys of Motherhood.* Ibadan: Heinemann, 1979.

Eshiwani, G. S. *A Study of Women's Access to Higher Education with a Special Reference to Science and Math.* Working paper no. 5003. Nairobi: Bureau of Educational Research, Kenyatta University College, 1983.

Etienne, Mona. "The Case of Social Maternity: Adoption of Children by Urban Baule Women." In *Gender in Cross-Cultural Perspective,* ed. Caroline B. Brettell and Carolyn F. Sargent, 32–38. Upper Saddle River, NJ: Prentice Hall, 2001.

Fafunwa, A. Babs. *History of Education in Nigeria.* London: Allen and Unwin, 1974.

Fapohunda, Eleanor R. "The Childcare Dilemma of Working Mothers in African Cities: The Case of Lagos, Nigeria." In *Women and Work in Africa,* ed. Edna Bay, 277–88. Boulder: Westview, 1982.

———. "Urban Women's Roles and Nigerian Government Development Strategies." In *Sex Roles, Population, and Development in West Africa,* ed. Christine Oppong, 203–12. London: James Currey, 1988.

Fatton, Roberts. "Gender, Class and the State in Africa." In *Women and the State in Africa,* ed. Jane L. Parpart and Kathleen A. Staudt, 47–66. London: Lynne Rienner, 1989.

Gladwin, Christina, ed. *Structural Adjustment and African Women Farmers.* Gainesville: University Press of Florida, 1991.

Goody, Esther. "Some Theoretical and Empirical Aspects of Parenthood in West Africa." In *Seminar of the International Sociological Association Committee on Family Research.* Lome, Togo: 1976.

Gordon, April. *Transforming Capitalism and Patriarchy: Gender and Development in Africa.* Boulder: Lynne Rienner, 1996.

Gunderson, Morley, and Craig Riddell. *Labor Market Economics: Theory, Evidence and Policy in Canada.* 2d ed. Toronto: McGraw-Hill Ryerson, 1988.

Guppy, Neil, Doug Balson, and Susan Vellutini. "Women and Higher Education in Canadian Society." In *Women and Education: A Canadian Perspective*, ed. Jane S. Gaskell and Arlene T. McLaren, 171–92. Calgary: Detselig Enterprises, 1987.

Guyer, Jane. *Family and Farm in Southern Cameroon.* African Research Studies, no. 15. Boston: Boston University, African Studies Center, 1984.

———, ed. *Feeding African Cities: Studies in Regional Social History.* Bloomington: Indiana University Press, 1987.

Hay, Margaret Jean, and Marcia Wright, eds. *African Women and the Law: Historical Perspectives.* Boston University Papers on Africa, no. 7. Boston: Boston University, African Studies Center, 1982.

Hayward, F. M. "Higher Education in Africa: Crisis and Transformation." In *Transforming Higher Education: Views from Leaders around the World*, ed. M. F. Green, 87–113. Phoenix: Oryx Press, 1997.

Heyzer, N. "Towards a Framework of Analysis, in Women and the Informal Sector." *IDS Bulletin* (University of Sussex, Institute of Development Studies) 12, no. 3 (1981): 3–8.

Hodgson, Dorothy, and Sheryl McCurdy, eds. *"Wicked" Women and the Reconfiguration of Gender in Africa.* Oxford: James Currey, 2001.

House-Midamba, Bessie, and Felix K. Ekechi, eds. *African Market Women and Economic Power.* Westport, CT: Greenwood Press.

Ihonvbere, Julius. "From Movement to Government: The Movement for Multi-Party Democracy and the Crisis of Democratic Consolidation in Zambia." *Canadian Journal of African Studies* 29, no. 1 (1995): 1–25.

Ikejiani, Okechukwu. "Education for Efficiency." In *Nigerian Education*, ed. Okechukwu Ikejiani, 83–92. Lagos: Longmans of Nigeria, 1964.

———, ed. *Nigerian Education.* Lagos: Longmans of Nigeria, 1964.

Ikejiani, Okechukwu, and J. O. Anowi. "Nigerian Universities." In *Nigerian Education*, ed. Okechukwu Ikejiani, 128–182. Lagos: Longmans of Nigeria, 1964.

ILO (International Labour Organization). *World Labour Report.* Geneva: ILO, 1989.

Isbister, John. *Promises Not Kept: The Betrayal of Social Change in the Third World.* West Hartford: Kumarian Press, 1993.

Iweriabor, Ifeyinwa. "Women in the Family, Labour and Management: What Can Be Done?" In *Women and the Family in Nigeria*, ed. Ayesha Imam, Renée Pittin, and H. Omole, 145–54. Dakar: CODESRIA, 1985.

Iyam, David. "'Full Men' and 'Powerful Women': The Reconstruction of Gender Status among the Biase of South Eastern Nigeria." *Canadian Journal of African Studies* 30, no. 3 (1996): 387–409.

Jakubowski, Marie. *Immigration and the Legalization of Racism.* Halifax: Fernwood Publishing, 1997.

Johnson-Odim, Cheryl, and Nina Mba. *For Women and the Nation: Funmilayo Ransome Kuti of Nigeria.* Chicago: University of Illinois Press, 1997.

Kalu, Anthonia. "Women and the Social Construction of Gender in African Development." *Africa Today* 43, no. 3 (July–September 1996): 269–88.

Kaplan, Flora, ed. *Queens, Queen Mothers, Priestesses, and Power: Case Studies in African Gender.* New York: New York Academy of Sciences, 1997.

Kasunmu, Alfred, and Jeswald Salacuse. *Nigerian Family Law.* London: Butterworths, 1960.

Katjavivi, P. "Empowering African Women through Higher Education." In *Women, Power, and the Academy: From Rhetoric to Reality,* ed. Mary-Louise Kearney, 59–70. New York: UNESCO/Berghahn Books, 2000.

Kelly, Grace P., ed. *International Handbook of Women's Education.* New York: Greenwood Press, 1989.

King, Lamont D. "State and Ethnicity in Pre-colonial Northern Nigeria," *Journal of Asian and African Studies* 36, no. 4 (2001): 339–60.

Lazreg, Marnia. *The Eloquence of Silence: Algerian Women in Question.* New York: Routledge, 1994.

Lee, Valerie E., and Marlaine E. Lockheed. "Single-Sex Schooling and Its Effects on Nigerian Adolescents." In *Women and Education in Sub-Saharan Africa: Power, Opportunities, and Constraints,* ed. Marianne Bloch, Josephine A. Beoku-Betts, and Roberts B. Tabachnick, 201–26. Boulder: Lynne Rienner, 1998.

Leith-Ross, Sylvia. *African Women: A Study of the Ibo of Nigeria.* London: Routledge and Kegan Paul, 1939.

Lewis, Barbara. "Fertility and Employment: An Assessment of Role Incompatibility among African Urban Women." In *Women and Work in Africa,* ed. Edna Bay, 249–76. Boulder: Westview, 1982.

Lloyd, Peter. *Power and Independence: Urban Africans' Perception of Social Inequality.* London: Routledge and Kegan Paul, 1974.

Luxton, Meg. *More Than a Labour of Love: Three Generations of Women's Work in the Home.* Toronto: Women's Press, 1980.

Mama, Amina. "Feminism or Femocracy? State Feminism and Democratisation in Nigeria." *African Development* 20, no. 1 (1995): 37–58.

———. "Khaki in the Family: Gender Discourse and Militarism in Nigeria." *African Studies Review* 41, no. 2 (1998): 1–18.

Mamdani, Mahmood. *Citizen and Subject: Contemporary Africa and the Legacy of Late Colonialism.* Princeton Studies in Culture, Power, and History. Kampala: Fountain Publishers, 1996.

Mamuddu, Katherine. "Gender Perspectives in the Transformation of Africa: Challenges to the African University as a Model to Society." In *Conference of Association of African Universities.* Legon: University of Ghana, 1992.

Mann, Kristin. *Marrying Well: Marriage and Social Change among the Educated Elite in Colonial Lagos.* Cambridge: Cambridge University Press, 1985.

Mba, Nina E. *Nigerian Women Mobilized: Women's Political Activities in Southern Nigeria, 1900–1965.* Berkeley: University of California, Institute of International Studies, 1982.

Mbiti, John S. *African Religions and Philosophy.* Garden City, NY: Anchor Books, 1970.

Mifflen, Frank J., and Sydney C. Mifflen. *The Sociology of Education: Canada and Beyond.* Calgary: Detselig, 1982.

Moghadam, Valentine M. "Development and Women's Emancipation: Is There a Connection?" *Development and Change* 23, no. 3 (1992): 215–55.

Mohanty, Chandra T. Introduction to *Third World Women and the Politics of Feminism,* ed. Chandra T. Mohanty, Ann Russo, and Lourdes Torres, 1–47. Bloomington: Indiana University Press, 1991.

Moore, Kofo. "Kofo Moore's Lectures." *West African Pilot,* November 29–30, December 1, 1937, 2.

Moshi, Liobi. Foreword to *Women and Education in Sub-Saharan Africa,* ed. Marianne Bloch, Josephine A. Beoku-Betts and Roberts B. Tabachnick. Boulder: Lynne Rienner, 1998.

Mosley, Katherine. "'Seizing the Change': Economic Crisis and Industrial Restructuring in Nigeria." In *Beyond Structural Adjustment in Africa,* ed. Julius Nyang'oro and Timothy Shaw. New York: Praeger, 1992.

Muhammed, Safiya. "Women, the Family and the Wider Society." In *Women and the Family in Nigeria,* ed. Ayesha Imam, Renée Pittin, and H. Omole, 29–36. Dakar: CODESRIA, 1985.

Nfa-Abbenyi, Julian M. *Gender in African Women's Writing: Identity, Sexuality, and Difference.* Bloomington: Indiana University Press, 1997.

Nigeria. *Annual Abstract of Statistics.* Abuja: Federal Office of Statistics, 1998.

———. *Annual Report of the Federal Ministry of Labour, 1952–1953.* Lagos: Nigerian National Press, 1953.

———. *Annual Report of the Federal Ministry of Labour, 1954–1955.* Lagos: Nigerian National Press, 1955.

———. *Annual Report of the Federal Ministry of Labour, 1960–1961.* Lagos: Nigerian National Press, 1961.

Nigeria. Commission on Post-School Certificate and Higher Education. *Investment in Education: Report.* Lagos: Federal Ministry of Education, 1960.

Nigeria. Education Department. *Memorandum on Educational Policy in Nigeria.* Lagos: Government Printer, 1947.

Nigerian Association of University Women. *Survey of Women's Education in Western Nigeria.* Ibadan: Branch, 1963.

Nigerian Institute of Bankers. *The Collective Agreement between Nigerian Employers Association of Banks, Insurance and Allied Institutions, and the Association of Senior Staff of Banks, Insurance and Financial Institutions.* Lagos: Headquarters, 1990.

Nnaemeka, Obioma, ed. *Sisterhood, Feminisms, and Power: From Africa to the Diaspora.* Trenton: Africa World Press, 1998.

Nnoli, Okwudiba. *Ethnicity and Development in Nigeria.* Brookfield, VT: Ashgate Publishing, 1995.

Nwabara, Zahra. "Women in Nigeria: The Way I See It." In *Women and the Family in Nigeria*, ed. Ayesha Imam, Renée Pittin, and H. Omok. Dakar: CODESIRA, 1985.

Nzomo, Maria. "Beyond Structural Adjustment Programs: Democracy, Gender Equity, and Development in Africa, with Special Reference to Kenya." In *Beyond Structural Adjustment in Africa: The Political Economy of Sustainable and Democratic Development,* ed. Julius Nyang'oro and Timothy Shaw, 99–117. New York: Praeger, 1992.

Nzongola-Ntalaja, Georges. *Nation-Building and State-Building in Africa.* Occasional paper no. 3. Harare: SAPES Books, 1993.

Obi, Sebastian M. *How to Solve the Osu Problem.* Owerri: Agape Education Resources, 1994.

Obikeze, D. S. "Son Preference among Nigerian Mothers: Its Demographic and Psychological Implications." *International Journal of Contemporary Sociology* 25, no. 12 (January–April, 1988): 55–63.

Ogundipe-Leslie, Molara. "Women in Nigeria." In *Women in Nigeria Today,* ed. Women in Nigeria, 119–31. London: Zed Books, 1985.

Ogunsola, Albert F. *Legislation and Education in Northern Nigeria.* Oxford: Oxford University Press, 1974.

Okehie-Offoha, Marcellina U. "The Igbo." In *Ethnic and Cultural Diversity in Nigeria,* ed. Marcellina U. Okehie-Offoha and Matthew N. Sadiku, 63–77. Trenton: Africa World Press, 1996.

Okehie-Offoha, Marcellina U., and Matthew N. Sadiku, eds. *Ethnic and Cultural Diversity in Nigeria.* Trenton: Africa World Press, 1996.

Okeke, Eunice C. A. "Nigeria." In *International Handbook of Women's Education,* ed. Grace P. Kelly, 43–64. New York: Greenwood Press, 1989.

Okeke, Philomina. "The Content and Research Base for Women's Education in Africa: Postcolonial Realities and Outcomes." *Journal of Postcolonial Education* 2, no. 1 (2003): 7–22.

———. "Female Wage Earners and Separate Resource Structures in Post Oil Boom Nigeria." *Dialectical Anthropology* 22, nos. 3–4 (December 1997): 373–87.

———. "The First Lady Syndrome: The (En)Gendering of Bureaucratic Corruption in Nigeria." *Council for the Development of Social Science Research in Africa Bulletin* 3, no. 4 (1998): 16–19.

———. "Interrogating Tradition on African Women's Status: Beyond the Critique of Western Feminism." *Black Studies Journal* 2 (1999): 65–76.

———. *Is Development a Good Thing? Women and Wage Labour in a Developing Economy.* Pearson Public Interest Series. Halifax: Pearson International Institute for Development, Dalhousie University, March 1993.

———. "The Labour Market Implications of Women's Education in Nigeria: The Case of Igbo Women." Summer working paper, School of Education, Dalhousie University, 1990.

———. "Negotiating Social Independence: The Challenge of Career Pursuits for Igbo Women in Postcolonial Nigeria." In *"Wicked" Women and the Reconfiguration of Gender in Africa*, ed. Dorothy Hodgson and Sheryl McCurdy, 234–51. Oxford: James Currey, 2001.

———. "Postmodern Feminism and Knowledge Production: The African Context." *Africa Today* 43, no. 3 (July–September 1996): 223–33.

———. "Reconfiguring Tradition: Women's Rights and Social Statue in Contemporary Nigeria." *Africa Today* 47, no. 1 (2000): 49–65.

———. "Women's Movements." In *Encyclopedia of Twentieth Century African History*, ed. Paul Tiyambe Zeleza and Dickson Eyoh. London: Routledge, 2002.

Okeke, Philomina, and Susan Franceschet. "Democratisation and 'State Feminism': A Comparison of Gender Politics in Africa and Latin America." *Development and Change* 33, no. 3 (2002): 439–66.

Okeke, Uduaroh. "Background to the Problems of Nigerian Education." In *Nigerian Education*, ed. Okechukwu Ikejiani, 2–17. Lagos: Longmans of Nigeria, 1964.

Okonjo, K. "The Dual-Sex Political System in Operation: Igbo Women and Community Politics in Midwestern Nigeria." In *Women in Africa: Studies in Social and Economic Change*, ed. Nancy J. Hafkin and Edna G. Bay, 45–58. Stanford: Stanford University Press, 1976.

Oladimejo, Alo, and Selina Adjebeng-Asem. "Women and National Development: A Socio-Cultural Analysis of the Nigerian Experience." In *Women, Development, and Change: The Third World Experience*, ed.

Francis M. Abraham, and Subhadra P. Abraham, 217–44. Bristol: Wyndham Hall Press, 1988.

Onimode, Bade. *Imperialism and Underdevelopment in Nigeria: The Dialectics of Mass Poverty.* London: Zed Books, 1982.

Oppong, Christine. *Marriage among a Matrilineal Elite: A Family Study of Ghanaian Senior Civil Servants.* London: Cambridge University Press, 1974.

Organization of African Unity (OAU). *New Partnership for Africa's Development (NEPAD).* Abuja, Nigeria: Organization of African Unity, 2001.

Otu, Deborah Oluwumi. "Nigerian Women and Education: Issues, Concerns and Prospects for National Development." In *Conference on the Impact of Colonialism on Nigerian Women.* Ibadan: Institute of African Studies, University of Ibadan, 1989.

Oula, Q. "The Academic's Dilemma: Coping with the Neo-Liberal Reforms and the Intrusion of Money at Makerere University, Uganda." Paper presented at African Universities in the Twenty-First Century: International Symposium, CODESRIA/University of Illinois, Urbana-Champaign, 2002.

Oyewùmí, Oyèrónké. *The Invention of Women: Making an African Sense of Western Gender Discourses.* Minneapolis: University of Minnesota Press, 1997.

———, ed. *Reflecting on the Politics of Sisterhood.* Trenton: Africa World Press, 2003.

Parpart, Jane L. "Wage Earning Women and the Double Day: The Nigerian Case." In *Women, Employment and the Family in the International Division of Labour,* ed. Sharon Stichter and Jane L. Parpart, 161–82. London: Macmillan, 1990.

Phelps-Stokes Commission. *Education in Africa: A Study of West, South and Equatorial Africa by the first African Education Commission under the Auspices of the Phelps-Stokes Fund in Cooperation with the International Education Board, 1920–1921.* New York: Phelps-Stokes Fund, 1921.

Pittin, Renée. "The Control of Reproduction: Principle and Practice in Nigeria." *Review of African Political Economy* 35 (1986): 40–53.

Rathgeber, Eva. "Women and Higher Education in Africa: Access and Choices." In *Women's Higher Education in Comparative Perspective,* ed. Gail Kelly and Sheila Slaughter. Dordrecht: Kluwer Academic Publishers, 1991.

———. "Women's Participation in Science and Technology." In *Women in the Third World: An Encyclopedia of Contemporary Issues,* ed. Nelly Stromquist, 427–35. London: Garland Publishing, 1998.

Reynolds, Cecilia. "The Educational System." In *Feminist Issues: Race,*

Class, and Sexuality, ed. Nancy Mandell, 233–48. Scarborough, ON: Prentice Hall Allyn and Bacon, 1998.

Robertson, Claire. "Developing Economic Awareness: Changing Perspectives in Studies of African Women, 1976–1986." *Feminist Studies* 13, no. 1 (1987): 97–135.

———. *Sharing the Same Bowl: A Socioeconomic History of Women and Class in Accra, Ghana.* Bloomington: Indiana University Press, 1984.

———. "Women's Education and Class Formation in Africa, 1950–1980." In *Women and Class in Africa,* ed. Claire Robertson and Iris Berger, 92–113. London: Africana, 1986.

Rodenberg, Birte. *Integrating Gender into Poverty Reduction Strategies: From the Declaration of Intent to Development Policy in Practice.* German Development Institute Briefing Paper no. 2, 2002.

Rogers, Barbara. *The Domestication of Women: Discrimination in Developing Societies.* London: Tavistock, 1980.

Sall, Ebrima, ed. *Women in Academia: Gender and Academic Freedom in Africa.* Dakar: CODESRIA, 2000.

Samarasinghe, Vidyamali. "The Place of the WID Discourse in Global Analysis: The Potential for a 'Reverse Flow.'" In *Color, Class and Country: Experiences of Gender,* ed. Gay Young and Bette Dickerson, 218–31. London: Zed Books, 1994.

Schecter, Tanya. *Race, Class, Women and the State: The Case of Domestic Labour.* Montreal: Black Rose Books, 1998.

Shettima, Kole A. "Engendering Nigeria's Third Republic." *African Studies Review* 38, no. 3 (December 1995): 61–99.

Shindler, J. "Labour Saving Appliances and Domestic Service." *Southern African Labour Bulletin* 6, no. 1 (1980).

Silvera, Nakeda. "Speaking of Women's Lives and Imperialist Economics: Two Introductions from *Silenced.*" In *Returning the Gaze: Essays on Racism, Feminism and Politics,* ed. Himani Bannerji, 242–69. Toronto: Sister Vision Press, 1993.

Smock, C. E. *Women's Education in Developing Countries: Opportunities and Outcomes.* New York: Praeger, 1981.

Smythe, Hugh H., and Mabel M. Smythe. *The New Nigerian Elite.* Stanford: Stanford University Press, 1960.

Snyder, Margaret, and Mary Tadesse. "The African Context: Women in the Political Economy." In *The Women, Gender, and Development Reader,* ed. Nalini Visvanathan, Lynn Duggan, Laurie Nisonoff, and Nan Wiegersma, 75–79. London: Zed Books, 1997.

Soyombo, O. "The Economic Contribution of Women to National Development in Nigeria: Focus on Participation in the Labour Market."

Seminar on Nigerian Women and National Development. Ibadan: University of Ibadan, 1985.

Staudt, Kathleen. "Gender Politics in Bureaucracy: Theoretical Issues in Comparative Perspective." In *Women, International Development, and Politics: The Bureaucratic Mire*, ed. K. Staudt, 30–34. Philadelphia: Temple University Press, 1997.

Stichter, Sharon B. "The Middle Class in Kenya: Changes in Gender Relations." In *Patriarchy and Class: African Women in the Home and the Workforce*, ed. Sharon B. Stichter and Jane L. Parpart, 177–204. Boulder: Westview, 1988.

———. "Women, Employment and the Family: Current Debates." In *Women, Employment and the Family in the International Divison of Labour*, ed. Sharon Stichter and Jane L. Parpart, 11–71. London: Macmillan, 1990.

Sudarkasa, Niara. "Female Employment and Family Organization in West Africa." In *The Black Woman Cross-Culturally*, ed. Filomina C. Steady, 49–63. Cambridge, MA: Schenkman, 1981.

Taiwo, C. O. *The Nigerian Education System: Past, Present, and Future.* Ibadan: Nelson, 1980.

Thaver, B. "Private Higher Education in Africa: Six Country Case Studies." Paper presented at African Universities in the Twenty-First Century: International Symposium, CODESRIA/University of Illinois, Urbana-Champaign, 2002.

Tripp. Aili. *Changing the Rules: The Politics of Liberalization and the Urban Informal Economy in Tanzania.* Berkeley: University of California Press, 1997.

———. "Women's Movements and Challenges to Neopatrimonial Rule: Preliminary Observations from Africa." *Development and Change* 32 (2001): 33–54.

Uchendu, Patrick. *Education and the Changing Economic Role of Nigerian Women.* Enugu: Fourth Dimension Publishers, 1995.

Umeh, Marie. "(En)Gendering African Womanhood: Locating Sexual Politics in Igbo Society and Across Boundaries." Introduction to *Emerging Perspectives on Buchi Emecheta*, ed. Marie Umeh. Trenton: Africa World Press, 1996.

UNECA (United Nations Economic Commission for Africa). *African Charter for Popular Participation in Development* [Arusha Declaration]. Addis Ababa: UNECA, 1990.

———. *African Platform for Action: African Common Position for the Advancement of Women, Adopted at the Fifth African Regional Conference on Women, Dakar, Senegal, 16-23 November 1994.* Addis Ababa?: UNECA, 1995.

———. *Economic Report on Africa.* Addis Ababa: UNECA, 1990.

———. "Women in Traditional African Societies." In *Workshop on Urban Problems.* Addis Ababa: UNECA, 1963.

UNIFEM. *Executive Summary.* www.undp.org/unifem/progressww/index.html. Accessed June 2003.

———. *Progress of the World's Women 2000.* At www.unifem.org/index.php?f_page_pid=123.

Urdang, S. *And Still They Dance: Women, War, and the Struggle for Change in Mozambique.* London: Earthscan, 1989.

Van Allen, Judith. "'Aba Riots' or Igbo 'Women's War'? Ideology, Stratification, and the Invisibility of Women." In *Gender in Cross-Cultural Perspective,* ed. Caroline Brettell and Carolyn Sargent, 513–28. Upper Saddle River, NJ: Prentice Hall, 1997.

Wambui Wa Karanja. "Conjugal Decision-Making: Some Data from Lagos." In *Male and Female in West Africa,* ed. Christine Oppong, 236–41. London: Allen and Unwin, 1983.

———. "'Outside Wives' and 'Inside Wives' in Nigeria: A Study of Changing Perceptions in Marriage." In *Transformations of African Marriage,* ed. David Parkin and David Nyamwaya, 247–61. Manchester: Manchester University Press, 1987.

Willey, Nicole. "Ibuza vs. Lagos: The Feminist and Traditional Buchi Emecheta." *Journal of the Association for Research on Mothering* 2, no. 2 (Fall/Winter 2000): 155–66.

Women in Nigeria (WIN). Editorial Commission. *Women in Nigeria Today.* London: Zed Books, 1985.

World Bank. *Education in Sub-Saharan Africa: Policies for Adjustment, Revitalization and Expansion.* Washington, DC: World Bank, 1998.

———. *Higher Education: The Lessons of Experience.* Development in Practice Series. Washington, DC: World Bank, 1994.

———. *Higher Education in Developing Countries: Peril and Promise.* Washington, DC: World Bank, 2000.

Zeleza, Tiyambe. "Gendering African History." *African Development* 18, no. 1 (1993): 99–117. Book review.

Index

Printed and bound by CPI Group (UK) Ltd, Croydon, CR0 4YY

09/06/2025

14685965-0002